AMERICA ANONYMOUS

Eight Addicts in Search of a Life

BENOIT DENIZET-LEWIS

SIMON & SCHUSTER   New York • London • Toronto • Sydney

SIMON & SCHUSTER
1230 Avenue of the Americas
New York, NY 10020

First Simon & Schuster hardcover edition January 2009

SIMON & SCHUSTER and colophon are registered trademarks
of Simon & Schuster, Inc.

For information about special discounts for bulk purchases,
please contact Simon & Schuster Special Sales at
1-800-456-6798 or business@simonandschuster.com

Designed by Dana Sloan

Manufactured in the United States of America

10 9 8 7 6 5 4 3 2 1

Library of Congress Cataloging-in-Publication Data
Denizet-Lewis, Benoit.
America Anonymous : eight addicts in search of a life /
Benoit Denizet-Lewis.
p. cm.
Includes bibliographical references and index.
1. Addicts—United States. 2. Compulsive behavior.
3. Substance abuse.
HV4998.D46   2009
616.860092/273 22
ISBN-13: 978-0-7432-7782-2
ISBN-10: 0-7432-7782-1

Page 343 constitutes an extension of the copyright page.

For the addict who still suffers

AMERICA ANONYMOUS

The Twelve Steps will be found on page 314.

AUTHOR'S NOTE

FOR THIS WORK of nonfiction, I immersed myself for two to three years in the lives of eight men and women from around the country struggling with addictions. Most requested that I change their names, and some asked that I not mention the town, city, or state where they live. I have obliged them.

To further protect their anonymity, in most cases I have changed the names of their family members and friends. I have also changed the names of most secondary characters.

There are no composite characters in this book. No scenes have been invented or embellished. I was present for much of what I write about, although I re-created some scenes with the help of those who witnessed them or were a part of them.

Except in the case of one addict (Bobby), no identifying characteristics have been changed. In Bobby's case, because I write specifically about the neighborhood where he lives, I have changed a handful of facts about his life.

While I tried to write about men and women who suffered from a broad range of addictions (and who were in different stages of recovery), this book is not intended to represent addiction and recovery in every form in this country.

These are the addicts I followed for this book (including their age and occupations when I started following them, and their primary addictions):

BOBBY, 34, unemployed. *Heroin.*

MARVIN, 80, retired. *Alcohol.*

TODD, 40, bodybuilder and male escort. *Crystal meth and steroids.*

ELLEN, 51, radio executive and DJ. *Food.*

SEAN, 20, college student. *Sex and pornography.*

JANICE, 55, unemployed. *Crack.*

JODY, 32, addiction counselor. *Heroin, crack, prescription drugs, gambling, and nicotine.*

KATE, 32, stay-at-home mom. *Shoplifting.*

INTRODUCTION

I AM AN addict—or, as my father prefers it said, I *have an addiction*. There's no need, he insists, to so thoroughly pigeonhole myself. I think I know what he means. If I *have an addiction*, then maybe one day I can throw it away, or misplace it, or refuse to be seen with it. But if I *am an addict* . . . well, that feels more permanent, more all-defining.

I did not consciously choose my particular manifestation of addiction (sex), nor did I make a concerted effort not to become enslaved to cocaine, or crystal meth, or craps, or any of the myriad ways addicts commit suicide "on the installment plan," as educator Laurence Peter once put it. For whatever reasons, my brain believes that sex is the best way to medicate loneliness, disconnection, shame, anger, and a core belief—only recently challenged—that I am inherently unlovable.

Perhaps my sex addiction was foreshadowed many years ago. When I was twelve, my favorite song was George Michael's "I Want Your Sex." In the shower I could be heard happily belting, *Sex is natural, sex is good, not everybody does it, but everybody should!*

Back then, it would have been inconceivable to me that one could think about sex—or, better yet, have sex—too often for one's own good. Sex was definitely not like crack, which I was hearing about with increasing hysteria on the news. Crack seemed very, very bad. Sex seemed like a great idea, especially as it was explained to me in the pages of the *Penthouse* magazines I found while snooping around my father's bedroom. (My parents divorced when I was six, and I divided my time between their houses.)

If you had told me when I was twelve that I would grow up to be a sex addict, I likely would have prayed you were right. My attitude at the time would have mirrored that of some grown married men whom I've told about my addiction. When I say that sex can "take over my life," I don't get much sympathy.

But lucky I am not. Like any debilitating addiction, sex addiction is about as fun as a self-imposed daily practice of water torture. What does sex addiction look like? It can take many forms, but for me a bad day in my active addiction looked something like this:

9:45 A.M.: Wake up later than intended (resolve to get up earlier the next day).

9:46 A.M.: Feel shame for having blown off my friends (again) in favor of spending five hours the previous night in a chat room on the Internet, followed by an hour of sex with someone I met there. Resolve to see friends that night.

9:47 A.M.: Think about eating breakfast.

10:02 A.M.: Decide that I'll wait until lunch to eat.

10:05 A.M.: Blow off checking my work e-mail. Check my other e-mail, to see who responded to one of my online profiles, some more truthful than others.

10:38 A.M.: Have phone sex.

10:59 A.M.: Remember that I hate phone sex. Resolve to stop having phone sex.

11:03 A.M.: Check my work e-mail—realize that I missed an appointment.

11:05 A.M.: E-mail said person. Apologize, make excuse.

11:08 A.M.: Call a friend and make plans for that night.

11:20 A.M.: Try to work.

12:09 P.M.: Give up. Resolve to work harder the next day.

12:23 P.M.: Make a sandwich. Watch TV.

1:15 P.M.: Spend five hours online looking for someone attractive to have sex with. Ignore repeated calls from friend with whom I have plans.

6:17 P.M.: Call friend. Lie about why I can't meet.

6:19 P.M.: Feel shame.

6:20 P.M.: Go back online. Eventually find someone attractive to have sex with.

7:10 P.M.: Take first shower of the day.

7:20 P.M.: Drive an hour to meet the person. Wait. Person doesn't show.

8:40 P.M.: Drive home, angry and hungry.

9:40 P.M.: Get back online—look for someone new.

10:02 P.M.: Mom calls (later than usual). Let it go to voice mail.

10:05 P.M.: Watch some porn.

10:45 P.M.: Have phone sex.

12:45 A.M.: Remember that I hate phone sex. Resolve to stop having phone sex.

12:46 A.M.: Feel shame.

12:49 A.M.: Finally eat dinner (leftover Chinese food).

1:08 A.M.: Check mom's message. Realize that I forgot her birthday.

1:09 A.M.: Feel like killing myself.

Fortunately, I can take or leave drugs and alcohol. I drink wine often (I'm half French), but I stop after a glass or two. I enjoy marijuana, but not nearly enough to go looking for it. I tried acid once in college, but by the third hour I had convinced myself that my two chess-playing, acid-dropping friends were conspiring against me with every move. I tried mushrooms once, enjoying them very much until I thought I was a character in a television show I was watching and deciding that I would be happier curled up in bed listening to Enya.

I also tried cocaine a few times, felt very good for about forty minutes, and then felt very annoyed. *What a stupid drug*, I thought. It seemed that the only way to enjoy cocaine—to avoid the depressing low that followed the short, exhilarating high—was to essentially be high *all the time*, and that sounded silly and expensive.

The only drug I've ever used regularly was ecstasy. Over the course of four years in college, I took one or two ecstasy pills every few weekends. For me it was the perfect substance, because it seemed to help facilitate intense emotional connections with other people, something I was not good at achieving while not on ecstasy.

If cocaine is a selfish drug, ecstasy is its spiritual opposite—a miraculous conduit for human compassion and love. Ecstasy has the astonishing effect of making you see the good in other people, even those you may not otherwise like. As Andrew Solomon writes in *The Noonday Demon*, on ecstasy you feel like "communicating enormous love to everyone within reach."

But there is some evidence that prolonged ecstasy use damages serotonin responsiveness in the brain, which can lead to long-term memory and mood problems. So on those rare occasions when I'm tempted to take ecstasy again, I simply choose not to. When it comes to drugs, rational thinking wins.

When it comes to sex, though, rational thinking loses in a landslide, and the consequences seem trivial. That's because my brain reacts to sex and pornography as a crack addict's brain responds to crack cocaine—there's never enough of it, and it's the only thing that matters in the world. Poet Michael Ryan said it best in his memoir, *Secret Life*: "My primary loyalty was to sex. No human relationship took precedence over it. Not marriage, not friendship, and certainly not ethics."

My sex addiction has cost me many things—friends, romantic relationships, a job, and, on many days, my self-respect. But it has also given me my recovery, and for that I am grateful. My recovery has been far from perfect (when it comes to relapsing, celebrities have nothing on me), but it has undoubtedly saved my life—and, on many days, made that life worth living.

————

I tell you about my addiction not because it pleases me to do so (it doesn't), or because this book is about me (it isn't). *America Anonymous* is about eight men and women from around the country struggling with different manifestations of addiction. My story is relevant because it inevitably colors the way I conceptualize this topic. As someone in recovery from this disease—or illness, or disorder, or problem, or bad habit, or moral failing, or whatever you believe it to be—I came to this project with my fair share of biases.

First, I believe in an expanded understanding of addiction. That is, I believe that gambling, sex, food, spending, and work (to name a few) can, for some people, be as *addictive* and debilitating as an addiction to drugs. This is not a radical idea—an increasing number of addiction experts and researchers agree with this—but it is an important one that shaped the scope of this book.

As I searched for men and women to write about, I chose to define addiction broadly, immersing myself in the lives of a radio DJ addicted to food, a bisexual bodybuilder addicted to crystal meth and steroids, a college student addicted to sex and pornography, an eighty-year-old retiree addicted to alcohol, an unemployed former boxer addicted to heroin, a housewife addicted to shoplifting, a grandmother addicted to crack, and a drug and gambling addiction counselor addicted to—in his own words—"virtually everything."

I agree with Howard Shaffer, the director of the Division on Addictions at the Harvard Medical School, when he calls for a "syndrome model" understanding of addiction. Each outwardly unique manifestation of addiction, he believes, is likely part of the same underlying disorder. There is ample anecdotal evidence for this. Many addicts are hooked on more than one thing, and many will switch addictions if they give one up—witness the scene outside some Alcoholics Anonymous meetings, where recovering alcoholics clutch a cigarette in one hand and a cup of coffee in the other. (AA co-founder Bill Wilson smoked until his death from emphysema and pneumonia in 1971.)

Science also backs up the syndrome model. By studying the brain's reward and pleasure systems, researchers—many of whom used to dismiss an expanded understanding of addiction as just another example of this country's addiction to calling everything an addiction—are discovering that drugs and behaviors like gambling, sex, and overeating affect the brain in some similar ways as drugs.

The best definition of addiction I've found comes from a pamphlet published by Sex and Love Addicts Anonymous: *The use of a substance or activity, for the purpose of lessening pain or augmenting pleasure, by a person who has lost control over the rate, frequency, or duration of its use, and whose life has become progressively unmanageable as a result.*

It's not a perfect definition. Cigarette smokers are hooked on one of the world's most addictive substances (nicotine), yet for those smokers who don't contract cigarette-related illnesses, it's a stretch to argue that cigarettes cause progressive unmanageability in their lives.

The same is true for someone hooked on the world's most abused substance—caffeine. Four trips a day to Starbucks likely constitutes an unhealthy dependence on coffee, but does it cause severe negative consequences? Probably not. As writer John Ernest McCann put it, caffeine "intoxicates, without inviting the police." (In one large-scale study, it also proved to be a lifesaving coping mechanism. Nurses who drank two to three cups of coffee each day were significantly less likely to commit suicide than nurses who abstained.)

Still, it would be foolish to claim that people reliant on nicotine or caffeine to get them through the day don't suffer from addictions. They may not need rehab, but they are undeniably hooked.

So what happens if we scrap *progressively unmanageable* from the above definition? Does that mean that anything we do in excess to lessen pain or augment pleasure constitutes an addiction? Can we be addicted to things that are *good* for us? Further complicating any attempt to define addiction is that it is undeniably a cultural construct—what's good or bad for us is in the eye of the beholder. Countries and cultures understand the problem of addiction, and propose dealing with it, in different ways.

In China, for instance, addiction is still widely viewed as profound moral failing demanding punitive action. Many Chinese drug abusers are sent to labor camps, where they receive little treatment. And until a few years ago, police in China would sometimes shoot heroin dealers in the head and send a bill for the bullet to their families. In recent years, the Chinese government has become fixated on preventing and treating Internet addiction, particularly video game addiction among its young people.

In France, meanwhile, "recovering alcoholics" are a rarity, and food and sex addiction are mostly mocked as silly American inventions. So are there fewer addicts in France, or is the country in deep, blissful denial? Having spent plenty of time there, my guess is that it's probably a combination of both. But it's difficult to say for sure, because the French have a staggeringly different (and, I would argue, generally healthier) relationship to food, alcohol, and sex than we do. If the French don't have a cultural framework for food or sex addiction, can we label their behavior *addictive*?

Here at home, we've been maddeningly inconsistent in our understanding of addiction and recovery. We've vacillated throughout our history on what constitutes an addiction, what causes addiction, and what can be done to treat addiction. We've also changed our minds countless times about which drugs are most problematic and addictive (we've been perhaps the most befuddled by cocaine, which has been considered everything from an addiction cure to the most addictive substance ever). Occasionally there was a scientific basis for why we stigmatized a particular drug, but just as often it was based on political or economic interests.

"Merchants, capitalists, and the political elites who tax them have long appreciated that drugs are seductive products and lucrative sources of revenue," historian David Courtwright writes in *Forces of Habit: Drugs and the Making of the Modern World.* "The clash between opportunities for profit and concerns about health forms the central moral and political conflict running through the history of psychoactive commerce. . . . The growing cost of the abuse of manufactured drugs turned out to be a fundamental contradiction of capitalism itself."

For most of the 1800s, there were no laws in this country regulating drug use, even as many Americans were hooked on opium and its derivatives. We mostly tolerated drugs, just as we tolerated—and sometimes celebrated—our cultural inebriety. Americans drank more alcohol per capita between 1800 and 1830 than at any other time in our history. While some sounded an alarm (journalist Anne Royall wrote in 1830, "When I was in Virginia, it was too much whiskey—in Ohio, too much whiskey—in Tennessee, it is too, too much whiskey!"), few thought of perennial drunkenness as anything approaching a *disease*.

One man who did was doctor and Founding Father Benjamin Rush, who in 1810 articulated the idea that alcoholism—although the word itself wouldn't be introduced until 1849 or used widely until nearly a century later—was a progressive illness, and that the only solution was abstinence. Rush believed that lasting sobriety could be achieved through "religious, metaphysical, and medical" avenues, and that addicts seeking recovery should be placed in a "sober house" where they could be treated.

Rush conceded that he had few backers in these beliefs. In an essay, he wrote, "I am aware that the efforts of science and humanity, in applying their resources to the care of a disease induced by a vice, will meet with a cold reception from many people."

But by the mid- and late 1800s, Rush's beliefs were gaining currency. Addiction was increasingly being understood as an illness that wasn't necessarily the result of vice (heredity probably had a lot to do with it). Many called for a compassionate response, prompting treatment centers to sprout up across the country.

Speaking at an 1842 meeting of the Washingtonian Society (a short-lived fellowship for alcoholics seeking sobriety), Abraham Lincoln argued that addiction should not be viewed in moral or criminal terms. "In my judgment," he said, "such of us who have never fallen victims [to addiction] have been spared more by the absence of appetite than from any mental or moral superiority over those who have."

But the winds of public opinion shifted again early in the twentieth century. As the word "addict" came into common usage, it resonated "around stereotypes of the opium-smoking Chinese immigrant, the 'cocaine-crazed' and sexually threatening African-American male, the marijuana-smoking and violent Mexican youth of the Southwest," Janet Farrell Brodie and Marc Redfield write in the introduction to *High Anxieties: Cultural Studies in Addiction.* "Medical professionals, police and criminologists, government bureaucrats, policymakers, and social reformers harnessed the mass media, the language of statistics and academia, and harrowing descriptions of newly discovered 'deviant subcultures' to mount campaigns against the perceived threats of racial minorities, the urban poor, and the foreign born. Anxieties about addiction meshed with wider American anxieties about lost autonomy and the dangers of the un-American."

In 1914, the federal government began regulating the sale and possession of narcotic drugs. Sixteen years later, the establishment of the Federal Bureau of Narcotics prompted the first of the century's drug wars. By then, most of the treatment centers founded in the 1800s had long closed. "The country eventually fell sway to the argument that, if alcohol and other drugs were effectively prohibited, there would be no need for addiction treatment programs," William White writes in *Slaying the Dragon: The History of Addiction Treatment and Recovery in America.*

How wrong we were. Today, nearly 23 million Americans—9.2 percent of the population twelve or older—are hooked on alcohol or drugs, another 61 million smoke cigarettes, and millions more are slaves to gambling, compulsive overeating, and sex and pornography.

Those men and women who don't die from their addictions clog our hospitals, courts, and prisons, and the neglected and abused children of addicts overcrowd our juvenile justice and child welfare systems. (More than 70 percent of abused and neglected kids in family court and child welfare agencies have substance-abusing parents.)

In 2007, the economic cost from alcohol and drug abuse alone was estimated to be $534 billion. But as Joseph Califano Jr. makes clear in his book *High Society: How Substance Abuse Ravages America and What to Do About It*, the real cost of substance abuse is practically incalculable: "What funds terrorism, spawns crime, drives up health care costs, breaks up families, spreads AIDS, promotes unwanted teen pregnancy, and frustrates so many efforts to eliminate poverty?" The answer, he correctly points out, is "substance abuse and addiction."

Remarkably, while untreated addiction triggers and exacerbates many of our country's most pressing problems, we seem uninterested in tackling it—or even talking honestly, intelligently, or compassionately about it. And, sadly, politics and profit seeking continue to have more to do with how we combat addiction than does science or rational thinking. (How else to explain that the two deadliest substances in America—nicotine and alcohol—are legal, while marijuana, which kills virtually no one, remains the obsessive focus of our staggeringly ineffective drug war.)

But effectively combating addiction would require more than a complete rethinking of our drug policies. It would necessitate nothing short of a radical cultural shift of consciousness. In his book *Addictive Thinking: Understanding Self-Deception*, Abraham J. Twerski points out that curbing addiction would demand that American culture establish a "tolerance for delay" and "ultimate goals in life other than sense gratification."

In 1948 author and Trappist monk Thomas Merton wrote, "We live in a society whose whole policy is to excite every nerve in the human body and keep it at the highest pitch of artificial tension, to strain every human desire to the limit and to create as many new desires and synthetic passions as possible."

Sixty years later, as we find more and more ways to distract ourselves—and as we obsessively search for new and innovative ways to escape the reality of the present moment and make ourselves feel "better"—we've created a schizophrenic culture where nothing is ever enough, where stillness is equated with boredom, and where we need increasingly intense experiences just to feel alive.

In essence, we've created a culture that supports and encourages addiction while at the same time shames, ridicules, and criminalizes those of us afflicted with it. As writer and addiction psychologist Stanton Peele once said, "Addiction is not, as we like to think, an aberration from our way of life. Addiction is our way of life."

But recovery is the American way of life, too. We are a nation of anonymous Twelve Step soldiers in a war against our insatiable appetites. Unfortunately, the collective recovery of these millions of men and women has had little impact on the stigma and confusion that still shape our cultural understanding of addiction.

Although the American Medical Association first defined alcoholism as a disease in 1956, a series of recent focus groups sponsored by the National Council on Alcoholism and Drug Dependence, and Faces and Voices of Recovery, makes clear just how far we are from accepting addiction as a true medical disorder.

Half the participants called it a personal weakness, and even most who saw addiction as a disease put it in a special category, along with AIDS and lung cancer, that people get by making poor choices. In a 2004 poll of the general public, two-thirds said they believe that a stigma—defined by the pollsters as "something that detracts from the character or reputation of a person, a mark of disgrace"—exists toward people in recovery.

Even the family members of addicts seem conflicted. In a *USA Today*/HBO drug addiction poll of adults with an addicted family member, 76 percent called addiction a "disease," but a majority of those same respondents identified "lacking will power" as the main impediment facing addicts. If those closest to addicts erroneously believe that willpower is their loved one's main problem, then it's no surprise that nearly half said they felt shame over having an addicted family member.

Ironically, people in recovery, many of whom have been sober for decades, are partly responsible for our cultural confusion and apathy surrounding addiction. By keeping our recoveries private and anonymous at all costs (except for the addicted celebrity, who often enters and exits rehab with great fanfare), we have unwittingly excluded addiction and recovery from the national conversation and cemented the popular belief that being hooked is something to be ashamed about.

But that may be about to change. Across the country, a growing number of people in recovery from drugs and alcohol are coming together to speak out. They're holding marches, lobbying Congress for more research and treatment funding, challenging a federal law that barred young people convicted of felony drug offenses from receiving federal student loans, and otherwise coming out of the closet as people in recovery—advocating with anonymity by not naming the specific recovery fellowship they belong to, in keeping with the Twelve Step traditions that have been so critical to the success of groups like AA.

"Can you imagine the power of millions of recovering addicts walking on Washington, demanding that the government devote as much money to addiction research and treatment as they do to breast cancer and AIDS?" wonders addiction expert Patrick Carnes. "I predict it will happen, but I wonder how many more addicts will have to die before it does."

I share Carnes's frustration. But I also worry about the millions of us who *won't* die, who will live out our lives convinced it's the only way to live, medicating our pain and trauma with whatever substance or behavior best does the trick. "Like a cattle prod jabbed into someone who is exhausted and dazed, an addictive hit jolted us into a temporary illusion that we were alive and really living," reads the main text of Sex and Love Addicts Anonymous. Those same words apply to active addicts suffering from many manifestations of addiction.

For the most part, the addicts I followed for this book aspired to a different life. Not an easy life, to be sure, but a life free of cattle prods and shackles. Sometimes they faltered, and sometimes they *really* faltered, but most never lost sight for long of the life they aspired to. I am privileged to have witnessed them on a portion of their recovery journey, and I am honored by the opportunity to tell their stories.

1 BOBBY

The drug is at once pain and relief, poison and medicine; to be an "addict" is to live this circularity, with nothing at the origin but a sickness that strengthens itself in curing itself.

—JANET FARRELL BRODIE AND MARC REDFIELD,
HIGH ANXIETIES: CULTURAL STUDIES IN ADDICTION

THE MAIN FLIGHT path into Boston's Logan Airport takes air travelers over the eastern edge of South Boston, an insular Irish Catholic community best known for its gangsters and addicts (and for its nickname, Southie). Today, the gangsters are mostly gone, but the addicts are as stuck in this neighborhood as they are on the drugs that make living here bearable.

"Sometimes I think God could do us a favor and crash a 747 into this fucking place," Bobby says, standing barefoot in the kitchen of his parents' Southie brownstone, smoking a cigarette and loading dirty glasses and plates into the dishwasher. A thirty-four-year-old heroin addict, Bobby didn't want me to come over until he got high. "I got some about twenty minutes ago," he shouts from the kitchen.

"That's all I've been thinking about since I woke up. How am I going to get what I need? That's all I ever think about anymore."

His younger brother, Dan, sits on a red couch in the living room clutching a copy of the book *Boyos*, a novel set in Southie's criminal underworld written by a former state trooper who started robbing armored cars. Dan can relate to good guys doing bad things. A few years ago, when Dan was twenty-five, he was arrested for holding up a pharmacy for OxyContin, although the charges didn't stick.

High on Oxys (as he is now), Dan, who is boyish and handsome, likes to read. "I can read ten books in a row on Oxys!" he tells me proudly, sitting upright on the couch in baggy blue warm-up pants and a blue-collared shirt. Oxys make Dan feel smart. On them, he's not some Southie loser with no college degree, no job, no apartment, and a daughter he never sees. On Oxys, the former two-sport varsity athlete is a *Southie intellectual*, even if he doesn't always have the vocabulary to back it up.

"You know, when Oxys first came out, a lot of people around here thought heroin was voodoo," he tells me. Dan says "voodoo" a few more times before his brother can't stand it any longer. "You mean *taboo*," Bobby shouts from the kitchen. "Not *voodoo*. *Taboo!*"

Dan ignores him. "So the kids that would never dream of sticking a needle in their arm, they thought Oxys must be okay, because a doctor made it, ya know? What they didn't realize was that it's basically heroin in a pill. And then when they ran out of money and couldn't afford the Oxys anymore, they switched over to heroin, because they needed *something*. So kids either went to treatment, or they started using heroin."

"Or they killed themselves," Bobby says, walking purposefully into the living room and scanning the area for any dirty dishes. He scoops up a half-empty glass of Sprite from the top of the television and sits down, his hulking body (6-foot-5, 250 pounds) sinking into a beige sofa. He's wearing jeans, a gray long-sleeve shirt, and a red beanie over messy blond hair. He looks like an out-of-shape professional football player.

"I remember when I first saw an Oxy pill," Bobby tells me. He pauses, then takes a drag from his cigarette. "It was '96 or '97, and I was down in the projects when this kid came up to me and had these rough-looking pills. They were forty milligrams of OxyContin, but I didn't know that at the time. He didn't know what he had, either. He had taken them from some old guy who was dying, and he had a whole fucking container of them! So I was like, 'All right, I'll buy a few of those.' So I bought like ten for $4, which is so cheap, because now they're $40 a piece. So then I did them, and I was like, 'Oh, shit, what the fuck is this?' I started calling them *super-perps*. So the next day I went back and bought every single one off the guy for $4 a piece. He found out later what he actually had, and one day he saw me and he was like, 'You fuckin' motherfucker.'"

OxyContin—a controlled-release pain formula approved in 1995 by the FDA amid the heightened awareness that millions of Americans were suffering from chronic pain—was supposed to be less addictive than other painkillers. But by the late 1990s, people in Massachusetts and in many other states had figured out that if they crushed the pill or dissolved it in water, it created a staggeringly powerful high.

Dan never drank or used drugs until he was twenty-two, and for two years he resisted offers from friends to try Oxys. But when his relationship with his longtime girlfriend soured, Dan moved back into his parents' house and worked odd jobs. With seemingly little to live for, trying the drug didn't seem like that big a deal.

"It started as a weekend thing, but then before I knew it I was craving it, and then I needed it to function," he says, in perhaps the most concise and accurate description of the progression from habit to addiction I've ever heard.

Dan stands up and then sits down again. He does this often when

he's high—occasional bursts of movement without really going anywhere. Bobby gets up, too, although he shuffles back to the kitchen.

"Fuck!" Bobby screams a minute later, kicking the dishwasher in
frustration. "Fucking thing won't work. Did you put the dishwasher
stuff in the dishwasher?"

"Yeah, Bobby, now let me talk to him, will ya? Relax, we can do
it later."

"I want to do it *now*," Bobby says, hunched over at the waist and
frantically pushing buttons on the machine. As is his pattern, he goes
from calm to enraged in the span of a minute. He grabs the cord-
less phone and starts jabbing at the number keys. "It won't work!
It won't go on! I'm trying to tell you it won't work!" he screams to
someone on the other end of the line. I'm curious to know who he's
talking to, but I'm afraid to ask. I've been warned by several people
who know Bobby well to stay out of his way when he's angry, or
when he's desperate to find drugs.

"He has mood swings," Dan explains. "He's just a totally different person on heroin. You should see him when he's sober. He's a
great guy!" (I already have. I met Bobby a few months ago at a community meeting about addiction, where he was a few days clean and
said he was finally ready to stop using for good. But when it came
time for him to get into a friend's car and be driven to a local treatment center, he changed his mind.)

"Fuck!" Bobby screams again from the kitchen.

"Bobby, relax," Dan says.

"I hate this stupid thing. I'm trying to fucking clean, you know?
Why won't this thing work? All I want to do is the fucking dishes."

And then, a miracle: The machine starts working. Bobby hangs
up the phone. "Okay, now who wants food?" he asks, opening the
oven where he's been heating up a frozen pizza. The rage is gone as
quickly as it came. He tosses the pizza on a plate and joins us in the
living room, plopping himself down on the sofa again.

"You can't really keep a job on Oxys," Dan says, picking up where he left off before Bobby's tantrum. "So now I don't do anything all day, really. And I'm stuck in this fucking town."

"Our parents are in denial about Dan's addiction," Bobby tells me, coughing loudly. "I'm the addict, I'm the fuck-up of the family. They must know about Dan, but it's like they don't *want* to know. You gotta understand, there's a lot of dysfunction and denial in our family. I can't think of any family around here where there isn't addiction. Parents are alcoholics. Kids are alcoholics and drug addicts. Look around Southie. What do you see? You see a fucking liquor store and church on every other corner. So people can drink their life away, and then they can go and pray and ask God to make it all better."

While Dan has never been to treatment ("It's just not my thing"), Bobby estimates that he's been in and out of some seventy detoxes and residential treatment centers. Space in treatment centers isn't always easy to come by, but Bobby has an advantage. His godmother, Margaret, works for a local anti-addiction community group. Margaret spends her days counseling Southie parents, shuffling their kids to treatment and drug court, and making sure her own kids don't start using.

Bobby's longest periods of sobriety have come in jail. He's been convicted of drug possession and assault, serving a total of three years. "In jail, I'm working out, I'm eating right, and I'm clean," he explains. "When I get out, I end up back in Southie, around the same people, places, and things. But I don't want to leave my kids." (Bobby has two sons—they're seven and ten—who live with his ex-girlfriend.)

I ask Dan and Bobby if it's possible to stay sober in Southie. "It's hard, but it's possible," Dan says, standing up and pacing around the couch. "Some of my friends go to AA meetings all the time, and they're clean. They're always like, 'Dan, you should come to a meet-

ing. Dan, you can change your life. Dan, come on.' But there's a lot
of cliques in AA and stuff. I'm not a person who deals well with
cliques and phonies, you know? Plus I've probably had a run-in with
half the people in the room at AA. Some stupid fight over drugs, or
a girl. But I can talk to people I know in AA and basically have a
meeting like I'm doing right now with you. You know what I mean?
This is sort of like an AA meeting right now, but without the fucking
cliques. You know what I mean?"

I don't know what he means. This is far from an AA meeting, and
while Dan desperately wants me to agree with him, I'm uncomfortable supporting his rationalizations. "I don't know," Dan continues.
"Maybe in the future I'll go. I want to get into the Marines, and I'll
have to be clean for that. But if I don't do the Marines, I'll probably
start going to AA."

Dan sits down and squeezes his book tight. Bobby takes a big bite
out of his pizza, smacking loudly as he chews. I ask Bobby if he has
plans to return to treatment. "I'll go back soon enough," he says.
"I'll get sick of this life, like I always do, and I'll go."

"When?" I ask him.

"I'll go when I go. I don't know."

2 MARVIN

Alcohol, and not the dog, is man's best friend.

—W. C. FIELDS

"HI, FOLKS, MY name is Marvin, and I'm an alcoholic."

"Hi, Marvin!"

As I survey the crowded room of gray-haired grandparents with hearing aids, walkers, and oxygen tanks, I have to remind myself where I am. This is not Friday night bingo. This is an AA meeting unlike any I have seen. Once a week, the Hanley Center in West Palm Beach—one of the few treatment centers in the country with a program designed specifically for seniors—hosts a Sober Seniors meeting, which is open to both current patients and addicts from around the area. At thirty, I'm the youngest person here by some twenty years.

It's Marvin's turn to hand out sobriety chips, and he gets right down to business. (Sobriety chips are coins signifying that a person has attained a period of sobriety.) First is the "surrender chip," meant for those who want to affirm their willingness to do whatever it takes to stay sober today.

"I picked mine up here two years ago," he tells the group of about thirty-five seniors. "And thanks to my higher power, I still haven't had a drink. I rub it every day! So, who wants to start a new way of life today?" An elderly woman with gray hair and a slow, defeated gait makes her way to the front of the room, where Marvin hands her a chip and a bigger hug than she anticipated.

(During AA's early years, many members didn't believe women could be "real" alcoholics. In an AA newsletter published in 1946, a male member specified eleven reasons why women shouldn't be allowed in meetings, including "women talk too much," "women's feelings get hurt too often," "so many women want to run things," "many women form attachments too intense—bordering on the emotional," and "sooner or later, a woman-on-the-make sallies into a group, on the prowl for phone numbers and dates." The wives of some early AA members were so threatened by single and divorced women attending meetings that they demanded that men and women sit on opposite sides of the room.)

Looking dapper in a green golf shirt and khakis, Marvin, who recently turned eighty and has a heavily wrinkled face and thinning gray hair, waves another chip in the air. "Anybody else?" he asks. "Where there's one, there's two!" When no one comes forward, Marvin moves on. "Okay, so the next chip is for thirty days. After thirty days, you're feeling pretty good, the mind is clearing a bit. It's a green chip, a *green light* if you will, to keep doing what you're doing." He hands out two thirty-day chips and two bear hugs.

"So after thirty days we have a chip for sixty days," Marvin says, to which he is promptly corrected by most people in the room. There is no sixty-day chip. "Right, right," Marvin says. "*Ninety* days. Anyone for a ninety-day chip? By this time your mind is really starting to clear. Your life is getting better. Things are looking up! Anyone for thirty days?"

The crowd corrects him again—he's on ninety days, not thirty—although this time most people in the room find the mistake hilarious. A woman who's been knitting quietly in a corner starts giggling uncontrollably, and a frail man slaps his knee.

It's not the first time this group has broken out into laughter.

In his book *Slaying the Dragon*, William White notes that the levity of many AA meetings can surprise—even offend—nonalcoholic professionals attending as an observer (some Twelve Step meetings are open to those wishing to learn more about addiction). "The laughter within AA is not the superficial tittering of the cocktail party or the gallows laughter of the actively addicted," White writes. "This is the boisterous, knowing belly-laughing of healing."

When everyone settles down, Marvin, who's still smiling, decides to use his forgetfulness as a life lesson. "See," he tells the group. "This is what happens when you drink too much in your life! Let me be a warning to you all."

Later that afternoon, Marvin invites me to the modest first-floor condo he shares with his wife, Mary, in a retirement complex. When I arrive, Marvin orders me to remove my shoes. "This is condo living," he says, pointing to the wall-to-wall white carpeting. Marvin is watching Fox News, but he turns off the television and invites me to the enclosed back patio, where we sit facing a grass courtyard.

"So, this is where a recovering alcoholic lives," Marvin tells me, holding his glasses in one hand and a crumpled piece of paper in the other. "A *damn old* recovering alcoholic." Mary joins us a few minutes later. She wears a yellow-collared golf shirt and checked pants and looks a bit like an older version of Susan Sarandon.

I ask the couple when Marvin's drinking started getting out of control. Mary doesn't hesitate—she says it all began after a serious heart attack forced him to retire at fifty-eight from his management position at an insurance company.

"Before that," Mary explains, "he would have his one cocktail at night, which was fine. He would sometimes drink too much on the weekends, but it wasn't anything unusual. When he stopped working, though, he started needing cocktails during the day, too. Eventually it got so bad he had to have it *all the time*. I could barely communicate with him, he wasn't taking care of himself, and he got nasty, really mean."

Marvin mostly drank at home, but he occasionally passed out drunk at social functions and had to be carted home. His alcoholism was obvious to everyone but himself. His doctor told him he had a problem ("So I fired him!" Marvin says), and his brother-in-law suggested he go to an AA meeting. "I thought they were all crazy—and I told them that, too! I said, 'You're all a bunch of crazy buffoons!'"

He eventually collapsed one night in his kitchen and was rushed to the emergency room, spending five days in an alcohol-induced coma. He was then referred to Hanley, where he still denied being an alcoholic. "Excuse me guys and gals," he defiantly told everyone in group therapy, "but *you're* the sick ones. I don't belong here. I'll be outta here tomorrow, once I talk to my lawyer!"

Marvin ended up staying for thirty days (he celebrated his seventy-ninth birthday in treatment), but by the end he still hadn't fully accepted the extent of his drinking problem. "When I was leaving they made me agree to call this guy who had graduated from Hanley before me, so he could take me to AA meetings," Marvin says. "I agreed, because I'm a man of my word. So I told him, 'Look, you're dealing with an old guy who's pretty flaky, so I'm going to do this AA thing at my pace, and I don't want you giving me a hard time.' He looked at me and said, 'Sit down, pop, and listen to what I'm going to tell you, because you do way too much talking.' That guy saved my life. He was the guy who got me to admit that I'm an alcoholic."

Unlike many alcoholics who start drinking heavily early in life, Marvin, who was born in Manhattan in 1925, didn't show much interest in alcohol as a teen. But Marvin says his father did enough drinking for the entire family. He was a functioning alcoholic—he never missed a day of work, but he also never came home sober.

"On holidays," Marvin recalls, "my mother would say, 'Go to work with your father and see if you can bring him home sober.' It never worked."

After serving three years in the Navy during World War II, Marvin returned home at twenty and bought a little house in Levittown, a suburb of New York City generally regarded as the model for postwar veteran communities. He married Mary and worked several part-time jobs, including one delivering beer to bars and liquor stores. Before heading off to Korea for the war, Marvin also worked for two years as a highway patrol officer.

"I got to meet a *lot* of alcoholics in that job—I pulled them all over!" he says with a laugh. "I worked the midnight-to-8 A.M. shift, and I had my own way of dealing with the drunks. I would say, 'Give me your keys, and I'll give them to you when I get off duty. You just sit in the car and sleep it off. When you get home to your wife, you'll have to pay your fine there.' I used to do that all the time. In fact, I was in an AA meeting once and I told my story, and this guy came up to me and said, 'I remember you! You pulled me over on the Southern State Parkway!'"

Today, Marvin has been sober more than two years, and he's structured his life around the six or so AA meetings he attends each week. He's even earned the nickname "Mellow Marvin" from his AA friends. "Before they called me *Mad Marvin*, because I had so much anger," Marvin tells me. "But Mellow Marvin works better. I'm a *lover*, not a fighter!"

He says his grandchildren actually like being around him now, and that they always ask him for words of AA wisdom. Marvin's recent favorite: *I no longer attend every argument I'm invited to.*

Mary chuckles at that. "He is a lot better since he stopped drinking," she says. "But don't get me wrong. He doesn't need liquor to be difficult."

3   TODD

A junkie is someone who uses their body to tell society that something is wrong.

—Stella Adler

TODD, A FORTY-YEAR-OLD bisexual bodybuilder and male escort, kisses his wife goodbye in the driveway of their small apartment complex on a stormy weekend afternoon in the major city where they live. Julie is twenty-five and wears a tight T-shirt and short shorts, showing off thick, muscular thighs the size of my chest. Todd is in jeans, a white visor, and a form-fitting T-shirt that barely contains his massive chest, shoulders, and arms. Except for his small hands, which seem miscast, everything about Todd is cartoonishly large.

Fittingly, Todd met Julie at the gym. They flirted by the bench press for a few weeks before going on a date, during which Todd flung open the door to his closet full of skeletons: He told Julie that he took steroids (although she could tell that by looking at him), that until recently he had abused crystal meth, that for the last decade he had had sex only with men, and that he still worked as an escort for other men. Four months later, they were married.

"She's one of the most loving and understanding people I've ever met," Todd tells me as he directs me toward a loud, festive, gay-owned and -operated restaurant where he suggests we have lunch. (It strikes me as an odd choice for a married man who, except for his escorting work, says he's cut his ties to the gay community.)

Todd hasn't dated women since his twenties. "In my thirties I really just focused on guys," he says. "But I'm attracted to my wife both physically and emotionally. I guess I'm actually bisexual. I don't know—it's really confusing. But the year I've been with her has been incredible. Sometimes I wonder, though, if I'm going to wake up one morning and say, 'Who the hell am I, and what the fuck did I do?'"

While I met most of the addicts for this book through treatment centers or addiction experts, I was introduced to Todd through a friend, Christian Matyi, who has competed in bodybuilding for more than a decade. Christian has never used steroids and was originally drawn to the sport after entering addiction recovery fifteen years ago. In 2005, he founded Next Level, a bodybuilding educational foundation, and has since coached and mentored hundreds of athletes. (Although Christian requires them to be drug-free, he does welcome those who may have used or abused steroids in the past; about a third of them have, he says.)

Christian tries to incorporate Twelve Step principles into his bodybuilding seminars—including assembling athletes into teams to mimic a recovery fellowship—and is particularly drawn to helping those who struggle with addiction. While he never coached Todd, Christian said he immediately recognized him as an addict.

"He is the perfect example," Christian told me, "of a deeply addicted bodybuilder who is psychologically hooked on how he feels—or thinks he feels—when he's on steroids: powerful, dominant, unapologetic."

Like Todd, some bodybuilders, including many who identify as heterosexual, will do whatever it takes to keep their steroid supply coming. Some star in gay porn; others work as escorts for muscle-obsessed men.

"It's the sad, dirty little secret of the bodybuilding world," Christian said.

Todd has long been infatuated with muscular men. When he was nineteen, he hired a bodybuilder escort for his first same-sex experience. But he didn't start using steroids until his early thirties. "I made such good gains in my twenties that people accused me of taking them, so I felt that it wasn't necessary back then," he tells me at the restaurant, where he orders two large cheeseburgers. We're seated at a corner table in the crowded outdoor covered patio, and we have to speak up to compete with the loud dance music and the rain crashing against the patio tarp. "But then I got bored," he continues, "and I wanted to make gains faster. So I thought, why not? If I get this big naturally, then what could I do on steroids?"

Todd put less thought into trying crystal meth. He was thirty-seven, it was 4 A.M., and he was in the bedroom of a man he had met an hour earlier on the Internet. Todd was tired, but the man had a cure for that. They snorted meth, and soon Todd felt awake and sexually aroused—so much so that he got right back online when he got home after having sex with the man. The sun was rising, but it didn't take long to find another guy looking to PNP, short for "party and play," meaning to use meth and have sex.

(While at least 12 million Americans have tried meth, the drug has particularly ravaged two very different populations—poor rural men and women, and urban gay men. In the 1950s, though, legal pharmaceutical versions of the drug were marketed as "an all-purpose cure-all for the anomie afflicting depressed housewives," Frank Owen writes in *No Speed Limit: The Highs and Lows of Meth*. "The ones who first turned America onto methamphetamine in a big way weren't the Hells Angels or Mexican drug traffickers, but doctors and psychiatrists working in tandem with the pharmaceutical industry.")

Soon Todd was in the new stranger's bedroom, and this guy had an insulin needle on his nightstand. "How far are you willing to go?" the man wanted to know. No stranger to needles because of his steroid habit, Todd agreed to inject the drug.

"And then I saw God," Todd recalls. "It was so much better than snorting it. The next thing I know two days are gone, I'm having the time of my life with this guy. So finally I realize it's time to go home. I get home and I look at myself in the mirror, and it's *not* pretty."

But if Todd caught his reflection at the right time, meth made him feel Herculean. For the first six hours after injecting the drug, he would sometimes stand in front of a mirror and flex his muscles, staring at his reflection. "It was obviously me in the mirror, but for some reason my brain saw someone different, somebody else, somebody much more than me," he says. "In those times I stopped being Todd, and I sort of became *Billy*."

Billy is the name of a staggeringly arrogant, freakishly muscled teenage cartoon character. Since Todd first saw sketches of Billy online (in a typical one, Billy belittles an opponent in a high school wrestling match while the opponent, overcome with lust, performs oral sex on him), Todd has been obsessed with the cartoon. So much so that Todd can "slip into Billy character" when he's feeling particularly youthful and powerful, when he's living without fear of consequence.

"I can sometimes go into Billy mode sober," Todd tells me, "but I've never been able to feel as much like him as when I looked in the mirror on crystal. Problem is, after twelve or twenty-four hours on it, it all turns ugly, and I could barely look at my body. There's so much loss of water and body weight. Then after three days on a binge, your body grossly changes." Todd's longest binge lasted nearly five days. By the end he was bleeding from his skin. "I had blood coming out of my pores. I was delusional, I was crying and laughing and shaking."

Todd's meth use progressed from once every few weeks to every weekend, which affected what had been a rigorous and consistent workout regimen. He had gone to the gym at least four times a week since he was nineteen, sometimes competing in bodybuilding competitions. He had experimented with drugs before, but before meth nothing had interfered with his workouts.

Todd shared so many needles and had so much unsafe sex (a common occurrence for gay men on meth) that after a few years of using he assumed he was HIV positive. But he didn't want to know for certain, so he didn't get tested. And not wanting to infect anyone, he started seeking out only other HIV positive men for sex. (Todd turned out to be HIV negative.)

Yet it wasn't meth that got Todd in trouble with the law. It was steroids. He was busted for possession by two cops who work out at his gym. That landed Todd in drug court, where he admitted to his addiction to meth. Todd has four months until he graduates the drug court program. Until then, he attends court every Wednesday morning and submits to regular drug tests, although the court doesn't test for steroids (it's too expensive).

Todd says he hasn't used meth in eight months and that his body has mostly repaired itself. He certainly seems comfortable with his body at the restaurant. When he's done eating, he leans back in his chair, spreads his legs wide, tilts his head slightly to the left toward me, and folds his hands near his crotch, where he keeps them for the next fifteen minutes. Is he showing off? Flirting with me? I don't know, but it strikes me as the exaggerated pose of a cocky teenager feigning I'm-better-than-you lack of interest. It's how I imagine Billy the cartoon character might sit.

I want to ask him what the pose is about, but it's my first day meeting him, and I don't want to scare him off. He's expressed some reluctance to let me write about him, although he says that most of it comes from Julie.

"I don't have any problem talking to you," he tells me. "Actually,

I think talking to you will help. For the first six or seven months without crystal I was on a pink cloud, really enjoying being sober. But now the last month has been really hard. The urges are strong, and I'm not doing what I need to do for my recovery. I'm not going to meetings. I don't have a sponsor. I think I'm relying too much on the fact that I don't live alone now, and my wife won't tolerate my using crystal, so I don't see how I could even start it again, because it's all tied into me being alone and online and looking for sex."

More than anything, Todd hopes his dedication to sculpting his body will keep him from using meth again. "I still go to the gym every morning with my wife," he says. "It's a funny scene, because the cops who busted me are there working out in the morning, too. And they're *pissed*, because not only do I continue to get bigger, but I also nabbed the prettiest girl in the whole place. They're totally confused. The nice little faggot they arrested has the hottest girl in the gym."

4 ELLEN

When we drug ourselves to blot out our soul's
call, we are being good Americans. . . . We're
doing exactly what our TV commercials and
pop materialist culture have been brainwashing
us to do from birth.

—STEVEN PRESSFIELD, *THE WAR OF ART*

SAM, A TEN-YEAR-OLD in pajamas emblazoned with thunderbolts, seems concerned as his mother, Ellen, handles the matzoh during the family's Passover dinner. "Mom, doesn't that have flour in it?" he asks. Ellen smiles. "Yes, it does, but don't worry, I'm not going to eat it. We're just going to say a prayer, and then you guys can eat it."

"She can't eat white flour," Sam tells me.

His younger brother, seven-year-old Jesse, nods vigorously. "If she eats sugar or flour," Jesse explains, "she turns into a werewolf!"

Ellen says the werewolf seemed like a good analogy, because if she eats sugar or white flour, she could end up looking like a different person—a person who weighs three hundred pounds. Back when she was that heavy, Ellen ate enough each day for a family of three.

On her ten-minute drive to her job as a radio executive and DJ in a Northeastern city, she usually stopped twice, first for a few slices of breakfast pizza, then for two bagels with cream cheese and two cheese croissants.

"I would shove everything in my mouth except for one bagel before I got to work," she tells me, "so that when I walked into the office, I just had my little bag with a bagel—like a *normal person.*"

Ellen often left work mid-morning to get another bagel at Dunkin' Donuts, and for lunch she'd have a sandwich and chips from the sub shop next door. On her way home in the late afternoon, she usually stopped at the McDonald's drive-through window and ordered three combo meals.

"But I would order them all with drinks so that they would think they were for three different people," she says. At night, Ellen cooked dinner for her husband and children. And before going to bed, she usually ate pretzels or chips.

A failure at "every diet known to man," Ellen says it wasn't until she started attending Overeaters Anonymous meetings—and seeing her problem as a physical and psychological addiction—that she's been able to keep the weight off. Today, she weighs 125 pounds.

Ellen has a friendly, easygoing rapport with her kids, and it doesn't take long at dinner before we're all engaged in a lively conversation about addiction that feels part adult, part kid. (Her husband is working late tonight.)

"You guys know what addiction is, right?" Ellen asks the kids.

"Duh, of course!" says Jesse's twin, Ellie, the firebrand of the siblings. "Mom, we're going to have chocolate-covered matzoh for dessert, right?"

"Ellie's totally a sugar addict," Ellen tells me.

"Mom!" Ellie protests. "No, I'm not."

"Ellie, you've even told me that sometimes you can't stop yourself."

"Nu-huh."

"Yes, you have."

"Nu-uh."

"*Uh-huh*," Ellen says, doing her best imitation of a seven-year-old. ("I hear all these people at OA meetings tell me about behaviors they had when they were young," Ellen tells me privately later, "and Ellie has a lot of them. She obsesses over candy and sugar. She's even picked up gum off the floor to try to chew it. I really hope it doesn't happen, but if I have any kid who gets addicted to drugs or alcohol or food, it's going to be her.")

"What are some things that people get addicted to?" Ellen asks her kids.

"Well," Sam says dramatically, "I'm addicted to my toys. I know I'm a toy addict!"

Talk eventually turns to drugs, gambling, cigarettes, and Ellen's addiction, food. "If I'm not careful about what I eat," Ellen tells them, "I can get really sick."

"But you're not addicted anymore, right?" Jesse wants to know.

"Well, I still have to be careful."

"I bet you I could have one cigarette and stop," Jesse says.

Ellen shakes her head. "They put chemicals in there so you *can't* stop."

But Jesse won't be dissuaded. "I bet you I could have one and stop!"

"Ah," Ellen says with a laugh. "An addict's famous last words."

After dinner, as her kids chase each other around the two-story wooden house on a chocolate-covered-matzoh sugar high, Ellen tells me how she first realized she needed help.

"I had a great job, a great marriage, but I was just a shell of a person," she says, stepping around the family golden retriever and lifting the family cat off the kitchen counter. "I had no emotions, except maybe anger. I didn't know how to feel. I never really cried, because overeating was a way that I stuffed all my feelings. I worked all the time so I wouldn't have to think about my life. For forty-seven years of my life, I was like a zombie. But the thing is, I didn't realize it. I just knew something wasn't right, that I felt empty even though I was always stuffing myself with food."

Desperate, Ellen finally went to see Dru Myers, a food addiction specialist who founded Food Addiction Chemical Dependency Consultants in 1990. Dru was different from any therapist Ellen had ever seen. "She told me what to do," Ellen recalls. "I don't normally react well to that, but in this case I just surrendered to the idea that when it came to food, I clearly didn't know what was best."

First, Dru told Ellen to stop eating sugar and white flour. "I did what she suggested," Ellen recalls, "but then I had a huge withdrawal around it. I was dizzy, nauseous, couldn't sleep." Next, Dru started chipping away at when Ellen could eat. Dru asked Ellen if she could wait fifteen minutes without eating after dinner. Ellen could do that, so soon Dru pushed it to thirty minutes after dinner. Then it was forty-five minutes, then an hour, and pretty soon Ellen wasn't eating after dinner at all.

"Then she told me that I could eat three meals of any size," Ellen says, "but that I couldn't eat anything in between."

Finally, Dru told Ellen that she needed to attend OA, a Twelve Step fellowship founded in 1960. Ellen bristled at the idea. "I told her she was out of her mind," Ellen recalls. "The last thing I wanted to do was to go sit in a room with what I presumed to be a bunch of fat losers talking about how sad their lives were. I assumed I was different than them. I was better than them. I was smarter. A lot of typical judgmental addict shit. And I didn't want to hear anything about God or a higher power. I just wanted to lose weight."

But Dru kept badgering her, and Ellen grudgingly agreed to go. At her first meeting in 2001, Ellen spent much of the hour wondering who was in charge. Like AA and other Twelve Step fellowships, OA meetings are run by "group conscience." Members lead the meetings, and while each meeting has a structure (there are speaker meetings, meetings focused on one of the Twelve Steps, and topic meetings), there are no leaders or group facilitators. (Singer Grace Slick called Twelve Step meetings a "true democracy.")

"It all seemed so haphazard to me," Ellen recalls. "In my head I was like, 'Who's in charge here? What's the hierarchy? Who's the *president*?' I'm a manager, and it wasn't run like any organization I had ever seen. But once I relaxed and started listening to people, I knew I was in the right place. For so many years, I thought I was the only one."

Ellen was comforted when others spoke of their addiction to food as an illness or disease. "I didn't struggle accepting those words at all," she tells me. "I've always believed alcoholism and drug addiction are types of diseases, and when I looked at my life and how I used food, I used it exactly like a drug addict uses a drug. Food is my drug. I have no control over it."

Ellen was less comforted initially by all the talk of spirituality and developing faith in a higher power. Then an agnostic and self-described "cynical know-it-all," Ellen, like many addicts, couldn't wrap her head around Step Two and Step Three—*Came to believe that a Power greater than ourselves could restore us to sanity,* and *Made a decision to turn our will and our lives over to the care of God as we understood Him.* (See Appendix for the Twelve Steps.)

"I had prayed before in my life, but they were usually desperate prayers, like, 'God, please let me eat anything I want and still be thin!'" Ellen says. Still, the more meetings she attended, the more open she became to the spirituality of the Twelve Steps. No one was telling her what to believe, how to believe, or even that she *needed* to believe. Other members urged her only to be open to a spiritual way of life, however she chose to define it.

"And what did I have to lose?" she says. "Everything I had tried, all my *rational* attempts at self-control, hadn't worked. I was willing to try whatever I saw working for other people. But it's been my biggest challenge in recovery. I still struggle with letting go and getting beyond my ego, which thinks it should be able to control everything. I still struggle with having faith. If I can't see it or touch it—or, better yet, *taste* it—I have a hard time accepting that it's real."

5 SEAN

Every addiction arises from an unconscious refusal to face and move through your own pain. Every addiction starts with pain and ends with pain.

—ECKHART TOLLE, *The Power of Now*

SEAN HADN'T PLANNED on the cute, nosy teller at Sovereign Bank in Boston. "Are you okay?" she asks, seeming concerned as he fumbles through his transaction, avoids eye contact, and finally mumbles that he wants $400 from his savings, please. And no, Sean isn't *okay*, but is a teller window really an appropriate place for confession?

"Have a nice night," she says, smiling as Sean stuffs the money in his wallet and walks out the bank's front door, stepping into Boston's muddy winter slop. It is 5:45 P.M. on a Friday, a few hours since I last spoke with him by phone, and while other college students are gearing up for a night of partying or hanging out with friends, Sean is planning to take his cash and binge on pornography and escorts. (He recently got rid of the Internet in his apartment so he wouldn't have easy access to online porn.)

He flips his sweatshirt's hood over his curly blond hair and begins the short walk toward Amazing, a porn and erotica store near Fenway Park, the home of the Boston Red Sox.

It has been ninety days since the shy, boyish twenty-year-old did anything like this. It's his longest period of sexual sobriety since his first meeting of Sex and Love Addicts Anonymous (SLAA) in January 2004. At the time, he confided to his college roommate that he thought he might be a sex addict. "Dude," his roommate said incredulously, patting Sean heartily on the back. "We're guys. We're in college. We're *all* addicted to sex!"

But Sean suspects that he has long crossed the line from typical teenage obsession to sex addiction. Since the age of twelve, he has spent between one and five hours virtually every night watching Internet pornography, talking in sex chat rooms, and, later, cruising escort Web sites. In high school in Florida, he stayed up until 2 or 3 A.M. most nights masturbating to porn. He tried to cut down, but he couldn't.

"People at school assumed I was stoned all the time," Sean told me, "but I was really just exhausted. I didn't drink or do drugs. My drug was porn." An only child raised by what he calls his "alcoholic, emotionally abusive" mother, Sean said that going on the Internet made him feel "safe, comfortable, kind of happy. It put me in this trance, and all my problems went away."

Soon there were new problems. Sean spent so much time online that he didn't have any real friends, and he had no clue how to interact with girls. It got worse in college, as he spent most days alone in his dorm room watching porn. He spent hours looking at escort Web sites and even met a few escorts in person, blowing his meager savings. And when he moved into his own apartment off campus, he stood several hours a day for two weeks by the window of his street-level bedroom, hoping a gust of wind would lift a woman's skirt as she walked by. He kept telling himself to stop, to go outside, to do anything but stand by the window. But he couldn't move.

A therapist finally suggested that Sean attend an SLAA meeting. The Twelve Steps of SLAA are essentially unchanged from AA's
steps, except for replacing "alcohol" with "sex and love" and changing the end of Step Twelve from "practice these principles in all our
affairs" to "practice these principles in all areas of our lives." For a
sex addict, *affairs* is a loaded word.

In addition to SLAA, there are a handful of other Twelve Step
sexual recovery fellowships in this country. But unlike in AA, where
it's agreed that one drink is too many, there is no such consensus
in most sex addiction meetings. One program, Sexaholics Anonymous, suggests that its members refrain from masturbation or sex
outside of marriage, but most, like SLAA and Sex Addicts Anonymous, encourage addicts to develop their own sexual recovery goals
(sometimes called a "bottom line"), based on whatever behaviors
are most problematic and addictive. Abstain from those behaviors,
and you're considered sober. Sean's bottom line is simple: no escorts,
no pornography.

As Sean listened to men in SLAA meetings talk about how sex addiction destroyed their lives (some lost their wives, others their jobs),
he felt fortunate to have found recovery so young. He attended an
SLAA or Al-Anon (for friends and families of alcoholics) meeting
every day and felt better than he ever had, managing ninety days
without watching porn or hiring an escort.

But two days ago he came upon some pornographic images as he
was cleaning out files on his computer. Yesterday, he started obsessing
about the images and other pornography he'd seen. Today, he's taking
the next step. But as he hurries toward the porn store, a voice in his
head keeps telling him to turn around. *Yes, I am going to turn around.
Right now. Turning around right . . . now.* Sean keeps walking. But
didn't he want to turn around? It occurs to Sean that he should reach
out, make a phone call, ask for help. First he calls his SLAA sponsor,
but there's no answer. Next he calls another SLAA friend.

"Hey," Sean says, clutching the phone to his ear.

"Hey, buddy, how are you?"

"Oh, I'm okay."

"That's great."

"Well, actually, not really. I'm walking to a porn store right now."

"Really? That's probably not the best place for you to be, man."

"I know, I don't want to go."

"You don't *have* to go."

"I know."

"It might feel like you have to, but that's bullshit. That's the addict talking."

"Yeah, I know."

"So, why don't you turn around?"

"Yeah, I should. I have ninety days of sobriety."

"That's amazing, man."

"I want to get an escort, too."

"Wow, you got quite a night planned. Can I tell you something, though?"

"Yeah."

"If you play the tape through, all the way until the end, how do you think you'll feel when it's over?"

"Horrible. Pathetic. I don't want to go. But it's like I'm saying that to you now, and I *mean* it, but my body won't turn around. It's like I can't stop, like I don't have control over my body."

"I know what that's like, man. How about I come get you."

"Really?"

"Yeah, man, really."

"Awesome."

Sean tells his friend to meet him at a nearby intersection, but as Sean stands there waiting, thinking of how to pass the time, a thought occurs to him: *I should go to the porn store anyway.* So there he goes, sloshing through the wet snow, his legs taking him somewhere he doesn't really want to go. Or does he? Sean isn't sure what he wants anymore. Across town, his friend gets in his car, one addict on his way to help another.

Standing outside the porn store's front door, Sean tries one last grasp at self-control. *No, I don't want to go in. Don't fucking go in!* But Sean's legs aren't listening. They propel him inside, and once there he feels a sudden calmness. *This is where I'm meant to be*, he thinks to himself. He takes his sweet time, mulling his pornographic options, and finally settles on three DVDs. Then he hurries home, ignoring his friend's phone calls.

Sean doesn't hire an escort, but he does spend the next five hours masturbating to pornography. When he's done, he curls up in his bed and cries. The next day, he calls me, depressed and inconsolable: *I'm pathetic. I'm such a fucking loser. What the hell is wrong with me?*

6 JANICE

*Over the past century, both the ruin and the
superabundance of culture have been symbol-
ized by the addict, who has proved capable of
evoking by turns an urban, racialized under-
class, the glitter of jet-set consumption, or the
hothouse bloom of Wildean aestheticism.*

—Janet Farrell Brodie and Marc Redfield,
High Anxieties

JANICE, A FIFTY-FIVE-YEAR-OLD African-American grandmother, leaves
the dark, musty crack house on 144th Street in Harlem with good
intentions. She's alone (I won't meet her for another month, and
the addicts in the crack house want no part of her plan), but Janice
doesn't feel lonely. It is a clear and sunny morning, a day for bold actions and new beginnings. It's the perfect day, Janice says to herself,
to go to treatment and get clean.

What does one wear to treatment? Janice isn't sure, but it's not
like she has much to choose from. She's been living in crack houses
and homeless shelters for the past two years, often wearing the

same clothes for days at a time. This week's uniform is a baggy pair of purple sweatpants, a purple blouse, and well-worn dirty white sneakers.

Janice has a short walk to the subway station on Lenox Avenue, where she plans to ride the A train downtown to a state-funded outpatient treatment center recommended to her by a friend who is two years sober from crack. Janice can't imagine going two years without getting high (except for a short stint in jail, it's been more than twenty years since she's gone a week without drugs), but she is desperate enough to try.

I will do whatever I have to do to get my life back, she tells herself as she walks down the crack house's front steps, the sun reflecting off a church and a welfare hotel across the street. (In the six months that Janice has lived in this crack house, she's made friends with some residents of the hotel, who come over to get high after cashing their welfare checks.)

As she walks toward the subway station, Janice thinks about the life she used to have. Before drugs, Janice had her own apartment, worked several jobs (as a nurse's aide, a chambermaid, and an office assistant), and was a good mother to her two kids. In fact, in Janice's twenties and early thirties, friends of the plump, friendly Baptist often poked fun at her for being too good for her own good. They wanted her to take more risks, to live a little. Eventually, that meant trying what it seemed like everyone in Harlem was trying in the 1980s: crack cocaine.

But Janice didn't drink or smoke cigarettes, and she watched with amusement at parties when some of her friends disappeared into a bedroom to get high and emerged ten minutes later with goofy looks on their faces. Everyone kept pestering Janice to try it. "Come on," her downstairs neighbor said. "It's not going to hurt you!"

As predictions go, it was not a good one. Janice finally did try it, and before long she was shipping her kids off to her sister's or a baby-sitter so she could smoke crack in peace. When a neighbor finally called Child Protective Services to complain that Janice could no longer care for her children, Janice sent them to her sister's permanently. She visited several times a week, until one day her family wouldn't let her inside the house. "Not until you get some help," her eldest daughter, then twenty, told her.

Instead, Janice immersed herself even further into Harlem's drug culture. She hung out only with other users, and she began selling. Still, she didn't see herself as an out-of-control crack head. "I wasn't one of those girls who would stand on a doorstep offering hand jobs for drugs," she would later tell me. "I had an apartment. I still worked some regular jobs. I had food in the house. As long as I had those things, in my mind I was okay."

That illusion was shattered in 1996, when Janice was arrested for selling a small amount of crack and sentenced to six months in Rikers Island, the mammoth jail in the East River between the Bronx and Queens. Janice started getting high again the same day she was released. She no longer could afford her apartment, so she went to live for seven years with a boyfriend in Queens. When he suffered a stroke, Janice was back out on her own for two years, sleeping in shelters and crack houses.

That is, until this glorious morning. Her adult son has been trying to get her into treatment for years, and today she's finally going to make him proud. But as she makes her way toward the subway, she sees a familiar face approaching. It's Shaunie, a crack addict and neighborhood regular (he's white, a rarity in this part of Harlem).

Shaunie is perennially broke, and Janice has helped him over the years by connecting him with a loan shark she knows. Grateful for the help, Shaunie—who calls Janice by the nickname "Broker"—has always promised to hook Janice up with crack once his back Social Security check arrived.

"Broker!" Shaunie says, a big smile on his face.

"Yeah, what's up, Shaunie?"

"Guess what I got?"

"I don't know, Shaunie. What you got?"

"I got $300!"

Back to the crack house they go. When the money's nearly gone, Janice ventures outside to get some food, buy candles for the house (there's no electricity), and find more drugs. She isn't outside five minutes before she runs into a local dealer she's never bought from before.

"Come on," the dealer begs, "buy somethin' off me. You always say you're gonna buy somethin' off me, and you never do."

Janice isn't in the mood to go looking for another dealer, so she slips him $20 in a phone booth and he leaves some cocaine in a plastic sandwich bag on top of the phone. Next she's off to a local fried food restaurant, where she buys a carton of chicken to go, and then to a local convenience store, where she plans to get some candles for the house. But she never gets there. Two police officers stop her in front of Fatou, an African hair braiding shop on Adam Clayton Powell Jr. Boulevard, where they kindly let her finish her piece of chicken before arresting her.

To Janice's astonishment, she's not being busted for buying crack. She's being busted for *selling* it. "Either the guy I bought the drugs from lied and set me up, or he paid them off and the cops are crooked," Janice would later tell me. "I had sold drugs before, but not that day."

The state offers her a choice: two and a half years in prison (of which she likely would have to serve about fifteen months), or fifteen to twenty-four months in inpatient treatment as part of the state's Drug Treatment Alternative-to-Prison Program (DTAP), founded in 1990 as the nation's first prosecution-run program to divert felony offenders from prison to treatment. The judge wants to know: *What's it going to be?*

7 JODY

People who claim not to understand why anyone would get addicted to drugs are usually people who haven't tried them or who are genetically fairly invulnerable to them.

—ANDREW SOLOMON, *THE NOONDAY DEMON*

JODY, AN ADDICTION counselor at the Comprehensive Addiction Rehabilitation Education (C.A.R.E.) treatment center in North Palm Beach, Florida, wants to show me something. "I'm going to show you who the real fucking terrorists are," he says, pointing the way toward the beach of Singer Island. "We're off fighting terrorists in Iraq and all around the fucking world, but the real terrorists are already here."

I'm not sure what he means. Do terrorists hang out at the beach? Are they poisoning the drug supply? "Just drive," he says, laughing. It's a sweltering afternoon, and I'm driving because Jody—a tall and athletic thirty-two-year-old recovering addict (drugs, booze, gambling) with wavy brown hair, a white Billabong T-shirt, and black wraparound sunglasses—insists that he "can't see shit."

He's legally blind, which he's sure to remind any angry addict threatening to deck him. "I'll be like, sure, go ahead and hit a *blind man*," he tells me. "That really pisses them off, because they *really* want to hit me, and maybe I even deserve it, but what kind of ass-hole punches a blind dude?"

In truth, Jody isn't completely blind. He has retinitis pigmentosa, an inherited disorder that often causes tunnel vision. But Jody says he has an unusual form of RP—he sees better peripherally than he does directly in front of him, which means that he'll stare at my right armpit when he's actually looking at my face. Or, seated in the passenger seat of a car, he'll look straight ahead but actually be eyeing me. Still, he can barely make out faces, and he can't read or drive.

Although you wouldn't guess it by looking at him—he has the tanned, athletic appearance of a professional beach volleyball player in the twilight of his playing career—Jody used to be a big name in South Florida's addiction treatment industry. He co-founded two treatment centers, including C.A.R.E., and started his own addiction consulting firm, helping families find the right treatment center for an addicted family member.

"My reputation was golden back then," he says, lighting a cigarette. "People were like, 'Man, if you've been to every treatment center and you can't stay sober, you gotta get with this guy Jody.' I started making a ton of money."

He also started abusing his patients' pain medication, particularly the ADD drug Adderall. When his patients confronted him ("Not exactly how a treatment center is supposed to work," he concedes), he took off for Virginia on a four-month crack and heroin binge. He didn't pay his staff, didn't pay the mortgage. Eventually his staff quit, and his patients were evicted.

Two years clean from that debacle, Jody is back at C.A.R.E., although now he's only an entry-level counselor. He lives where he works, in a tiny apartment on a palm-tree-lined block of modest one-story homes, a handful of which were converted into apartments for the sober living community he manages. Addicts can stay there for up to a year or so after completing inpatient treatment at C.A.R.E. or another rehab center.

As we drive toward the beach and the mysterious terrorists, Jody's cell phone rings constantly. One call is from Melanie, a young woman Jody knows who's having trouble staying clean.

"What's up, Melanie? How are you? Are you still sober?"

I hear her say "Yes."

"Oh, what do ya got, ten days?" Jody asks her.

"Don't make fun of me, Jody," she says.

"I'm proud of ya. I'm not making fun. Are you ready to go to Wayside house yet?" (Jody has been trying to get her into a treatment center that specializes in trauma and addiction.) "I care about you and I think it would be helpful. I think it would change your life, but you probably don't want that, so I understand."

"Don't say that, Jody. I want that."

"You do want that? You want me to call them right now? I'll call right now." Silence. She doesn't say anything. "Ah, I see, so you don't want it right now, you want it *later*?"

"Jody, I mean—"

"So you're saying you might want to change your life *later*? You're okay with your life being a fucking mess right now?"

"It's not a mess," she says, sounding defensive and hurt.

"Listen, Melanie, I'll call ya tomorrow. Okay?" He hangs up. "Obviously, she ain't ready," he says. The exchange is typical Jody. If an addict is willing to do the work to get sober, Jody will stand by her through all of it. But he has little patience for people who won't accept help. "I'm not going to go chasing after her and try to convince her that she needs treatment," Jody says. "I'm busy enough with the people who *want* to get better."

A few minutes later, Jody tells me to stop the car in a half-empty outdoor parking lot a block away from the beach. He turns up the air conditioner and points toward a yellow, three-story hotel about fifty yards away. Although it's a gorgeous day, the drapes are drawn in most of the hotel's windows.

"That over there is a crack hotel," he says. "The dealers, and the people who run hotels like that, are the real fucking terrorists. They have destroyed more families and killed more people than Osama bin Laden killed on 9/11. Man, we're off in Iraq and Afghanistan trying to kill terrorists, but the terrorists are already here! We're fighting the *wrong war*."

"There is a war on drugs," I remind him.

"And what a waste of fucking money that is," he says. "We're fighting it in the stupidest way. Of the thousands of addicts I've met through the years, I've never had one tell me that the reason they got clean was because they couldn't find drugs anymore. Not one."

Jody's cell phone rings again. This time it's Frank, a former resident at Jody's sober living community.

"How you doing, man?" Jody asks him. "You still sober?"

"Yeah, pretty much," I hear Frank say.

"Pretty much?"

"Yeah, not really."

"Huh? You aren't making any sense."

"I'm doing good."

"You smoking crack?"

"Nah, none of that."

"So how are you *pretty much* sober? You drinking, smoking weed?"

"Yeah."

"Well, it's better than smoking crack, but that ain't sober, man. Hey, let me call you back."

"Okay."

Jody opens the passenger-side window and lights another cigarette. "So you know how we talk about the first step of recovery being breaking through the denial and admitting you have a problem?" he asks me. "Well, that's not just for addicts like Frank who's smoking weed and drinking but who thinks he's *pretty much sober* because he's not shooting dope. We're a fucking country in denial, man, and we won't admit that we have a massive fucking problem. Not just in some neighborhoods. In *all* neighborhoods. But the politicians won't touch it, except to say that we need to build more jails and be tougher on crime. We still have the idiotic notion that addicts somehow brought their addiction upon themselves, that addicts are dangerous fuck-ups who just need to grow some willpower and pull themselves up by the boot straps and get their shit together. And the politicians and insurance companies and corporations like to keep it that way, because as long as addiction is only the person's problem, and not our collective problem, then they don't have to do anything about it."

He takes a long drag from his cigarette. "Man, we need accessible treatment," he says. "We need to have treatment centers like we have 7-Elevens. They need to be all over the fucking place, and they need to be affordable. Treatment works. Maybe not the first time, but it works if you do it right, if you give it the time it needs. For that, you need to fucking fund it. But we don't do that. We'd rather build jails and spend millions of dollars cleaning up the messes of addicts, when we could spend much less and help them stop making messes!"

Jody laughs as he says this, but it's an exasperated laugh, a laugh of disbelief. How, he wants to know, could we be getting addiction recovery so wrong?

"It's almost like we set out as a country to make it as difficult as possible for people to recover from addictions," he says. "The ones who come to my sober living community are the lucky ones, because they get the time that's needed to really begin recovery. Most people who get treatment get thirty days, and that's if they have the money. Many people don't even get that, either because they can't afford treatment, they can't afford to leave their job for thirty days, or they're too ashamed to even ask for help."

Insurance companies don't pay for addiction treatment as they do for other chronic conditions, many of which are, of course, caused by untreated addiction. Of the more than 23 million people in this country who needed treatment for drugs or alcohol in 2006, only 2.5 million received it. Joan Ward, a mother of a drug addict from Pennsylvania, summed up the problem this way when she testified before that state's legislature about the lack of affordable addiction treatment: "We can build a better system, or we can continue to bury our children."

But in Jody's view, the blame doesn't belong only to politicians. He's frustrated by the lack of advocacy among addicts with long-term recovery. Turning in his seat and staring intently at my right shoulder, he asks, "Where is the massive movement, like we see with other illnesses, demanding that we do something about this problem?"

8 KATE

Shame is the motor behind compulsive behavior.

—Anonymous

KATE'S THREE-YEAR-OLD SON, Patrick, stands upright in the massive Costco shopping cart, his little arms reaching for toys and CDs and whatever else he *absolutely* needs. "I want it! I want that! Gimme that!" he whines as Kate, a thirty-two-year-old stay-at-home mom from a small town on the West Coast, pushes bravely along, trying to focus on her shopping list on a sunny weekday a few months before I will meet her. "Oh, Mommy, I want that! Can I have that? Oh, I want that! No, that! Mom, I want that. Please, Mommy?"

Patrick nearly leaps out of the cart when he spots a DVD of Dora the Explorer, the Nickelodeon show about Dora and her entourage of animal friends who journey through Crocodile Lake, the Spooky Forest, and other scary places. "Oh, Mommy, please? Please? I want that!"

Kate stops the cart. Getting him the DVD would be rewarding his whining, but at this point she doesn't care. She grabs the DVD and looks at the price. *What a rip-off.* She tears the shrink wrap, takes the DVD container out of its cardboard box, and places it in the cart. Patrick jumps up and down with excitement. Kate throws the shrink wrap and the cardboard box in a wastebasket at the end of the aisle.

She resumes her shopping—she still needs soda, paper plates, and barbecue sauce for an upcoming Father's Day cookout. When Kate reaches the last aisle, she looks around to make sure no one is watching. Then she takes the Dora the Explorer DVD, lifts her fleece pullover, and stuffs it in her waistband. She doesn't feel scared. She doesn't feel anything.

Kate pushes the cart toward the register, but before she can get there, a store security guard approaches her. "I'm going to need that back," he tells her. Kate feels sick—her throat closes up, her mouth goes dry, and she's afraid she might vomit right there. The manager tells Kate to leave the cart where it is.

"Can I buy what's in it?" she asks him.

"We'll see," he says.

Kate scoops up Patrick from the cart and follows the manager to a back office. *Does Patrick know what's happening?* Kate doubts it, but she can't be sure. Either way, the guilt is paralyzing. *What am I doing to my son? What kind of parent does this?* And then there's her husband, who still doesn't know about Kate's shoplifting problem. *What would he think? Would he want to be married to a thief?*

Inside the sparse back office, the manager calls the police. And then he asks Kate a question she doesn't know how to answer: "Ma'am, why did you try to steal this?"

Because I always have? Because I can't stop? Because I'm addicted to it? Kate doesn't know what to say. She isn't convinced her problem is an addiction (calling it that feels like a cop-out), but she can't deny that she's shoplifted several times a week for most of her life, that she's tried hundreds of times to stop on her own, and that she's never been able to stop for long.

Kate has shoplifted for herself, for her friends, for her relatives, for her husband, and for her son. She's switched tags on clothing, slipped toys in her pocket, stuffed picture frames in her son's stroller, and marched out of J.C. Penney with a comforter. And she didn't really need any of it. Kate and her husband aren't rich, but they aren't poor, either. Still, the consequences of not stopping—arrest, humiliation, probation, jail—haven't prevented her. She's been arrested three times and been caught eight times and let go, usually after a reprimand and an order never to come back.

While many compulsive shoplifters report a feeling of excitement and adrenaline as they're stealing (some describe it as similar to a sexual rush), Kate says she doesn't feel that kind of high. She doesn't consciously feel anything while she shoplifts, but once she's made it safely home, she usually feels some relief.

"Temporary happiness," is how she puts it. "But that's usually followed right away with the usual beating myself up. I'll think to myself, 'I can't believe I just did that again. I don't need this. Why did I do that? I'm so stupid. I could have been arrested. Is it really worth it? Why am I so stupid?'"

Since her arrest, Kate isn't so sure her problem is stupidity. She's read every book she could find about shoplifting and has joined an online shoplifting and fraud recovery community organized by Terry Shulman, a therapist and recovering shoplifter who believes that, for some, shoplifting is a true addiction. In 1992, Shulman founded Cleptomaniacs and Shoplifters Anonymous (CASA). In 2000, he started the shoplifting recovery online group.

While there are Twelve Step–oriented recovery programs for other behavioral compulsions (sex, overeating, gambling, shopping, spending), there are few meetings around the country for shoplifters, so Kate receives most of her support by communicating with others on the Internet.

A few weeks before her sentencing, Kate posts this message:

I have not been keeping count of my shoplifting free days (maybe 2 or 3 weeks); however yesterday I had to make 3 store stops and I resisted temptation.

The reason I post today is to let y'all know this: For whatever reason the feeling of forgetting something was not as strong as in previous non-stealing store stops. In the beginning I noticed each time I made the decision not to shoplift, I would experience a feeling of loss or of "forgetting something" when I left the store with only my purchases. Perhaps this is a good sign.

My psycho ladies (I see one for therapy & one for counseling + meds) are working with me on the whole stealing issue. Also, they want to go back into my growing up years to resolve some destructive issues I have not dealt with in my 31 years of life. They suggest that somehow the two are connected. Heck, I'm willing to try anything at this point to stop the habit for good.

Real shitter is that I haven't told my friends and family about it. I can't escape the stigma and shame of being a thief long enough to "confess my sins." Despite having been arrested and appeared in court for an arraignment, it is still my dirty little secret.

9 SEAN

The spiritual life is not a theory.
We have to live it.

—ALCOHOLICS ANONYMOUS

A DOZEN MEN, including Sean (the sex addict) and myself, stand in a semicircle around a small grave at the East Dorset cemetery in Vermont. Behind us, an occasional car rumbles by on a two-lane country road, temporarily drowning out the chorus of chirping birds.

Dave, Sean's SLAA sponsor and a former major player in the entertainment industry, kneels down in front of the small white marble tombstone of AA co-founder Bill Wilson, where recent visitors have left flowers, two small American flags, and sobriety chips and coins. Dave has recently lost sixty pounds, and I almost don't recognize him. He looks ten years younger. He also looks fragile and slightly defenseless, in that way that men do when they suddenly have less of themselves to throw around.

When I first met Dave at a Twelve Step meeting five years ago, he told me that he was addicted to virtually everything: sex, food, alcohol, drugs, power, control, and work. I asked him if that was all.

He laughed. Then he said that when he gets control of one addiction, another will rear its ugly head and take over his life. He called that dance "switching seats on the *Titanic*."

Dave says a prayer while the rest of us stand in silence. Everyone is here to do Step Three—*Made a decision to turn our will and our lives over to the care of God as we understood Him*—as part of this weekend Twelve Step retreat at the Wilson House, the birthplace of Bill Wilson and now a homey, three-story inn geared toward people in recovery. We aren't literally praying to Wilson, but there is something moving about saying the Third Step at his grave.

Aldous Huxley, the philosopher and author of *Brave New World*, wasn't overstating it when he called Wilson—who co-founded AA in 1935—"the greatest social architect of the century." With its focus on anonymity, group conscience, spiritual connection, rigorous honesty, amends making, and helping other alcoholics, AA has stayed true to its original purpose, survived consistent attacks from outsiders, and helped millions of Americans get sober and lead meaningful lives. Today AA has more than a million members in this country and nearly two million members worldwide, and its Twelve Steps are used by dozens of other addiction fellowships.

AA owes much of its success to the hard lessons learned from previous mutual aid sobriety groups, including the Washingtonian Society. Founded in 1840, that group enjoyed some initial success but was mostly dead a decade later, the result of internal squabbling, political disagreement over outside issues, and damaged credibility when some of its most visible and outspoken proponents relapsed.

Eighty-five years later, Wilson and the earliest AA members would heed those lessons. They created a fellowship with "no opinion on outside issues," a public relations policy "based on attraction rather than promotion," and a focus on anonymity as a spiritual exercise in ego reduction and as a way to protect the privacy of its members and safeguard against any member diminishing the group as a whole.

Like many addicts, I didn't take to the Twelve Steps quickly or easily. Step Three, in particular, struck me as preposterous. It's inextricably linked to Step Two (*Came to believe that a Power greater than ourselves could restore us to sanity*), which has been known to turn off newcomers with its implication that they are not sane.

"Hey, just because I drink too much doesn't mean I'm *crazy*," is a typical response to a first reading of the Second Step.

Personally, I didn't struggle accepting my insanity (my addictive behavior was clearly insane), but I wasn't so sure that God—if God even existed—had any inclination to fix it. Fortunately, the Second Step doesn't ask us to believe in God. It asks only that we accept that we're not Him.

The Third Step seemed scarier. I was supposed to surrender my will and my life over to the care of something that I wasn't sure I even believed in? And what kind of loser just hands over his will, anyway? The first time I read Step Three, I thought it sounded weak, ludicrous, almost un-American. I remember asking my first sponsor if I could skip Steps Two and Three and go right to Step Four, *Made a searching and fearless moral inventory of ourselves*, which also sounded excruciating but at least didn't involve God. My sponsor chuckled and told me to focus on Step One, which I had yet to complete.

Next up to say his prayer at the cemetery is a family doctor from a Southern state. Short and thin, with gray hair, big ears, and a mouse-like face, the doctor always speaks methodically, as if he's expecting everyone to take notes. Yesterday, he told us how he used to try to solve his addictions to liquor, sex, and food on his own.

"I would dump all my liquor and pornography and doughnuts in a Dumpster," he said, "but the next day I would be standing in that Dumpster, in my tie and coat, frantically trying to get them back. It was like I was taken over by an alien."

Sean stands next to me in the circle. He's wearing jeans and a blue T-shirt, and he looks serene. I'm feeling serene, too, because this morning Sean taught me Transcendental Meditation, a practice that promotes deep relaxation. Sean gave me a mantra, which I repeated to myself, and before long I was in a powerful, comforting trance.

"They made me sign something promising not to teach it to anyone, but fuck that, I don't care," he told me on our drive up from Boston. "It's unreal. I've never done drugs, but my friend who used to be a drug addict says it's like taking the best parts of pot, mushrooms, and ecstasy, all combined into one. But it's healthy for you! I do it twice a day for thirty minutes, and afterward I feel so relaxed, so okay in my skin. It's helping me stay sober."

It's been a few months since Sean went to the porn store on that cold winter night. He's been doing well since; his only slip was looking at pornography once on his cell phone. (Frustrated, he went to a T-Mobile store the next day to buy a phone without Internet access, but it was standard on all the models for sale. So Sean walked to the back of the store, where there was a big bin overflowing with recycled phones. On top of the pile, he found an older model without Internet capability. He picked it up, turned it on, and casually walked out.)

Sean isn't typically one for retail theft, but the cell phone story didn't surprise me. Since first meeting him in 2004, I had come to admire Sean's perseverance. Like many sex addicts in recovery, he struggled to stay sober, sometimes relapsing with pornography or an escort. But he never gave up.

He went to an SLAA meeting nearly every day. He made telephone calls and asked for help when he wanted to act out sexually. When he started accessing porn on his laptop in the school library, he surrendered his laptop Ethernet card to an SLAA friend, only to buy another one a month later when the urge to act out became too great. He repeated this drill two more times ("I've given away a lot of Ethernet cards!" he joked) before finally just getting rid of his laptop altogether.

And it said a lot about his desire to recover that he came to this weekend retreat. "My mom never did anything like this for herself," he tells me.

Growing up, Sean says he bore the brunt of her dysfunction and anger. "In third grade," he recalls, "I would always be the last kid to be picked up at after-care. She was usually at the bar, and she would show up all tipsy to pick me up, and then she would take me *back* to the bar with her to hang out. When we got home, if she was in a bad mood she would yell and scream and throw shit around. I would cry, and she would be, like, 'Why are you crying!' I didn't know what the hell was going on."

When she wasn't yelling, Sean says she was treating him like a close friend or surrogate spouse, involving him in her relationship drama. And when she worked, slept, or nursed a hangover, Sean says he spent most of his time alone. He played the piano, zoned out on video games, or made up elaborate fantasy games in his head. He had few friends, and his anger manifested itself in fights with other kids at school.

(When I spoke with Sean's mother by phone to get her perspective on his childhood, she denied being an alcoholic or mistreating him. "I don't know where he gets that idea," she said. When I relayed to Sean what she told me, Sean wasn't surprised. "She's always been in denial about her problems or how bad things were for me," he said.)

When he was eleven, Sean started spending more time at his grandparents' house. They had recently gotten the Internet, and it didn't take him long to find sexual chat rooms. "I remember the first sexual image I ever saw online," he says. "It was these two lesbians 69ing, but it didn't actually show their breasts, so I was like, 'Damn, this sucks.'"

But soon Sean found hard-core chat rooms and pornography sites, and he spent hours watching and masturbating after his grandparents went to sleep. One afternoon his grandmother caught him, and his grandfather sat Sean down for a talk. He was humiliated, but he couldn't stop.

When he was sixteen and had moved permanently into his grandparents' house, Sean found girls online who performed Web cam sex shows for money. Before he knew it, he had charged $2,000 to his grandparents' credit card.

"I would never keep track of how much I was spending," he says. "I would look at cam shows for hours, and then I'd wake up the next morning feeling so guilty for spending their money. Sometimes I would cry. But then the night would come and it was like I *had* to do it. At some point it stopped being a choice. I think I was so sad and in so much pain that the porn was the only way I knew to make myself feel better. I was like a zombie. This addiction turned me into this person with no life, no energy, no friends. It was like I was nothing, like I was totally worthless."

After saying our Third Step prayer at the cemetery, Sean and I walk along rusted railroad tracks near the inn. It's dusk, and we're procrastinating. We're supposed to be working on Step Four, but Sean says he's feeling neither searching nor fearless.

He points to a fenced-off pasture to our right. "Look at those cows!" he says excitedly. "They're running. I don't think I've ever seen cows run before."

I've seen cows jog, but these are in a full-on sprint. "I think we pissed them off." he says as they take a sharp right, heading toward us. Fortunately, we're protected by a wooden railing, and the cows stop about twenty feet away. We stare at them. They stare at us. "What's up with cows in Vermont?" Sean says with a laugh.

The cows eventually lose interest, and Sean and I move down the tracks. "I can't believe I haven't had sex in *a year*," he tells me, kicking a rock through the dirt. "How fucked up is that? It happens in my mind ten times a day, so I don't even realize it sometimes. But it's been a year."

Since Sean lost his virginity at seventeen to a girl he met on the Internet, he's had sex with only two women who weren't prostitutes. He's told me many times that he feels awkward around "normal" girls that he's attracted to—he doesn't know what to say or how to act. (It's not only girls. He's socially awkward around many people, particularly those he doesn't know well.) And it's only recently that he learned that men could look at women as anything other than sexual objects.

"I remember this friend in high school who described to me what a healthy relationship was," Sean recalls. "She talked about mutual respect, love that wasn't about control or jealousy. I couldn't comprehend it. I was like, 'What the hell are you talking about?' I didn't know that I could see a girl as a *real person*. But lately I'm starting to have glimpses of that. If I'm in a good space, I'll see a cute girl on the street and I'll think, 'Oh, she's cute, I'd like to get to know her,' as opposed to before, when I would just fantasize about having sex with her."

Since coming to SLAA, Sean has learned to recognize when he's "triggered" to act out. A few months before our trip to Vermont, he told me about one of his most intense urges.

"I was in an underground parking lot," he said, "and I couldn't find where the elevator was, so I asked this group of girls how to get out. They were drunk, and this one girl was laughing at me like I was stupid, like I was too dumb to know how to get out of the parking lot. I was embarrassed and angry, and right then I wanted to go see an escort or look at porn. But what I realized was that the girl who was drunk and condescending reminded me of my mom, and that triggered these bad emotions, and when I have emotions, I want to look at porn or have sex. My mind will unconsciously start to feed me pornographic images, adrenaline pumps through my body. It's like my body creates these drugs inside me that make me want to act out. But that time I just sat with the feelings instead of numbing them. It was hard. I cried."

Back at the Wilson House, an AA meeting is letting out as we arrive, and a dozen people stand or sit in rocking chairs on the front porch. Just about everyone is smoking, drinking coffee, or both. "Alcoholics are funny," Sean mumbles to me as we walk into the main meeting room, where framed AA slogans (*Easy Does It, First Things First, But for the Grace of God*) and recovery-inspired license plates (12AA12, STP Twelve, We OWEAA, Step 3) adorn the wooden walls.

"We sex addicts are pretty funny, too," I remind him.

Later, in our room, Sean sits cross-legged on his bed and starts working on Step Four. We won't have time to do so thoroughly before tomorrow, but the retreat leaders want us to start looking at our fears and resentments. They also want us to highlight our personality strengths, lest the exercise send us sprinting toward the nearest tall bridge.

"I don't get this thing about resentments," Sean says. "I don't feel like I have any resentments."

"Oh, really," I say.

"You think I have resentments?"

"We all have resentments. I can think of three you have right off the bat."

"Seriously? Like what?"

"Well, you resent your mother. You resent women. And you resent guys that are more comfortable talking to women."

"Oh, yeah," he says sheepishly. "I guess I do have some resentments." A few minutes later, he says, "I think I have a lot of anger toward people that I'm not even aware of. It's like I don't want to even look at my anger, because I think it scares me. I'm not sure I want to go there."

After thirty minutes, Sean shows me his list of character strengths and weaknesses:

STRENGTHS

1. Always trying to improve and learn about myself—Ever since I was seventeen and listened to Tony Robbins tapes, I've thought that growing and improving (emotionally, spiritually, artistically) are most important.
2. Extremely open-minded. Willing to listen and take in what other people have to say.
3. A lot of willingness to reach out for help.
4. Creative and talented.
5. Want to help others in the world and contribute. Also want to help others through music.
6. Usually honest.
7. Have a drive to be successful and have a family.

WEAKNESSES

1. Insecure, shy, scared.
2. Selfishness.
3. Judgmental. I criticize instead of having compassion.
4. Not very giving and loving. I live in isolation, then I wonder why I'm so lonely.
5. Masochistic in my mind. I'll visualize myself being hurt or punishing myself. Cutting.
6. Use women, sexualize them.

When I'm done reading his list, Sean leaps off his bed. "Let's go get some junk food at the town store," he says. "If we can't stuff our feelings with sex, let's stuff them with food!"

10 JODY

Who could even imagine the advent of modern literature without the addictive, visionary excesses of writers like Baudelaire, Rimbaud, de Quincey, Poe, Burroughs, Ginsberg, or Artaud; or, for that matter, modern culture without its perennial outsiders, its incorrigible addicts, its defaced subjects: the smokers, tokers, overeaters, the alcoholics, the insane and "eccentric," and so on?

—Anna Alexander and Mark Roberts,
*High Culture: Reflections on Addiction
and Modernity*

JODY, THE ADDICTION counselor, smokes a Marlboro under a bright, nearly full moon on a muggy Monday night on Singer Island in West Palm Beach. He's wearing a T-shirt and shorts and sitting on a white garden chair in front of a beat-up Dodge in the driveway of his street-level apartment. Except for chirping crickets and occasional laughter emanating from a nearby apartment, the block is quiet.

Across the street, Jody's new co-counselor, Max, knocks loudly on doors for his head count. It's nearly midnight, and by now the fifteen residents of C.A.R.E.'s sober living community should all be accounted for. They don't literally have to be in their apartments, but they do have to be somewhere on this block. Most of the addicts in the community graduated from C.A.R.E.'s inpatient center; others came after completing treatment centers around the country.

"This is not like inpatient treatment, where you're being watched all the time," Jody tells me, fiddling with his lighter. "When you come here, you're ready for a bit more freedom. You get a job. You cook your own meals. You slowly learn how to do all the things you weren't doing because you were too busy getting fucked up."

Finished with his head count, Max meanders over to where we're sitting. He's short and middle-aged, with thick glasses and a Hawaiian shirt that strains to cover his protruding belly. "Have you seen John?" he asks Jody, looking concerned. John, a drug addict and former professional football player who's been living in the sober community for a few months, is nowhere to be found.

"I might be a little worried about him," Jody says. "He rented a car today."

"He probably hooked up with some girl," Max says, leaning on the car. "All it takes is eye contact for him, and he's golden."

Jody laughs. "John just starts whipping out that football 'I played in the NFL' shit, and girls can't resist that. I wish I had that kind of mojo."

"So what do you think he's doing?" Max wonders aloud.

"He might have gone to a meeting and went out to eat and just forgot to call," Jody says, leaning back in his chair and stretching his legs. "Or, he could be smoking crack. At least he has money, so I don't have to worry about him stealing the fucking TV."

Max's cell phone rings. While he takes the call, a neighbor who's renovating some of the community's apartments across the street walks briskly toward us. He's tall and gangly, with stringy brown hair and many missing teeth.

"Hey, Jody," he says. "I'm getting my teeth done soon!"

"Is that right?"

"Yes, sir, all my bottoms are getting done. It costs $6,500 for the bottoms, and the top ones are only $9,500."

"Fifteen grand? Man, you need to start flossing."

"Why? I don't got to now."

"Lazy fuck."

"This ain't typical, everyday work. I told them I want *movie star* teeth."

"You gonna look like Julia Roberts?"

"That would be *hot*," says Mark, a twenty-eight-year-old alcoholic and crack addict who joins the gathering on Jody's driveway. Mark is clean-cut, Jewish, and seems plucked directly from an investment banking job. He's been living here for eight months, and when he's not working the front desk at a nearby resort hotel, there's a good chance he's fishing. Yesterday morning, he and Jody took me out on a packed commercial fishing boat, where we caught a dozen bonita.

"Man," Jody says, shaking his head, "ya'll need to move along. This is my night off." It's one of the hazards of living where you work. Unless he leaves the area, Jody never really gets a break.

"Hey, before you forget," Max tells Mark, ignoring Jody's plea, "put my number in your phone. You need to start calling me, too, not only Jody."

"Max is new," Jody whispers to me, "so he's taking his job *real* serious."

"Max, you want me to call you when I want to *drink*?" Mark says, a grin on his face. (Everyone, it seems, likes pulling Max's chain.)

Jody chuckles. "Calling Max when you want to get loaded is like calling your girlfriend when you're about to fuck her best friend," he says. "It probably ain't gonna happen."

"So what am I supposed to call Max for?" Mark says, trying to suppress a laugh.

"If you need something," Max suggests, seemingly unaware that he's being made fun of. "If the girls are fighting next door, or if they're having a pillow fight or something."

Mark shakes his head. "Nah, Max, I'll be peeking in the window if that's happening. But, hey, I will *definitely* call you if my roommate blows himself up with the turkey fryer."

There's a lull in the conversation, which Jody uses to again remind everyone that they should move along. "I'm trying to relax here," he demands, more forcefully this time. But no one seems in a hurry to go to bed. "Okay, come on," Mark finally tells the group. "It's late, and Jody needs his beauty rest. It's been a fucked-up week around here."

The drama started a few days ago, when Jody received a phone call at 1 A.M. on Saturday from a resident manager at C.A.R.E.'s inpatient center. Two young men who had graduated from the program that day and were supposed to transition to Jody's sober living community were caught in the apartment of a female patient.

"I suppose they were hoping to get laid," Jody tells me, "but no one realized they were drunk, so they just sent them over here. The first guy gets here, and he's being drunk and stupid, throwing around attitude, and I'm like, 'Dude, sorry, but you can't live here. Nothing personal, but you broke the rules.' So he starts getting all redneck on me—he's out in the street with his shirt off, ranting and raving, screaming 'Fuck it, I don't give a fuck, fuck you!' I'm like, 'Dude, *chill*, you can't be out here screaming like a maniac.' So he gets on his cell phone and calls his grandma, of all people. He starts going off on her, 'That's right, Grandma, I fucked up! Fuck it, I'm just a fuck-up. I'm a fucking crack head, Grandma! If anybody offers me fucking crack, I'm gonna beat those niggers' ass!' And that's not the smartest thing to say, because we have a few black guys in the community, including John, who could fuck this kid up."

The guy eventually left, but a few minutes later Jody heard shouting coming from the other end of the street, in front of a run-down house where an American flag hangs meekly from a short pole. Jody assumed the guy had walked around the block and was coming back for more.

"But it was actually the *other* guy who was in the girls' room with him," Jody says, chuckling as he recounts the story. "So he's hollering, 'Fuck you, fuck this,' and he walks right by me, walks into one of the apartments he doesn't live in, and I'm like, 'Dude, you can't go in there.' But he goes in the bedroom and sits down like he fucking owns the place. I follow him in and tell him to get out. He says, 'Fuck you! I don't give a fuck!' I'm like, 'What are you talking about, *fuck me*? Fuck *you*!' And I know the guy's story. The whole reason he's in treatment is so he doesn't go to jail. But he's still hollering, 'I don't give a fuck, you can call the fucking police!' So I call the cops, and he just sits there. I'm like, 'You moron, the cops are coming!' He finally ended up leaving a few minutes before the cops got there."

The drama continued the following day when a counselor at a sober living house down the block from Jody's community kicked a resident out for sneaking a girl into his apartment. After unsuccessfully trying to sway the counselor with promises of good behavior, the young man followed him toward Jody's front lawn and tried a new tack. "I hope you pay taxes on this place," the man said.

The counselor, who looks like a cross between Nick Nolte and Jimmy Buffett, couldn't believe what he heard. "What did you say?"

"You heard me. I hope you pay taxes on this place."

"Are you threatening me?" the counselor wanted to know.

"I'm not fucking threatening you. I just hope you pay taxes on this place."

"Oh, really?" he said, hustling across Jody's front lawn and punching the guy in the face, effectively ending the conversation.

The following day, things got much more serious. Leon Crutchfield—a forty-year-old former resident of Jody's community whom Jody had recently kicked out for using drugs—forced his way inside the Palm Beach Assisted Living Facility. A police spokesperson later told the *South Florida Sun-Sentinel* that Crutchfield was "screaming and yelling that somebody was trying to kill him."

Four police officers surrounded Crutchfield when he left the facility through a fire exit. Concerned for their safety—Crutchfield was acting erratically, yelling, and dripping with sweat—officers shot him three times with a Taser gun. Moments later, Crutchfield died. It was the state's twenty-seventh death following Taser shocks. At least twenty of the victims had drugs, including amphetamines or cocaine, in their system. (The State Attorney's Office later cleared the officers of any wrongdoing, stating that Crutchfield died of acute cocaine toxicity.)

According to the *Sun-Sentinel*, Crutchfield had been arrested at least twenty-one times since 1993, mostly for misdemeanor thefts. "He was not always the person I wanted him to be, but he was turning his life around," Crutchfield's mother told the paper, adding that he was a longtime drug addict who had spent much of his life in and out of treatment.

His last stint was in Jody's community, where he was well liked. "He was a good guy," Jody says. "He's like most addicts. When he's using, he turns into a different person, an *insane* person." Jody knows all about that. "I'm an addict, not any different from any of the guys in this community," he tells me. "It's a fucking miracle that I'm here, that I'm sober, and that no one ever Tasered me."

The oldest of three, Jody was born and raised in Chesapeake, Virginia. His father, Bill, was only twenty-one when Jody was born. In his mid-twenties, Bill made good money as the president of a construction company, and the family lived at the end of a cul-de-sac in a nice suburb. But all was not well. Jody's parents fought often, in part because Bill drank heavily and started using drugs.

Bill and his wife divorced when Jody was seven, which exacerbated Bill's drug use—he started abusing cocaine and heroin. It was the late 1970s, when President Jimmy Carter was considering decriminalizing marijuana, and cocaine was the drug of choice for hard-partying young men with plenty of cash: professional athletes, Hollywood players, and hotshot young businessmen like Bill. Even the country's drug czar, Peter Bourne, couldn't keep his hand out of the cookie jar, sniffing cocaine at the National Organization for the Reform of Marijuana Laws annual Christmas party in 1977. (Bourne resigned when the news came out.)

Jody's father soon lost his business (he was too high to function), and, without a better idea, he planned to move to California with a girlfriend he used drugs with. But a day before the move, Bill and the woman were shooting cocaine when she went into cocaine psychosis and had to be rushed to the hospital. The doctors, though, were more concerned about Bill. There were abscesses on his arm, and an infection was heading toward his heart. The only way to stop it was to amputate the arm. The surgery was scheduled for the next day.

That night, Jody's grandmother arrived at the hospital with a preacher in tow. They prayed for him, and that night Bill made a deal with God. As he tells it, he said, "God, man, if you're up there, and you get me out of this, I promise I will go to work for you."

The next morning, as a doctor prepped Bill for the surgery, he looked at the soon-to-be-amputated arm. Then he looked again. Then he went to get more doctors. They couldn't believe their eyes—neither could Bill. The arm was fine. "When my dad got home from the hospital," Jody says, "he sure was fired up about God. All he knew is that he made a deal with God, and things were looking up!"

Bill was a different man when he wasn't using, and soon he remarried Jody's mother. But Bill didn't know much about addiction and recovery, and he never attended AA or NA—Narcotics Anonymous—meetings. Instead, he rebuilt his business and threw himself into church life, certain that his using days were behind him. Three years later, he started using pain medication for a bad back, and soon he was hooked. "And eventually he started up with the heroin again," Jody recalls. For the next two years, Bill was in and out of treatment centers and detox centers trying to get and stay sober.

Jody, meanwhile, was developing his own addiction. A popular and well-liked skateboarder and surfer in high school, Jody started smoking weed and dropping acid at fifteen and using heroin at sixteen. By seventeen, he was venturing into the nearby projects to score heroin and crack for himself and his friends. Suburban white boys buying crack were rare (they usually preferred powdered cocaine, which was easier for them to get, carried less of a stigma, and was less severely criminalized), but Jody's experience would have fit nicely into the drug narrative of the time.

It was 1989, the zenith of the crack scare. Politicians and the media eagerly portrayed the drug as the most addictive substance ever (each decade has its "most addictive drug ever"—ours has been the decade of crystal meth), one that was fast spreading from the ghettos to suburban America. To prove the point, in his first primetime television address George H. W. Bush sat in the Oval Office in September of 1989 and held up a clear plastic bag of crack. It was seized, he dramatically told the country, "in a park across the street from the White House." That was technically true, but the seizure may go down as one of the most orchestrated minor drug buys in American history.

For one thing, there were no crack dealers in Lafayette Park, because crack users at the time were almost exclusively in poor black neighborhoods. DEA agents couldn't find anyone selling drugs near the White House, so they manipulated a black high school senior, who didn't even know how to get to the White House, to come to Lafayette Park.

Combined with the media's addiction to crack stories and politicians' tough talk on drug-related crime, Bush's prime-time performance succeeded in making illegal drugs the country's biggest issue that year. Nearly two-thirds of Americans thought illicit drugs were the most important problem facing the country (compare that to 1985, when fewer than one percent did). Representative Thomas Hartnett, a South Carolina Republican, summed up the mood at the time when he said that drugs were now "a threat worse than any nuclear warfare or any chemical warfare waged on any battlefield."

Jody knew that smoking crack was risky—some users call it "sucking on the devil's dick." But like so many of his generation, he grew up mocking "This is your brain on drugs" commercials and Nancy Reagan's pleas of "Just Say No." And, besides, for a while he thought his life was manageable.

"I had friends, a girlfriend, and I could put down a drug for a few days," he says. But when Bill, then sober and a regular at NA meetings, caught Jody at seventeen with cocaine and some Valiums in his backpack, he sent him to outpatient treatment.

The next year Jody left home for college, where he spent his time smoking weed, popping prescription drugs (mostly Valium and Xanax), chasing girls, and playing drums in a band. "It was basically as manageable as I ever got," he says, "because I wasn't doing any coke or heroin. But I couldn't function without pills."

The summer before his sophomore year, Jody started to lose his vision. It worsened for three months, and finally he couldn't read or drive. He quit school and focused on throwing parties and selling drugs. But the panic was always there. Would any girl want to date him now? How would he make a living? And is a blind man really a man at all?

He could still play the drums (that talent depended more on instinct and practice than on perfect vision), and in 1993 he and his band hit the road. They spent the next two years touring, shooting heroin every chance they got. "This was that whole Nirvana, Smashing Pumpkins time," he recalls. "Everyone in that scene was doing heroin. It was just what you did. And we were a great band. But I was a fucking mess."

In a halfhearted attempt at "growing up," Jody left the band when he was twenty-four and returned home, going to work for his dad's construction company. He wasn't home a week before all hell broke loose. "My dad comes in my room," Jody recalls, "and there are needles everywhere and three girls, who look like whores, in my bed. My dad's like, 'Jody, this ain't working. We're so tired of your bullshit rock 'n' roll lifestyle. You need to get some help.'"

By that point, Jody was starting to agree with him.

11 KATE

I would distrust anyone who says they can cure addiction.

—NEUROLOGIST AND ADDICTION
RESEARCHER WALTER LING

IN THE MONTHS following her shoplifting arrest, Kate—who received a ninety-day suspended sentence, on the condition that she not be caught stealing for one year—posts many messages to the online shoplifting recovery support group.

Kate is more open and self-reflective in writing than she is on the telephone or in person, and I eagerly await the new posts she sends me every few weeks.

On Valentine's Day this year, Grandma Bev (my husband's grandmother) died. Cancer in her brain took her from us. Peaceful death for her, but tragic for me. Then, just last night, Momma Rae (his mother) died. Cancer of her spine took her from us. A peaceful death for her, also, but tragic for me as well. I loved their hearts and souls, and treasured, or worshiped really, characteristics of their personalities which I myself do not possess.

Progress: After I left the grieving family to begin a long drive home, I stopped for caffeine and candy. At the gas station I saw a frog lighter. I picked it up, I ALMOST put it in my pocket while the clerk looked away, then I put it back on the counter, paid for my purchase, got in my car, turned the music up loud, rolled the windows down, and hit the highway. Momma Rae was a heavy smoker and she actually owned a frog lighter. Did I want to steal it to remember her? Did I want to steal it to strike back because she had died? Did I not steal it because she would have been disappointed in me? Or because I would have been disappointed in myself? Fact is, I did not steal. That, my friends, feels like progress. I feel that each day presents an opportunity to begin anew. Screw up today? Will there always be a tomorrow to do it right? I would like to think so . . . or else, why would I get out of bed at all?!

So I was at the shrink's office the other day and she asked how I was doing on the shoplifting thing, and I thought I'd share my answer with my CASA friends. About 95% of the time, I can recognize the urge to shoplift and avoid doing it. It's the 5% of the time that I need to work on. When I do shop without shoplifting, I do not feel good about it and have conflicting feelings of pride and disgust. I have such a hard, hard time paying full price for things. One of us said that shoplifting was like getting a discount on the purchase . . . that's how I looked at it for a long time.

Last week I had to make 2 stops, Safeway and Wal-Mart. We parked, and my son asked if I had my "list." I didn't but asked him to climb in my lap and we'd make one before we got out of the car. Three years old, God bless him! On a scrap of paper we made a list together of the things we needed and something he wanted to look at. We got everything and got out safely . . . twice.

While I was at Wal-Mart, I checked out the new Lionel Richie CD. They wanted like $16 for it. Before now I would have just compromised the packaging with my fingernail or car key and removed the security tag and stole it. I started talking to myself (not outwardly, I'm not crazy!) about the risk of stealing. I decided that I didn't want it enough to pay $16, or to go through the humiliation of being stopped for shoplifting it. I didn't know if I would like it once I got it home, and if I did like it and I stole it, then I wouldn't like it as much as if I had come by it honestly and paid the price. So I didn't steal it. I repeated the same situation again a few days later at Target. Maybe I will never buy the CD, but I won't steal it either!

Sometimes I think my son and my husband are my internal security devices. In times of temptation, I reach over into the shopping cart and touch my son. Sometimes I pick him up and give him a hug or carry him around for a while. If my arms are full of his 40-pound body, what or how can I possibly shoplift? He's a good deterrent, and I love him even more for it.

So, while I am not completely shoplifting free, I AM TRYING. I am not shoplifting at every store stop anymore. I am not dreaming about ways to outsmart the security systems anymore. I still look around at the cameras in the ceilings, but less often and for different reasons, I hope. I feel more rational about not shoplifting and talking myself down from the ledge when I feel the urge. I'm better, but not by any means "cured." I bless this group when the messages reflect recovery and stories of specific successes. We should promote healthy thinking and not discourage sharing. I hope the messages posted return to a place of peace and support. Thanks everyone for reading and sharing in my day of strength.

12 JANICE

Like the alcoholic, the junkie can never start to cure himself until he recognizes and accepts his true condition.

—MALCOLM X

"LET'S TALK ABOUT those maxims on the wall," says J.R., a lanky, sixty-three-year-old African American counselor at Odyssey House, a long-term inpatient treatment center only a few blocks from the East River in Harlem. J.R. stands in front of about thirty black and Hispanic addicts—including Janice, the crack addict—seated on chairs with arm desks, and he gestures rather dramatically toward the far white wall, where a lifetime of wisdom hangs for everyone to see: *It Works if You Work It; No Free Lunch; Honesty Is the Key; Responsible Love and Concern; What Goes Around Comes Around; Personal Growth Before Vested Status*; and so on.

While most high-priced treatment centers are purposely secluded away from temptation, Odyssey House, like many rehabs catering to low-income addicts, is not far from where some of its patients got high. The neighborhood has markedly gentrified in recent years, but crack houses still blight the area. If the addicts here want to leave and score drugs, they don't have to walk far.

Janice, who recently turned fifty-six, sits next to me in the front row, twiddling her thumbs. She's wearing black tennis shoes and a white cotton dress with flowers on it, and when she smiles or laughs, which she does often, I can see she is missing her two front teeth. Janice is overweight, with a puffy, freckled face carved with laugh lines. Her nails are cut short and painted light pink, and her hair is pulled back and matted down on her head with gel.

Janice is in her sixth month at Odyssey House—when offered a choice between prison and treatment, she didn't hesitate. She's one of the youngest addicts in the elder care unit, sharing a bedroom on the fourth floor with three women in their sixties. There are two floors for adult men, and two others are shared among women and single mothers with young children. (The Odyssey House staff agreed to let me drop in on Janice periodically during her treatment.)

Odyssey House residents are fortunate to be here. The vast majority are low-income minorities who committed drug crimes, but instead of joining the half-million Americans incarcerated for drug offenses (that's ten times as many as in 1980 and more people than Western Europe incarcerates for *all* criminal offenses), they're court-mandated to stay in long-term treatment as part of the Drug Treatment Alternative-to-Prison Program (DTAP).

DTAP works differently from traditional drug courts, many of which target first-time drug offenders. DTAP enrolls only repeat offenders who face significant prison time (often three to six years) for nonviolent drug felonies under the state's mandatory sentencing guidelines. Those who complete treatment have their charges dismissed. Those who don't are sent to prison.

A five-year study of the DTAP program by the National Center on Addiction and Substance Abuse (CASA) at Columbia University found that DTAP graduates had significantly lower recidivism rates than comparable offenders who were sent to prison. (Those results were achieved at about half the cost of incarceration, CASA found.) "This program in which failure is a one-way ticket to prison shows the effectiveness of coerced treatment," said CASA president Joseph A. Califano Jr.

(For addicts like Janice who don't have health insurance but need addiction treatment, it often pays to get arrested. "The way to get the intensive substance abuse treatment that you need is to commit a crime," said Eric Goplerud, an expert on insurance policies and addiction.)

"Sometimes," J.R. continues, "I think you all try your best not to read these maxims. So we're going to read them now."

Another counselor, whom everyone calls Mr. Ricks, stands to the right of J.R. and leans on a cane. "If you spent more time taking those maxims in," Mr. Ricks tells the group, "then maybe you wouldn't be so interested in playing the victim role. There's been a whole lot of that lately around here. But you know what? We're not victims. Are we victims?"

The room is silent—the elder care patients are lethargic today. "I said, are we victims?" Mr. Ricks asks again.

"Hell, no!" a man shouts from the back row.

"Okay," Mr. Ricks says. "So let's stop acting like victims. We've gone through our life blaming everyone else for our problems, and where did that get us? It got us here, and here isn't much fun. We go through our life saying, 'No one understands me.' Well, you know what? A dope fiend is a dope fiend. And the only reason you're in here is because you got tired of being a dope fiend, or the police got tired for you. And you want to save your own life. So don't come in here playing the victim role, because it's only going to slow down your recovery."

"And it slows down everyone else's, too," J.R. tells the group.

"Exactly," Mr. Ricks says. "I've been noticing that a lot of you are tolerating others in this community being a victim. But we can't do that anymore. Maybe we do it because they're like us—they're Puerto Rican, Dominican, black, and we let them get away with this shit because they're like us. Don't do that! We have to look out for one another, challenge each other, and confront each other even if it's hard. Stop being a victim!"

"So, let's talk about a maxim that relates to this—Responsible Love and Concern," J.R. says. "Who wants to talk about responsible love and concern?"

A few hands shoot up, but J.R.—who was addicted to heroin for nearly thirty years before getting sober and becoming an addiction counselor—doesn't call on anyone. Instead, he sighs and takes a seat, waiting for a petite woman slumped in her chair and napping in the front row to notice that she's holding up the lecture. She doesn't.

"Here's a perfect example of responsible love and concern," J.R. tells the group. "If I'm acting with responsible love and concern, I would say"—he gets up and knocks on the sleeper's desk, startling her—"'What's up? Do you need to get some air? Do you need to splash some water on your face, or do you want to miss everything that's going on?' That's an act of responsible love and concern."

Though not a particularly effective one. The woman still looks groggy, and she's still slouched in her seat, her chin practically resting on her chest. "Do you need to leave?" J.R. asks her.

"No," she says.

"Then do you need to apologize to the group?"

"I'm sorry, family," she says, sitting up straighter in her chair. (Patients refer to the community as "family.")

"Okay," J.R. says. "So let's talk about some examples of responsible love and concern on the outside. If I've got some money in my pocket, and my woman says to me, 'The baby needs some milk,' and I leave the house with every intention of getting some milk but go to the crack house instead, is that being responsible?"

"Nuh-uh," Janice says loudly. "Shoooot, that's being selfish!"

"Right," J.R. says. "That's not showing any love and concern to the baby, your wife, or yourself. And what if I have some money in my pocket and I go buy a Cadillac that I probably can't afford? Is that responsible? Is that love and concern? No, it's not. It's idiocy. It's selfishness. It's *addiction*. That's my wants coming before my needs. Because if I was responsible and looked at my budget and looked at what my family needed, then I would realize I could get a Suburban wagon and make the payments without hurting my family. These maxims, they're important. They're what we need to follow in order to stay clean and sober." He turns to face the wall. "So, what other maxims up here do you all want to talk about?"

Talk turns to *Honesty Is the Key*. "In order to recover, you gotta *uncover*," a tall black man in his fifties tells the group. "You gotta tell on your disease. You got to break through the denial. A prime example of denial is someone saying, 'Well, I smoked crack, but I didn't *inhale*.'"

The room erupts in laughter. "And what do we have to do when we tell a lie?" J.R. asks.

"Tell another!" several addicts shout in unison. The room is energized now.

"If we're not rigorously honest," J.R. says, "we can't recover. It's impossible."

A few minutes later, a short black man wearing a cross necklace over a long-sleeve shirt brings up the maxim, *No Free Lunch*. "That's my favorite," he tells the group. "It means that I have to work for my recovery. Nothing will get handed to me. There's no free lunch." He chuckles. "I have a funny story about that maxim. I remember one girl who came here, and on her first day she looked up and saw *No Free Lunch* on the wall, and she jumped out of her chair and was like, 'I have to pay for my lunch?'"

After group, Janice and I take the elevator up to her tidy room, where her twin bed is positioned parallel to a window that looks out onto the small backyard where some patients congregate to smoke cigarettes. Janice sits down on the edge of her bed and starts laughing at nothing in particular. "Shoooot," she says, "I've been laughing all day."

That's a significant improvement from the last time I visited a few months ago. Then, she rarely opened her mouth and cried herself to sleep most nights. "My counselor keeps trying to get me to talk," she told me at the time, "but I don't say much."

Finally, after about two months, Janice started talking. "And then everyone was wishing I would just shut up!" she tells me. "Shoooot, I just keep talking and talking and talking. When I first got here, I would never cry in front of people. I had too much false pride, so I would just cry in bed. Now, I cry all the time. But it's a *good* crying, because it means I'm feeling some feelings and I'm just being myself. I cry in group, I cry watching TV. Mmm-hmmm, in here I'm either laughing or crying!"

Lately, though, she hasn't been laughing at her favorite television show, *Charmed,* about three well-meaning witches who battle evil warlocks and demons in San Francisco. (She's so obsessed with the program that some at Odyssey House nicknamed her after it.)

"Everybody in the building is on restriction," she explains. "Too many people got in trouble and weren't doing what they were supposed to be doing, so now we can't watch TV, can't play cards, can't get no soda from the machines, can't do nothing fun. A lot of us did nothing wrong, and we're mad. We call it Peter paying for Paul."

As Janice tells it, the infractions were varied: One patient's urine came back positive for marijuana after he returned from a weekend pass, but he wouldn't admit to using. Two younger patients were caught having sex in a stairwell. ("Whaaaat? No sex in the stairwell up here in elder care!" Janice says.) One guy was hoarding hundreds of bags of popcorn in his room. And two men "went LACA," which stands for when a patient leaves the program against clinical advice.

"One guy left Friday, came back on Sunday, then walked out again, and then came back last night," Janice tells me. "The poor guy can't make up his mind. So now he's on a last-chance contract. If he leaves again, they won't let him back." Janice says that she's never seriously considered leaving the program, because that would mean going to jail.

Janice is well liked by her Odyssey House peers—particularly the men, with whom she flirts playfully. While she can become depressed or argumentative at times (usually over "immaterial things," her counselor says), she's a fairly consistent source of humor and joy in treatment.

Every day at the morning meeting, she and three other elder care women—they call their group the Golden Girls—sing songs to the community. They belt out "We Shall Overcome," "Amazing Grace," and "Lay Down Your Weary Tune," although they sometimes change the words to fit the context of their recovery. "In 'Lay Down,'" Janice says, "we sing, 'Lay down your crack stem,' or 'Lay down your bag of dope.'"

Five days a week, Janice also rides the bus to another Odyssey House building on Ward's Island, where she takes classes in preparation for her GED test next month. "I'm passing that test," she tells me with certainty. "I *know* I'll pass."

I'm not so sure, and neither is the Odyssey staff. Janice never got past the ninth grade, and it's been forty years since she was in a classroom.

The tenth child in a family of seventeen, Janice was raised on a farm on the Gulf Coast of Florida, where her family grew tobacco, corn, tomatoes, watermelon, and sugarcane. She was shy and overweight as a kid ("I was born heavy") and didn't make friends easily. Janice mostly spent time with two of her sisters, Angelina and Joyce, who were prettier and more popular.

When she was nine, Janice was raped by a relative in his late twenties. Janice told her mother (her father was gone most of the week working on the railroads), but she didn't believe Janice. Janice's sisters confronted the man, but he denied it. "And then people just forgot about it," Janice tells me.

Early in the ninth grade at her segregated, all-black school, Janice met her first boyfriend, an eighteen-year-old named Perceil. He was four years older than Janice, but he was as shy as she was. "He was very respectful, very nice," Janice recalls. "He was quiet, like me."

They started dating, and within months Janice was pregnant. Deeply embarrassed, Janice's mother sent her to New York City to stay with family and have the baby. "I couldn't understand why my mom would send me away," Janice says. "I didn't want her to be ashamed of me, but she was."

A year later, when her mother became seriously ill, Janice returned home to take care of her. After her mother died, Janice moved back to New York City. With no money, Janice ended up on welfare before finding a job as a hotel chambermaid and having another child. A devoted mother until she tried crack when she was thirty-two, Janice used to spend all of her free time with her two kids.

At Odyssey House, I sat down with Janice's counselor, Robert Harven, who outlined the challenges facing her in treatment. For addicts like Janice—poor, uneducated, and in trouble with the law— treatment is about more than "feeling your feelings" and going to Twelve Step meetings. Those won't much matter if she graduates the program without a job or a place to live. So Janice will spend much of her treatment time developing workplace skills. After taking the GED, she'll spend three months interning in a cafeteria kitchen, and she won't be discharged from the program until she secures an apartment and enough money for two or three months' rent.

But Robert also wants Janice to look at what she was medicating by using crack for most of her adult life. He hopes Janice will grieve for the childhood she never had and unlearn the negative messages she internalized growing up—messages that still affect how she sees herself.

"The bottom line is that if people treat you like crap all the time, which is what happened with Janice, you start feeling like crap and thinking you're crap," Robert told me. "Janice has a serious case of the 'Ugly Duck' syndrome. Growing up, Janice got a lot of ridicule, had a lot of people who neglected her feelings. She was overweight, considered unattractive. She had sisters who made fun of her and a mother who abandoned her, who sent her away. She was raped and then told it didn't happen. She has so much trauma that she's never dealt with, and we're going to try to deal with some of that here. Because she's bought into the idea that she's ugly, that she's worthless, that she's expendable. Those internal tapes that play in our heads are tough to change. But if Janice is going to stay sober when she gets out of here, hers *need* to change."

13 TODD

Drug dealers are to dopamine what pornographers are to testosterone or food engineers are to taste buds or plastic surgeons are to reproductive fitness. They are all profit-seekers who have managed, with the assistance of technology, to plug into internal reward or regulatory systems that evolved under circumstances radically different from those of the present. That such exploitation can be physically dangerous and morally subversive is apparent enough. What to do about it is a recurring political dilemma, one that grows more urgent with the wiring of the world.

—DAVID COURTWRIGHT, *FORCES OF HABIT*

TODD STANDS NEXT to a small table heaped with apples, bananas, protein powder, and muscle-building supplements (creatine, glutamine) in a nondescript hotel room in Somerville, west of Boston. He's in town on business—he has more than a dozen escorting clients to see during this five-day trip. But he has most of today off, and this morning we spent an hour at a nearby Gold's Gym, where he worked out in tight silver shorts, a blue tank top, and a Corona baseball cap.

(It's fitting that Todd prefers working out at Gold's. In the late 1970s and early 1980s, the chain's Venice Beach location was a veritable circus of muscle and steroids and a second home for "The Steroid Guru" Dan Duchaine, who wrote the *Underground Steroid Handbook*.)

I didn't think it was possible, but at the gym Todd looked more muscular than when I last visited him a few months ago in the city where he lives. He was also more agitated; his hands shook slightly, and he kept complaining that it was too hot. It wasn't, but Todd was in no position to accurately gauge much of anything.

In the last few weeks he had turned into a steroid fiend, injecting himself nearly every other day. As part of his current twelve-week steroid cycle, Todd is supposed to inject himself only twice a week. Even among heavy steroid users, Todd's behavior is unusual—most tend to follow their planned cycles.

"I'll be feeling good looking in the mirror, and I'll think, 'Well, more will make you look and feel even *better*,'" he tells me in his hotel room, where a lone ray of sunlight makes its way through the closed curtains. "The other day, I was like, 'Why are you fucking up the plan? You're not supposed to inject today!' But I did. And then"—he shakes his head—"I had too much in my system. My throat was constricting, and my hands and feet were burning. I'm doing this more and more, and it's not good. I'm starting to use some of the same behaviors and rationales with steroids that I used with crystal, and that's really scary."

I'm surprised to hear Todd comparing steroids to meth, because until recently he dismissed the idea that steroids could be physically or psychologically addictive. The first time we spoke on the phone, Todd told me that he never craved steroids the way he craved meth, and that steroids didn't make his life unmanageable. He's not so sure anymore. "I don't like this feeling that I'm getting that I *need* to take more steroids, that I'm not taking enough."

If the hamsters in steroid studies could talk, they might have said the same thing. Most showed a preference for a testosterone-laced solution, whether they received it orally, intravenously, or directly into their brains. (Testosterone is the original anabolic steroid.) But unlike with classic addictive drugs, there was no corresponding dopamine spike in the hamsters' brains.

Ruth Wood, a steroid researcher and professor in the Keck School of Medicine at the University of Southern California, told me that there's something fundamentally different about how steroids cause their reward. "It's not the immediate kind of sensation that you get with cocaine," she said. "Testosterone doesn't really give you a rush. It appears to produce more of a long-term sense of well-being." (It also leads to aggressive behavior in hamsters, just as it does in some human users.)

Wood added that one of the advantages of studying steroid use and dependence in animals is that they don't care how they look in the mirror. "In humans, steroid use is complicated by athletic performance and body physique and image," she said. "It's clear that some steroid users have a psychological dependence on them. But it's hard to separate the muscle-building effects, and the positive feelings they generate, from the direct effects of testosterone on the brain."

Experts aren't sure what those direct effects are, but there is increasing evidence that steroids "tickle the same part of the brain" as opiates, said Harrison Pope, a professor of psychiatry at Harvard Medical School and co-author of *The Adonis Complex*. Give an animal a drug that blocks opiate receptors in the brain, for example, and it will no longer self-administer testosterone. Human steroid users are also disproportionately likely to go on to abuse opiates. In a large study of opiate-dependent men in a Boston-area treatment facility, Pope found that 25 percent reported steroid use (among those admitted for other substance addictions, the rate was only 5 percent).

Steroid users also have high rates of abuse of other illicit substances, including cocaine and ecstasy. Meth is less common, although it's a popular choice for some gay and bisexual steroid users who are introduced to the drug in the gay party scene.

It's been a year since Todd last took meth, but in its place he's now dependent on ephedra, a dietary supplement and performance-enhancing drug that causes a mild sense of euphoria. A naturally occurring botanical, ephedra contains ephedrine, the primary ingredient in some illegally synthesized drugs—including meth. A recovering meth addict regularly taking ephedra is a little like an alcoholic eating rum cake every night.

"I know it's probably playing with fire," Todd concedes. "Plus, it wears off and makes me edgy if I take it for too many days in a row."

Todd changes into a camouflage T-shirt with the number 3 on it and opens a suitcase on the hotel room bed. He's going to spend the night with a client, Fred, who lives an hour away.

"How much do you weigh now?" I ask Todd.

"Oh, I don't know," he says, folding a pair of shorts and placing them gently into his suitcase. "I won't get on a scale. I'm one of those bodybuilders who have body dysmorphia to the largest degree, and I'm afraid of seeing something on the scale that doesn't agree with all the hard work I've done in the gym." (First recognized by the American Psychiatric Association in 1987, body dysmorphia is a mental disorder involving an obsessive preoccupation with a physical defect, real or imagined.)

I ask him if he'll inject today. "No," he says. "Most likely tomorrow I won't, either. I can't do two days in a row again. It *has* to stop.

The benefit is that I'm getting hyper muscular growth, but what's being sacrificed is mood and my sex life. I have an erection in the middle of the night, but tomorrow night I won't. I'm horny one day, and nothing the next. I'm tired of that."

"So are you thinking you might stop taking steroids completely?"

"I may. It all depends on how I respond when I take a break. The problem is the temptation that comes from being around body-building. And I'm thinking of doing some bodybuilding competitions soon, and it's hard to compete if you're not on them. But man, as I get older, what I'm realizing is that I want to be normal."

Todd disappears to the bathroom to get his toiletries together. I sit on the bed, next to the open suitcase. He wants to be *normal*? I'm not sure what he means by that. Everything about Todd—his body, his job, his marriage—seems intentionally abnormal, and I don't really believe he'll stop taking steroids anytime soon. Not only can he not afford to (his clients love his steroid-induced size), but quitting steroids would likely mean giving up his alter ego, Billy, too.

Back from the bathroom, Todd shows me the small bottles at the bottom of his suitcase where he keeps the two injectible steroids that make up his current cycle. Like some steroid abusers, Todd gets a portion of his stash legally. Physicians can prescribe testosterone for people suffering from muscle wasting caused by old age, HIV/AIDS, or injury. (Testosterone can also be prescribed for young men with low levels and older men who complain of a lack of sexual drive or energy.)

"My doctor knows what I use them for, but he's kind enough to allow this," Todd tells me. "There are doctors who think it's unethical and don't want any part of it, but then there are doctors who don't care."

Later, across the street at a diner, Todd orders a turkey club sandwich on wheat bread and some fries. "French fries are evil," he tells the young waitress with a grin, "but I love them."

The waitress, who seemed smitten with Todd from the moment we walked in, smiles and cocks her head to the right. "Oh, honey," she says, "you look like you work out enough. I'm sure you can handle *a few little fries.*"

"Okay, okay, you convinced me!" he says.

Once the waitress leaves, Todd tells me that his wife would kill him if she knew he was eating fries. "She's a Nazi when it comes to eating right," he says. "Once I had some M&Ms in the kitchen, and she found them and threw them away! She fights over a quarter for laundry, but she threw the damn M&Ms away. I said, 'Honey, you could have sold them to some kid!'"

Todd invited Christian (the bodybuilding coach who introduced us) and Fred (the client he's spending the night with) to join us for lunch, but neither is here yet. While we wait, he calls his wife. "She was at the gym—I want to make sure she got home all right," he tells me as he dials. It's a quick call; he tells her that he's meeting a client later today, and she urges him to spend thriftily during his last few days in Boston.

"Do you want me to bring you *receipts?*" he asks her, half joking. "Okay, baby, I love you. I'll call you later." (By now I'm used to the fact that Julie doesn't seem to mind what Todd does for a living, but it's still odd to hear them talking about it so nonchalantly.)

Todd will make about $3,000 on this trip. Ideally, he likes to see three or four clients each day, although he can't squeeze in that many "if they're all into doing crazy things," he says. He leans in over the table and lowers his voice. "You wouldn't believe the guy I met yesterday," he tells me. "When I got to his hotel, I called his room, and he said there was a little bag for me at the front desk, some things I needed before I came upstairs. So I get the bag, and inside there's scrubs and a pair of plastic gloves. I called him again from the lobby, and he said, 'Oh, is that you, *doctor?* Do you make *house calls?*' I played along and told him I did, and then he said, 'Good, because doctor, there's something very wrong with my *pussy*. It's very, very tight, and I can't seem to get it loosened up.'"

Todd put the scrubs on quickly outside the man's door. "Then I walked into his room," Todd continues, "and he's sitting there on a chair wearing nothing but panties. I sat in the chair, he sat in my lap, and I did what he wanted me to do. Every now and again you'll encounter unusual people, and they can be a little taxing."

About half of Todd's clients are only into what he calls "muscle worship." They usually just want Todd to flex and show off. Some don't even want to touch him. Todd says that most of the clients into muscle worship claim to be bisexual or straight. "It's just a fetish for them. Over time, I've seen them have successful marriages with their wives. They seem to be very happy, from what I can tell."

Some of Todd's other clients want him to play a more active and dominant role, to boss and toss them around or pretend to be their "daddy." But then there are also guys who want the roles reversed. "In those cases, I'm the *bitch*," he says. "I'm nothing but muscle trash."

"Muscle trash?" I ask.

"Yeah, where you're an *object*. You're a *rag*. And that's the client's fantasy, and you have to respect it and go along with it. When it's over, I can laugh to myself and say, 'Well, that's not true. I'm not trash in real life.'"

Todd has a few clients into hard-core S&M, and one recently paid him $1,000 to whip him. Two days after the whipping, Todd flew to another state to meet a client who likes to "abuse" him. "I'm there taking gut punches," Todd recalls, "and he's beating me and punching me and slapping me around, and I'm not enjoying it sexually, but I am enjoying the fact that I can take what he's dishing out. It's like I had to prove that I'm a man. I even spit in his face and said, 'You're no fucking master!' So he slaps me, and when it's all over, I'm thinking to myself, 'Okay, did we really have to prove anything? You're an old man, Todd. You don't need this.'"

I suspect that part of him does need it. He could probably do without the punching and the spitting, but I wonder if his escorting is itself a kind of addiction.

Todd looks up to see Christian walking toward our booth. It's a hot day, and Christian's wearing a white tank top and khaki shorts, showing off his strong arms and staggeringly large calves ("Many a man wishes he could be blessed with Christian's calves," Todd told me earlier). But while Christian is certainly big, his muscles don't look like Todd's. That is, they don't look like separate attachments.

Fred arrives a few minutes later wearing a polo shirt, shorts, and a baseball hat backward. He's middle-aged, and his limp walk and lazy eye give him a slightly sinister affect. But Todd doesn't seem to mind; he says he considers Fred a friend.

"I think of him as a friend *and* a client," Todd told me earlier at the gym. "You can only have so many of those, but he and his partner are very generous. I can use their guest room to meet another client, and they'll let me borrow their car. Fred's partner accepts the situation very nicely. Fred will hang out with me, and his partner will go to a bathhouse."

A self-described "muscle worshipper," Fred can hardly contain his excitement at our table. After all, he's having lunch with *two* attractive bodybuilders. "You don't understand how hard it is to find guys like these," he gushes to me, in a rare acknowledgment of my presence at the table. "It's just so hard to find beautiful muscle men in gay circles who don't act like big girls. It's very, very depressing. At the gym where I live, it's *so ugly*. So ugly! The two guys who are cute and jacked at my gym, I'm afraid to ask them if they're into muscle worship."

Fred met Todd in 1998 after reading his ad in a local gay newspaper. Todd was living as an out-of-the-closet gay man at the time, and he had posted the escort ad only at the urging of some friends. "They said, 'You're muscular. You could do this!'" recalls Todd. "But I was so nervous, and I didn't meet any of the first guys who responded.

So finally Fred calls, and he says, 'Are you what you say you are in the ad? Because I've already sent three guys away.' So now I'm even more scared, because what if he sends me away, too? But I thought this would be a test. If I could satisfy this guy, then I had what it took. So I go to his hotel room, he opens the door, and he's like, 'Hi iiiiiiiiiiiiiiiiiiiiiiiiiiiiii!' He went nuts."

Fred nods in agreement. "Todd was a definite find," he tells Christian and me. "If he had taken my advice, he would be rich today. I told him to quit his job right then and make a career out of escorting, but it took him a while to really start doing it regularly." Fred eyes Christian. "Now, tell me about *you.*"

Poor Fred—he doesn't realize he's barking up the wrong tree. Christian enjoys healthy flattery, but he champions bodybuilding as a kind of spiritual practice, and little irritates him more than men who treat it only as a sexual fetish.

"I coach young athletes and bodybuilders," Christian tells him. "But it's more than just about bodybuilding—"

"Lucky you!" Fred interrupts. "I would *love* that job."

"I bet you would," Todd says, laughing.

"Can I come and *watch*?" Fred asks Christian, who avoids the question, covers his face with his menu, looks at me, and rolls his eyes. "So why aren't more young people into competitive bodybuilding?" Fred continues, undeterred.

"Maybe because some people have helped give bodybuilding a bad rap," Christian tells him, dropping a not-so-subtle hint. "Of course lots of young guys are attracted to the idea of bodybuilding; it's a chance to be strong, heroic, and express your sense of masculinity. But when they get involved without someone to help them navigate the sport, it's not long before they stumble on all sorts of criminal and tawdry sexual elements. With that kind of association, of course they're apprehensive."

"What's wrong with a little bit of tawdry?" Fred interjects with a disbelieving laugh. "A little tawdry never hurt anybody! I don't understand this younger generation with their baggy shorts and loose-fitting T-shirts. Why are they trying to hide everything? If you ask me, nothing's better than a hot guy in tight pants, where you can see everything. Now"—he slams his fist on the table—"*that's* a man!"

Todd takes a big bite out of his sandwich. "A lot of people think bodybuilding is gay," he says. "I've heard comments like, 'Muscles are *so gay.*'"

"Yeah," Christian says, "and the Internet has helped fuel the myth that bodybuilding is gay. If you type 'bodybuilder' in Google, many of the sites that pop up are sexual fetish sites. And in our culture, if anything seems even the slightest bit gay, then it's automatically deemed contrary to being a man, and that freaks out a lot of young guys. Kids are trained to say, 'Keep me far away from gay stuff, it will feminize me.' God forbid, right?"

Talk eventually turns to women and their lack of appreciation for bodybuilders. "Yesterday I was walking around Boston," Todd tells us, "and I noticed that the women worked really hard not to look at me or make faces. But the guys were looking. They were intrigued."

"I called one of my athletes out the other day on this," Christian says. "I told him, 'It's obvious you're more into improving your body to impress all your boys, your guy friends, and not for the benefit of girls.' He is a totally heterosexual guy, so naturally his first response was like, 'Nah, man, no way.' But I really believe that a lot of young guys who lift seriously are trying to impress their guy friends with how strong and masculine they are, more than they're trying to impress women. Women usually tend to shy away from big bodybuilders."

Fred smiles. "Good," he says, sounding like a kid whose best friend just decided he didn't like playing with GI Joes anymore. "That just leaves more for us."

14 MARVIN

Who cares to admit complete defeat? Practically no one, of course.

Every natural instinct cries out against the idea of personal powerlessness. . . . When first challenged to admit defeat, most of us revolted. We had approached AA expecting to be taught self-confidence. Then we had been told that so far as alcohol is concerned, self-confidence was no good whatever; in fact, it was a total liability.

—*Twelve Steps and Twelve Traditions*

DURING MY FLIGHT to visit Marvin in Florida (and to meet with counselors at the Hanley Center, where he was treated in the older adult program), an elderly man in the middle seat next to me orders a highball on the rocks. I check the time. It's 9:45 A.M.

"A little early for a highball," I mumble to the flight attendant.

"Son," the man says, his hearing aid apparently functioning, "it's *never* too early for a highball." Besides, he's earned it. "After a week with my kids, I really need a drink," he tells me and everyone else within earshot.

The flight attendant smiles and reaches over me to hand him a plastic cup with ice cubes and whiskey. He pays his $7, but he's not happy about it. "At home," he says once the attendant moves down the aisle, "I can go to the bar and get drunk for seven dollars."

"And I bet you do," I tell him, picturing him poolside at his Florida retirement community, downing highballs and complaining about his grown children.

"Of course I do," he says. "I'll get good and drunk if I want to!"

And what would be so wrong with that? Sure, he probably drinks too much (most people who order highballs at 9:45 A.M. do), but he's made it this long, right? He's no apparent menace to society. Odds are he doesn't drive anything other than a golf cart, so it's unlikely he can do much damage drunk behind the wheel. And even if he is a full-fledged alcoholic, what would be the point of intervening this late in the game? He looks to be about seventy-five or eighty, maybe older. Shouldn't he be allowed to golf, drink, and die in peace? Isn't that, in some ways, the *point* of a Florida retirement?

The flood of questions surprises me. Here I am on my way to visit Marvin, and I'm busy rationalizing why the man next to me should be allowed to drink himself to death. During our descent, he asks where I'm heading. I tell him the truth—a treatment center for elderly addicts. There's an awkward silence, during which he turns to talk to the even older man to his right, who's been staring blankly out the window for most of the flight. Maybe his hearing aid isn't working just then. Or maybe, as I was beginning to understand, we were both more comfortable ignoring his problem.

I recount the story the following day to Carol Colleran, the director of older adult services at Hanley. A tall, energetic seventy-year-old with twenty-five years of sobriety from alcohol, Colleran is one of the leading experts on the elderly and addiction in America.

"Up until recently, nobody was talking about this," she tells me, sitting in an office with counselor Juan Harris, a youthful fifty-four-year-old black man with dreadlocks. (A heroin addict with long-term recovery, Harris likes to joke that when he went through treatment a decade ago, he had so many enemies that he was essentially entering the "treatment-protection program.")

Colleran isn't surprised by my airplane story. She says that my rationalizations, and my seatmate's denial, are typical. "Older adults suffer from denial, their friends suffer from denial, their adult children suffer from denial," she says. "As a society, we're in complete denial that older adults can be addicted to anything other than sleeping pills."

John Benshoff, a professor of rehabilitation at Southern Illinois University, calls it the "Little Old Lady" or "Nice Old Man" syndrome. "Even if we do accept that granny might be addicted," he told me, "we rationalize why we shouldn't do anything about it. We say, 'Oh, she's so old, what's the point *now*? Why take away the one pleasure she has in life? She's not hurting anybody."

She's hurting herself, of course, but we tend to tolerate addiction in other people as long as there is little collateral damage, and older adults are the quietest, least disruptive, most unthreatening addicts in America. Those over sixty-five rarely work or commit serious crimes, meaning they have little contact with two of the primary referrers to treatment: the workplace and the criminal justice system.

As the oldest baby boomers reach their early sixties and the elderly population continues to grow (the U.S. Census Bureau says it will be the fastest-growing age group for the next quarter century), some addiction professionals worry that we're grossly unprepared for the onslaught of older adults who will need help getting off drugs and alcohol.

The face of addiction is already aging. Between 2002 and 2005, illegal drug use increased 63 percent among people in their fifties. For those in their forties and fifties, overdose deaths from illicit drugs increased by 800 percent between 1980 and 2006. And according to the federal Substance Abuse and Mental Health Services Administration, the number of people older than fifty needing treatment will double from 2.5 million in 1999 to five million in 2020.

"Very few people have thought about the implications of all this," said Peter Provet, CEO of Odyssey House, where Janice is in treatment. "Most of the addiction field is focused on young people, because it's believed that if you keep someone away from drugs early in life, they're unlikely to start using later. But we're seeing more and more baby boomers in trouble, and we're seeing some other people—we call them 'late-onset' addicts—who never abused alcohol or drugs and then start later in life. What's going on *there*? We don't really know, because we've never studied it. Everyone is in denial."

Even doctors seem unwilling, or unable, to see their elderly patients as addicts needing treatment, often mistaking symptoms of alcoholism and drug abuse for those of depression and dementia. In an extensive report on substance abuse and older women by the National Center on Addiction and Substance Abuse, four hundred primary care physicians were provided with the clinical symptoms of early alcohol addiction in an older woman. More than 80 percent made a diagnosis of depression, while only one percent considered the diagnosis of alcohol abuse.

Colleran and Harris are firm believers that elderly people—although they never use those words, preferring "older adults"—need specialized treatment. In 1998, Colleran created Hanley's older adult program after complaints from patients over sixty-five who didn't feel comfortable around younger addicts. "They couldn't deal with the foul language, the disrespect, the endless drama," Colleran says.

Hanley structures its older adult program in unusual ways. For one thing, Colleran and Harris don't push elderly patients to accept that they're alcoholics, or even that they're powerless over their addiction, both considered by most treatment centers as the first steps toward recovery.

"Older adults—especially those in their seventies and eighties—don't react well to the word *alcoholic*," Colleran explains. "They grew up at a time when an alcoholic was a horribly negative word. The alcoholic was the town drunk or the homeless person under the bridge. Alcoholism still has a stigma attached to it, but when these older adults grew up, it was seen as a humiliating moral failing, something to be deeply ashamed about. So we try to get them to accept how alcohol and drugs have caused problems in their lives, without using the word alcoholic or addict, because many older adults will shut down if you call them that right away."

If getting an older man to admit he's an addict is difficult, try getting him to admit he's *powerless*. One of the great paradoxes of the Twelve Steps is the notion that admitting powerlessness over an addiction—surrendering to the idea that you can't beat it with sheer willpower—is the first step toward acquiring the strength to get sober.

"Admitting powerlessness is difficult for most people, but men of that generation grew up admiring John Wayne, Ted Williams, men who were strong, forceful, and never asked for help," Juan Harris says. "So we slowly have to teach them that admitting that maybe you can't beat your addiction by yourself is okay, that it's okay to ask for help, and that it's okay, and even beneficial, to talk about your feelings. But that isn't easy. They come into treatment and we say, 'How are you feeling? Let's try and get in touch with your *feelings*.' They'll say something like, 'I feel good.' And to that I'll say, 'Good is not a feeling. Good is a hamburger.'"

Even group therapy has to be reconceived when dealing with elderly addicts, who are often too civil for their own therapeutic good. Unlike younger adults and many aging boomers who eagerly confront the denial of others in group therapy, most addicts in their seventies and eighties seek to avoid confrontation and often sidestep difficult issues. Colleran tells me that counselors are generally taught that if they leave a group therapy session tired, then they worked too hard, and the patients didn't work hard enough.

"In other words," Colleran says, "you're supposed to let them do the talking. But with many older adults, their value system is that they speak when spoken to. So you have to draw them out. If you just sit there and let them do the talking, they'll go to sleep." (Or they'll go to the bathroom. The active bladders of older adults make it difficult to create an intimate group therapy setting.)

While older adults certainly pose challenges to addiction specialists, those who work with them say they do better in treatment than younger addicts—and stay sober longer once they leave. Older adults show up to meetings and therapy sessions on time and have a deep respect for authority, a refreshing change for counselors used to working with volatile younger addicts. Elderly men, in particular, are eager to be thought of as "winners" at recovery, and once they set their mind to battling their addiction, very little can stop them.

There's another advantage to working with elderly addicts: They don't pose much of a flight risk. "Our staff can usually catch up to them and convince them to stay before they get too far," Colleran says. "Once we had a seventy-five-year-old man who took off with a young woman from the women's program and never came back, but that's not typical. He was rich and she wasn't, so we know what that was about."

What Colleran and others don't fully understand is why men like Marvin, who drink relatively normally (if at times excessively) for most of their lives, lose control later in life. Were they not addicts for most of their lives but then turned into addicts later? Or were they always addicts who simply needed a trigger to start acting like one?

Marvin's wife, Mary, has little doubt that Marvin's addiction was prompted by the loss of his job. "When he was working," she told me the first time we met, "he put his heart and soul into it. When he couldn't work anymore, he had all this time on his hands, and I think he felt really useless, like he didn't have a place in the world."

At Hanley, Colleran says, the common denominator among late-onset addicts is a loss of purpose—a sense of not being needed or wanted. "You really don't find people who are going great in their sixties and then just start abusing alcohol or drugs for the heck of it," she tells me. "What I'm seeing are a lot of older adults who live the American dream, maybe they run a business up in Ohio, then decide to turn over their business to their son, and they move to Florida to relax and play golf where the sun always shines. What they don't realize is that not only does the sun not shine all the time, but when you have nothing special to do, and you're not accountable for anything, and you don't feel needed, and maybe your spouse dies and you have grief issues along with it, then it can lead to you medicating with alcohol or drugs."

For some late-onset addicts, their addiction is triggered by the death of a spouse or child. At Odyssey House, I met Moses, a strong and reserved fifty-seven-year-old who rarely drank and had tried only marijuana before his wife died in 2001.

"When I lost my wife," he said in a group therapy session I attended, "I also lost my best friend. All I could do was think about her, and I needed something to help me control my thoughts." He chose heroin. Moses quickly started abusing it, and then selling it. "I sold it to be around it," he told the group. "It was all I lived for." When he sold to an undercover cop, he ended up in prison.

At first glance, Moses doesn't seem to fit neatly into the disease model of addiction, which argues that addiction is a chronic and progressive illness. There appears to be nothing chronic in Moses's story, nor does his addiction seem to have progressed so much as *appeared*. If he does suffer from the disease of addiction, could it have been dormant for most of his life? Yes, argue many addiction researchers, who liken addiction to other chronic diseases—Type II diabetes, cancer, and cardiovascular disease—that have a genetic component and an onset and course that vary depending on behavior and environmental factors.

"Do we know that there is a degree of genetic pull in some addictions? The answer is, without a doubt, yes," Odyssey House's Provet told me. "Do we know definitely how predisposition mixes with environment to create an addict? No. We're not at the point where we can draw a clean curve, or graph, and explain why someone can take or leave drugs for most of his life but then start abusing them in his fifties. That's still a mystery."

———

After sitting down with Colleran and Harris, I accompany Marvin to an AA meeting, where he tells the group how grateful he is for his more than two and a half years of sobriety. "It's mind-boggling how much my life has changed," he says. "I have a new way of life today. I have new friends. My drinking friends, I don't know where the hell they are, and I don't miss 'em!"

"And I bet they don't miss *you*, Marvin," a fellow AA member jokes.

After the meeting, Marvin and I grab a late lunch at an outdoor café near his condo. He's in good spirits, although he says his wife isn't very happy lately.

"I think she's jealous of my recovery," Marvin tells me. "Basically, my life revolves around AA meetings. I socialize with people from the meetings, and I'm always out doing stuff for my recovery. I think my wife's mad that I'm focusing so much on AA. She won't go to Al-Anon, because she doesn't think she needs it. So what am I supposed to do?" He shakes his head. "After fifty-seven years together," he continues, "we mostly stay out of each other's way." (Yesterday, though, Marvin did take her to Home Depot, where she looked at new kitchens. "She kept badgering me to take her," he says, "so I gave in.")

I'm surprised that Marvin divulged this much about his marriage. He's generally uncomfortable talking to me about anything other than the basics of "his recovery," and as much as he respects and lives the AA program, I'm not sure he's capable of the introspection required to work all of the Twelve Steps.

For instance, when I ask him if he's worked Steps Eight and Nine (*Made a list of all persons we had harmed, and became willing to make amends to them all*, and *Made direct amends to such people wherever possible, except when to do so would injure them or others*), he tells me that he skipped them.

"I can't do those," he explains, "because the only person I harmed was my wife."

"Have you made amends to her?" I ask.

"I can't think of anyone that I personally have to make amends to," he says, ignoring my question. "I have a good relationship with my four kids. They're all grown and have their own kids. My friends are mostly dead. And I don't remember hurting anyone intentionally."

But Steps Eight and Nine say nothing about *intent*. We're supposed to make amends—with the guidance of a sponsor—to those we've harmed, regardless of whether we meant to harm them, or, most vexing at times, whether they also harmed us. And I'm skeptical that he's harmed only his wife. We addicts end up hurting virtually everyone who's close to us. Writer Joyce Rebeta-Burditt may have put it best: "Alcoholism isn't a spectator sport. Eventually the whole family gets to play."

(That might explain the popularity of Al-Anon, a Twelve Step–based fellowship for the families and friends of alcoholics. Co-founded in 1951 by Lois Wilson, the wife of AA co-founder Bill Wilson, there are now some 26,000 Al-Anon and Alateen groups in

115 countries. Lois realized she needed help after Bill got sober and began devoting his life to recovery. "My life's purpose of sobering up Bill, which had made me feel desperately needed, had vanished," she wrote in Al-Anon's main text. Lois hit her "bottom" when Bill invited her to a recovery meeting. "Damn your old meetings!" she yelled, hurling a shoe at him.)

Marvin's reluctance to make amends doesn't make him unique. There's a joke about an alternative Eighth Step that some addicts may secretly prefer: *Made a list of all the people we had harmed, and asked God to remove them.*

Many elderly addicts, in particular, have trouble with Steps Eight and Nine. "They don't connect that their drinking or drug use is related to many of the problems in their friendships and relationships," Colleran told me. "Why is this more common with older adults? I don't know, but it's normal to find older addicts who don't really *get* those steps. Still, it is really critical for *all* addicts to try to do them."

That can have unintended consequences. As part of his Ninth Step, an AA member named William Beebe wrote a letter of apology in 2005 to a woman he had raped more than twenty years before at a University of Virginia fraternity party. In return for his amend, Beebe was sentenced to eighteen months in prison. Prosecutors claimed that Beebe's amend was selfish, and that it had retraumatized his victim. Essentially, they argued that Beebe had failed to heed the warning spelled out at the end of Step Nine—*except when to do so would injure them or others.*

It is one of the most difficult caveats to navigate with integrity. As addicts in recovery, we're supposed to make amends to clean up our side of the street and enhance our own healing, not to receive absolution or sympathy from the people we harmed (or, worse yet, to try to fix and heal *them*). At the same time, we're told to consider and predict their feelings and emotional states, even if they've long been out of our lives. In some cases—if the person we need to make amends to is dead, or if it's likely that contacting the person would cause further hurt—we're advised by our sponsors that the best amends we can make is to stay sober and to try not to cause harm today.

Still, the book *Twelve Steps and Twelve Traditions* urges recovering addicts to make sure we aren't avoiding an amends out of fear: *For the readiness to take the full consequences of our past acts, and to take responsibility for the well-being of others at the same time, is the very spirit of Step Nine.*

For Marvin, fear seems to be at the root of his reluctance to tackle many of the Twelve Steps. It especially took a lot of convincing (from his sponsor and others in AA) for Marvin to do his Fourth and Fifth Steps—*Made a searching and fearless moral inventory of ourselves,* and *Admitted to God, to ourselves, and to another human being the exact nature of our wrongs.*

"I used to piss and moan so much about those," Marvin tells me. "My friends in AA would say, 'Marvin, we're so sick of your baloney. Stop with the B.S. Do the damn steps and get them over with!'" (Marvin is definitely not alone there, either. Many addicts put off Steps Four and Five for years.)

Working with his sponsor, Marvin finally did them, focusing on his anger and resentments. "I wrote them all down and then read it to him on the beach," he says. "I was ranting and raving about my character defects, about my anger, my temper, my resentments. I was totally honest with him. I got it all out, and it wasn't that bad. I'm only human, after all."

As we're leaving the café, Marvin grabs my arm. "I know I have to work the steps," he tells me. "My compulsion to drink isn't gone. The urge is still there. If I get tired or ornery, I sometimes want a drink really bad. And I'm old, so I get tired and ornery a lot!"

15 BOBBY

I admire addicts. In a world where everybody is waiting for some blind, random disaster, or some sudden disease, the addict has the comfort of knowing what will most likely wait for him down the road. He's taken some control over his ultimate fate, and his addiction keeps the cause of death from being a total surprise.

—Writer Chuck Palahniuk

"I THINK BOBBY'S going to die," Margaret tells me, slumped in her chair and crying in the cramped ground-floor office of the South Boston anti-addiction community organization where she works. Margaret was in a good mood when I arrived, but after thirty minutes of talking about her heroin-addicted godson, she's staring blankly around the street-level room, her voice soft and defeated.

"I've been able to help so many people who walked through these doors," she says in her thick South Boston accent, "but I can't help my own godson. I don't know what else to do. I've done everything I can. I don't want to give up, because so many people have already given up on Bobby, but at some point this just becomes too painful."

I came here hoping Margaret would know where Bobby is, but she hasn't seen him in three months. I haven't seen him or talked to him in nearly half a year. I left dozens of messages on the answering machine at his parents' house, where he and his brother usually stay. They went unreturned. I also dropped by the house a handful of times, but either no one was home, or no one wanted to talk to me. I called Tina, his ex-girlfriend and the mother of his two sons, but when I told her I was working on a book about addiction, she passed the phone to a man who said never to call again.

Finally, I visited the South Boston Drug Court, where Bobby is well known—and not particularly beloved. "Of all the addicts in Southie to write about, you choose *him*?" a court employee said, shaking his head. "Bobby has been causing trouble around this neighborhood for a long time."

Assistant Chief Probation Officer Jack Leary (whom Margaret calls the "Jesus Christ of South Boston" for his tireless work helping Southie addicts get clean) could at least confirm that Bobby was alive. "Yeah, I picked him up a few weeks ago," he told me recently. There had been a warrant out for Bobby's arrest. He still owed $150 as part of his sentence for stealing cases of baby formula from a pharmacy, which he intended to sell to bodegas and use the profits to buy heroin.

"We were actually after someone else," Leary continued, "but we had knowledge that Bobby was also in the apartment. So we went in there early. I call them 'underwear raids,' because everyone's still asleep."

According to Leary, there was a large knife at the base of the bed where Bobby and the girl Leary was after were sleeping. Bobby was lying on his stomach, so Leary said he grabbed his hands and cuffed him. "That's the way you want to find Bobby—asleep, on his stomach," Leary said. "He's a big, physical guy, and he can't put up much of a fight that way." (Bobby ended up in jail for five days.)

Probation officers aren't the only ones with a healthy fear of Bobby. Doug, a drug addict from Boston's South Shore, has seen Bobby when he's using drugs and when he's sober. They were once roommates in a halfway house.

"I'm not scared of many people, but he scares the shit out of me," Doug told me. "When he's sober he's a great guy. He'll give you the shirt off his back. But you put him in a position where he's out of shit, and he wants some shit, and he's got to go through you to get the shit, then you're in a fucked-up position. I've seen him like that. He doesn't see you as a human being. You're an obstacle. Many addicts are like that, but he's just so physically imposing, and he's not scared of anybody. You'll be sitting with your family having dinner, and he'll walk into your house, grab your TV, and walk out saying, 'What are you going to do about it?'"

Southie addicts know to hide their drugs when Bobby comes around. About a year after they roomed together at the halfway house, Doug relapsed and was getting high on crack and heroin with some friends when Bobby unexpectedly showed up.

"I was just chillin' at this kid's apartment on the love seat by the window, which looked out into an alley," Doug said. "All of a sudden I see this big head peer inside. It's Bobby. In this deep voice he's like, 'WHOOOO HAAAAS DRUUUUGS?' So we're all freaking out. We're like, 'Fuck, he's going to come in here and take our drugs!' So he came in, and we sat there pretending like we weren't high and didn't have any drugs until he went away. I'm still not sure how the fuck we pulled it off."

Margaret knows about Bobby's reputation, but she has a hard time believing it. "A lot of people are afraid of him, think he's a no-good person," she says. "And I guess he's done plenty of things to earn that reputation, but I just don't see it. He doesn't scare me or intimidate me. I know the real Bobby. I remember what Bobby was like *before* the drugs."

Back then, Bobby was a shy, oversized twelve-year-old—he was already six feet tall—who avoided fights with older neighborhood boys who picked on him. "Believe it or not," Margaret says, "when Bobby was young, I thought he would grow up to be a singer. He used to go to barrooms and sing this long, tear-jerker Irish song. It was a real weeper, and Bobby would have everyone crying."

When Bobby was sixteen, he took up boxing, mostly to make his father proud, but also because excelling in sports is a surefire way to get respect in Southie. Margaret tried to convince Bobby to go to college, but there was too much pressure on him to stay home and box. Bobby took a cycle of steroids to get stronger, and he kept getting better. But by eighteen, he started drinking heavily on weekends. By twenty, he was partying and using cocaine. Those are late starts in Southie, where many kids start drinking around eleven or twelve and abusing illicit drugs by thirteen or fourteen. Still, by the time Bobby was twenty-seven, he was a full-fledged heroin addict. And his promising boxing career was over.

———

In 1997, a headline in the *Boston Globe* screamed, HEROIN DIGS ITS HOOKS INTO SOUTH BOSTON. That year, a rash of teen overdoses and suicides brought unwelcome attention to this proud neighborhood. But like a good addict, the community's denial ran deep, and when OxyContin soon flooded the area, there was nothing to stop it.

By 2001, gangs of gun-wielding kids from Southie and other Boston-area neighborhoods—they wore bandannas and baseball caps to cover their faces—were holding up pharmacies for Oxys. In 2002, nearly 90 percent of the pharmacy thefts in New England took place in Massachusetts.

"In Southie today," Margaret tells me in her office, "most kids start real young with alcohol, then they move to weed, then they dabble in ecstasy and coke, and then they graduate to Oxys. But soon Oxys become too expensive to keep up with the habit because they're so addictive. So they switch to heroin."

The numbers started bearing that out early this decade. Between the summers of 2001 and 2002, South Boston residents sought treatment for heroin more than eight hundred times, an astonishingly high number for a neighborhood of only thirty thousand. Southie has more fatalities directly attributable to substance abuse than any other Boston neighborhood. In January of 2004, Jim McCay, a former youth worker in Southie, told the *Boston Globe* that he had never seen the drug problem so bad. "I feel kind of hopeless," he said.

Boston shatters the myth that drug addiction disproportionately affects racial minorities. The city's per capita rate of drug-related deaths is highest in South Boston and Charlestown, both predominantly white neighborhoods. And in many mostly white and rural Massachusetts communities, heroin and OxyContin abuse are also raging. Between 1993 and 2005, drug overdoses in Massachusetts skyrocketed six-fold.

The increase coincided with a dramatic reduction in state spending for substance abuse treatment. Between 2001 and 2004, $16 million was cut from the Bureau of Substance Abuse Services, and the number of detoxification beds plummeted.

"I don't think we could be handling this problem in a worse way," Massachusetts State Representative Ruth Balser told me. "What happens when the state cuts all these services is that addicts who need treatment end up dead, committing crimes to support their addiction, or in jail." (Of the nearly 25,000 people in the state's correctional facilities in 2005, 80 percent reported having a substance abuse problem.)

Nowhere in Massachusetts is the drug problem worse than in

South Boston. Even the gentrification of the once homogeneous neighborhood that fought court-mandated school busing hasn't slowed the epidemic of drug abuse. To grow up in Southie is to grow up feeling trapped, Bobby's brother, Dan, told me the first time we met. "When you feel like you're stuck here and you're not going to become anything, which is how a lot of kids around here think, getting high is the only way to feel any kind of freedom," he said. "It takes you out of Southie for a while."

To make it to eighteen without abusing drugs is nothing short of a miracle, Bobby told me once. "Out of the kids I knew growing up," he said, "I can think of *one* who didn't have problems with drugs or alcohol. The rest are dead, in jail, still using, or went to treatment and got sober."

When I ask Margaret what makes Southie so ripe for addiction, she points to the community's culture of low expectations. "When you come from the mafia background we came from, where it's basically a bunch of struggling Irish Catholics trying to come here and survive and learn every kind of technique to do that, you end up learning that scamming and putting one over on people are essential to survival," she says. "Growing up in Southie, you think it's cool to use your connections or kiss the ass of some city employer to get a summer job where you won't have to do too much actual work. And you think you're pulling a fast one, but you get in this mind-set where you're not expecting much of yourself. So you're surrounded by a bunch of other people who don't expect much, people who inevitably abuse alcohol and drugs, and you get caught up in that, and before you know it you're caught in this cesspool, and you're addicted."

Hoping to rewrite the script, in 2001 a group of Southie mothers with kids addicted to heroin and other drugs formed the anti-addiction organization where Margaret works. The mothers quickly made a splash, publicly airing the dirty laundry of a neighborhood that had long pretended there wasn't a problem. They called community meetings, rallied the press, started weekly support groups for parents of addicted kids, and lobbied state politicians to fund addiction treatment.

"If we're so ashamed as a community that we can't even talk about the problem," Margaret says, "then our kids are going to keep dying, and I'm not prepared to let that keep happening for the sake of *appearances*."

Margaret's organization has helped hundreds of Southie residents, many of them teenagers, find treatment. "Some people need two, five, ten tries at treatment before it works," she says. "But then there are those, like Bobby, who've been to hundreds of detoxes and treatment centers and can't seem to stay sober. He's been to every known detox and treatment center around. I've also sent him to Chicago and Florida for treatment. I'm not lying when I tell you that he's been to hundreds of different places."

That hasn't left him much time to be a dad to his two sons. They live with their mother, Tina, who friends of the family have told me battles an OxyContin addiction. Tina has also spent time in jail for her part in a professional shoplifting ring. Tina and several other women reportedly stole expensive items from stores and then handed them over to a male accomplice, who sold the items on the Internet.

"Tina isn't in a much better position than Bobby to be taking care of their kids," a friend of Bobby's told me. "How much do you want to guess those kids grow up to be addicts, too? It's heartbreaking, but if we're good at anything in South Boston, it's passing addiction on to our children."

16 ELLEN

A good meal ought to begin with hunger.

—French proverb

A FEW MONTHS after the Passover dinner at her house, Ellen sends me her First Step, which she wrote and presented to her sponsor soon after she began attending Overeaters Anonymous in 2001. While there are different ways to formally work the step with a sponsor, some addicts choose to write a chronology of their life, focusing on their powerlessness over their addiction and the unmanageability it caused in their lives.

The exercise is meant to help addicts break through denial, or what some call their "built-in forgetter." Denial is one of the primary symptoms of addiction, which differentiates addiction from many other illnesses (cancer patients, for example, rarely deny they have cancer once it's been diagnosed). That's why many addicts choose to say the First Step out loud every morning, and why addicts at Twelve Step meetings begin their sharing by saying, My name is _____, and I'm a _____ addict.

"This ritual undermines the alcoholic's propensity to redefine his or her problem as something other than alcoholism as soon as the acute pain subsides," William White writes in *Slaying the Dragon*.

For Ellen, writing her First Step was a deeply humbling process, but she persisted. "I wanted to get it over with," she told me. "Once I started, it wrote itself; the words just flowed out. I didn't edit. I just wrote from stream of consciousness. And before I knew it, it was done."

This is a portion of Ellen's First Step . . .

Step 1: Admitted I am powerless over food, that my life had become unmanageable.

When I started the program of Overeaters Anonymous, my life had definitely become unmanageable. I weighed almost 300 pounds (my highest ever was 304) and couldn't tie my shoes. I had difficulty fitting behind the steering wheel of the car and needed seat belt extensions on airplanes. Just walking around the mall took all the wind out of me, and it was getting difficult to reach certain areas I needed to wash in the shower. I hated sex because it was so uncomfortable, wanted to partake in no physical activities, and viewed myself as a disembodied mind . . . a mind with no connection to a physical body. I'd lie in bed in the middle of the night in a panic, knowing I was headed for death and resolving that the next day I'd start dieting. Of course when the next day arrived, I lost all resolve and continued to overeat. How did I get to this desperate place?

As far back as I can remember, I've turned to food as my first love. One of my fondest childhood memories is of smelling pizza cooking after I'd gone to bed and getting up to share the pizza that my mother had made for herself as a compensation for my father's absence. I thought about food and eating all the time. I snuck food from a very young age—there are many "cute" photos of me as a young child caught in the act of sneaking cookies.

I don't have a lot of early memories other than loving to read and loving to eat, usually at the same time. I started to be aware of this fact that I was overweight when I was almost eight. I took dance classes from my cousin and despised them. I was larger than the other girls in my tutu, and I felt like a clumsy elephant. When the school nurse came into the classroom to weigh all the kids, I dreaded the moment when she would announce my weight out loud to the entire class. In fact, I tried to stay home sick on those days.

At age eight my mother took me to her doctor, who put me on a diet. I was also put on amphetamines and an exercise plan that was originally developed by the Canadian air force. I felt so horrible on the speed that I determined I'd rather be fat than feel like that. Meanwhile, I continued taking great comfort in food, especially carbohydrates. I loved buttered noodles, chili on noodles, hamburger casserole . . . these foods made me feel happy (numb).

When I reached adolescence and started to interact with boys, I was so full of shame over my weight. I recall pictures of me standing next to my best friend and feeling like a hippopotamus next to her. At Bar Mitzvah parties, I was the one playing with the boys, not dancing with them. I was desperately unhappy and convinced myself, and my parents, that if I got a nose job every-thing would be better. All the while I continued to eat huge amounts of food, primarily in private, because I was too ashamed to let others see me eat.

I was the girl with the "good personality," the one all the boys were friends with. I always used self-deprecating humor, because that's what fat girls did. I spent my teenage years feeling desperately unhappy. I escaped into books whenever I could, and of course into food. I can remember feeling ultimately comforted when I had a huge plate of chili and noodles and sat eating it while reading.

I was always a good student in school even though I hated it. Fortunately I was bright, so I could do well despite being as damaged as I was. When I was 17, I convinced my parents to let me drop out of school and start a "free school." It was a geographical fix, but it worked for a while. In fact, I set my sights on the art teacher, who was 26, and after sleeping with every other teacher and student (looking for the answer in sex—it was 1970), moved in with Patrick, my first dissipated artist. I continued to eat everything in sight, getting fatter and fatter.

Shortly after I moved in with Patrick, I got hired at my first radio station. Radio was a perfect job for a fat person because you could be anyone you wanted and no one could see you. I began to fall out of love (lust) with Patrick after a year or so, and split up with him, much to his dismay. He beat me up one night and that was that. I moved in with some friends and never saw him again.

Around that time, I began my first serious diet. I went at it very compulsively. I was working overnights at the station, and when I got off the air, I would head to the health club and work out for an hour and a half, swim a mile, go home and bike 15 miles, and then go to sleep (no eating of course—some mornings I was so weak I could barely lift my arms to shampoo my hair). When I woke up, I ate a dry chicken breast and a wedge of lettuce. That was all I ate for months. I wished I could just go to sleep and wake up thin. I knew that once I was thin, I would be happy. I spent those months lost in a fantasy of how I would be thin, wear a green velvet blazer, tight jeans, and Frye boots, meet a DJ at a competing station that I liked, and fall in love and be happy.

I did lose the weight. My mother had never given me so much positive reinforcement before. It was fantastic. Even though I was very thin, I didn't like my breasts. They were too big and saggy, and my mom said she and my father would buy me a breast reduction. After the reduction, my mother and I shopped for bikinis. I was incredibly happy. I spent all my time suntanning, smoking pot, doing cocaine (which had the wonderful benefit of taking away my appetite). For my 21st birthday, I was thin and beautiful and my mom asked what I wanted for my birthday dinner. I requested lasagna, and ate until I was so sick I had to lie down in pain.

My affections had turned to another DJ, and I finally did meet him. I looked perfect—tan, thin, beautiful. He took me on a picnic on his motorcycle, and we fucked all night. It was heaven. I was in love. But he never called me again, my heart broke, and I started eating. I vividly recall one starry night, standing outside my house, feeling the warm breeze, and feeling so empty. I was full of longing, but I didn't know for what.

I went through a series of relationships, none of them healthy, continued to gain weight, and met Tom. I wasn't attracted to him at first but he pushed hard to be friends. All my girlfriends talked about how gorgeous and nice he was, and I began to let him in. We were soon in a relationship (or so I thought—he continued to see other people). He moved into my house as a "roommate." I wanted him as a lover, but he continued to withhold from me and brought his other girlfriend home with him to my house. I can't express how much that hurt. I ate and ate, turning to my old friend, food.

He told me that he and another friend were going to Europe in the fall, and I invited myself along. Thus began my next period of starving. I had to be thin to go to Europe! Once again, I exercised compulsively and ate anorexically. I do remember one night, though, when I just lost it and drove to the all-night convenience store and binged my head off. When I got to Europe (Tom and his friend had gone a month before me), I was looking thin and beautiful. Of course when I got there, Tom was involved in a relationship with a thin, gorgeous, South African marathon runner. I started eating again.

Tom and I decided to go to Africa to visit a former roommate who was in the Peace Corps there. We stayed at his house, and Tom would not be my lover. The pain was palpable. I returned to Paris alone and was so lonely, I would spend every night in my hotel room with huge amounts of cheese and baguettes.

I wanted to stay in Paris and found a job as a masseuse. I was more and more into the food and remember my boss telling me I'd better lose some weight if I wanted to keep my job. I desperately wanted Tom to join me in Paris and sent him money to return and told him he would share my apartment. Only one condition . . . he had to have a relationship with only me. He returned, and finally we lived together as lovers. I had pushed hard enough and won.

Eventually, I tired of life in the massage world. Tom and I returned home, got an apartment, set up housekeeping, and he promptly proceeded to take up with his former girlfriend, Joyce, the one who had caused me all the pain when we lived there before. I looked for a geographic fix and found a job in another city. I'll never forget the general manager of the radio station telling me when he hired me that I should lose a little weight, so I could be more like Mary Tyler Moore. Tom drove out there with me and then, after helping me get settled, flew back to Minneapolis and moved in with Joyce. I was so unhappy and lonely. I gorged myself with carry-out Chinese food and chili Polish sausages.

Before I could ever really get settled, I was offered a job in another city, and there was no decision. Better city, better situation. I was gone. I made some friends at work but still was calling Tom and begging him to move out and join me. I tempted him with my good job and a nice apartment. He skipped out on Joyce in the middle of the night and joined me.

About this time, I should have realized that he was an alcoholic fully into his disease, but good codependent that I was, I lived in denial. Instead I stopped at the sub shop every day on the way to and from work and ate a huge loaded sub. I was so unhappy. I would drive in the car and cry. I looked toward another geographic fix and quit my job. The plan was that we would go to Florida and stay in my grandparents' vacation trailer, then head to Boston.

I started eating again and gained back the weight I had lost. Tom and I decided to get married, so of course, I needed to lose weight for my wedding. I once again went on a crash diet, knowing that once I could fit into a size 6 wedding gown, life would be bliss. I never made it to size 6 but did make size 10. We were married in Minneapolis, took our booty, and drove back to Boston. Tom was working as a bar manager for an Indian restaurant and we found a beautiful apartment. On the surface, life was good. We had good jobs, a lovely home, a great city. I was unhappy, though. Tom was drinking heavily and staying out partying till all hours of the night.

I was eating like there was no tomorrow. At one point I hit 250 pounds and my mom made the very hurtful comment that she didn't know how Tom could love someone so fat. When Tom had a ruptured appendix and was hospitalized for twelve weeks, I ate pint after pint of Ben & Jerry's chocolate chocolate chip. Even writing that name now gives me comfort in some perverse way. When he got out of the hospital I made up a story about how I had been mugged in the alley and we had to move out of Boston. (Another geographic fix.)

We moved, but he still was at the bar, and I was lonely and getting fatter and fatter. I didn't have to worry about sneaking food because he was never home. Tom was more heavily into the booze than ever. I got a job at the station where I work now. I focused on losing weight and once again began to exercise compulsively. It was getting harder to diet though, and although I lost weight, it came back on very quickly. We bought a house and I wanted to have children. Tom said I was too fat. I weighed about 140 and wasn't really too fat.

I decided that if he wanted me to be thinner in order to "give" me a baby, I'd lose weight. I starved and exercised compulsively, walking miles around the cove and doing weight training. Of course, once again I just wanted to go into a deep freeze and wake up when I was thin. I got down to about 115 pounds. Of course Tom still wouldn't have sex or a baby, so I started eating. I also finally came to the conclusion that he was an alcoholic. I'll never forget the day I said to his mother, "I think Tom is an alcoholic." She said, "Of course he is."

Things had gotten very bad between us. We were having knock-down, drag-out fights. He would pin me down and say that I was a "fat fuck," and I would throw things at him and call him a drunk.

I was living in total isolation. I had no friends, and no one knew what was going on. I was so ashamed. I gained sixty pounds in one year and went to a therapist. I told her that I didn't know why I couldn't stop eating, that except for the weight gain, my life was fine! With her help, I extricated myself from my marriage and struck out on my own. Through this my assistant at work, Alan, was my best friend and was so supportive. I don't know if I could have done this without him.

Alan and I grew closer and fell in love. I wanted to have children. Thus began a quest for children that lasted four years. During this time I didn't focus on my weight or eating because I was too focused on my fertility. Either I was trying to get pregnant, was pregnant, or was breast-feeding. All the while, I was stopping at every fast food place in town, ruining my clothes with ketchup and mustard stains from dripping food in the car. Every morning on the way to work, I would stop at Mr. Bagel and get two bagels with cream cheese, and two fruit cream cheese croissants, which I would eat before I got to work.

During my pregnancy, I had gestational diabetes and could have no sugar. All I thought about was cake. The night he was born, I stuffed my face with cake. Alan was supportive and always loved me unconditionally so I felt free to eat large amounts of food in front of him, but I also still snuck food at every opportunity.

After I was done having kids I weighed 300 pounds. I was miserable and desperate. I could not get down on the floor with my kids because I could not get back up. I could not stop eating. I'd lie awake in the quiet of the middle of the night knowing I was going to die. Every night I'd resolve to start dieting the next day. Every day I'd fail. I was a failure. I was desperate. There was no hope . . . until I found Overeaters Anonymous.

———————

OA wasn't the first major recovery fellowship for overeaters. That distinction belongs to Take Off Pounds Sensibly (or TOPS), which was founded in 1948 by Esther Manz, a wife and mother from Milwaukee. As far as Manz was concerned, she was as addicted to food as any AA member was to alcohol. A skilled promoter, Manz succeeded at getting the *Milwaukee Journal* to write an article about her new group, and soon so many people showed up that Manz said she "could hardly get through the crowd to our meeting room!"

By 1958, TOPS boasted thirty thousand members and an admirable penchant for self-deprecation. Its local chapters had colorful names (Invisi-Belles, Thick 'N Tired, Inches Anonymous, Shrinking Violets) and comical props, including pig bibs, pigpens, and a piggy bank for fines if you violated group mandates. There was also the *pig song*—"We are plump little pigs / Who eat too much / Fat, Fat, Fat."

Rozanne S., a copywriter in her thirties, took a more sobering approach when she founded OA in 1960. With the support of the founder of Gamblers Anonymous, Rozanne and two other women—

one the wife of a GA member, the other a neighbor of Rozanne's—formed the first OA group after attending GA and AA meetings for inspiration. (The wife of the GA member soon dropped out. "My doctor says that dieting makes me nervous," she told the others.)

Rozanne initially set out to rewrite the Twelve Steps. "I believed that I was not so weak that I had to turn my life and will over to the care of any God, whether he existed or not," she once wrote in OA's main text. Rozanne eventually changed her mind and decided not to tinker with the Steps, replacing only the words "alcohol" and "alcoholic" with "food" and "compulsive overeater."

While OA membership grew rapidly, the fellowship was divided over how to define "abstinence" and whether to sanction an official food plan. In 1972, Rozanne was stripped of her position as the group's national secretary for not being a "physical example of recovery"—in other words, she was too fat.

That year, OA approved three "disciplined" food plans for its members. One, called the "Grey Sheet" because it was printed on grey paper, called for low carbohydrates and no refined sugar. Five years later, OA scrapped the Grey Sheet, causing some members to defect and start a splinter group, GreySheeters Anonymous. Over the years, other OA members have left to start separate food addiction fellowships with stricter food plans.

By 1993, when addiction researcher Mark Gold arrived at the annual American Society of Addiction Medicine (ASAM) conference arguing that the organization should officially recognize compulsive overeating as a real addiction, there were thousands of food addiction recovery meetings around the world. But while anorexia and bulimia were hot topics of research and debate, compulsive overeating was largely ignored by scientists and the media. All the while, Americans kept getting fatter.

Gold had his work cut out for him at ASAM, where he urged his fellow addiction researchers and treatment providers to see food addiction as similar to cocaine addiction. He reminded them that only a decade before, many had discounted the belief that cocaine was addictive.

The conventional wisdom in the early 1980s was that there could be no addiction without physical withdrawal symptoms, and cocaine didn't cause many (unlike heroin and alcohol). Singer David Crosby spoke for many people when he said, "We all knew—because it was common knowledge, accepted knowledge—that cocaine was not addictive." (There was even a time when some thought that cocaine could *cure* addictions to alcohol and morphine. In the 1880s, Sigmund Freud claimed that addiction treatment centers "can now be entirely dispensed with because of cocaine's curative powers.")

By the late 1980s, as cocaine abuse became impossible to ignore, many addiction researchers were using a new model to explain addiction. Perhaps being hooked was less about fatal withdrawal than it was about *fatal attraction*. Cocaine was a perfect example of a substance without satiety. People who abused it took as much as they could until they ran out, even as their lives fell apart.

At ASAM, Gold argued that food was similar. "I had virtually no science to back up what I was saying," Gold told me, "but to me it was common sense." For some people, there was clearly never enough food. These were not men and women who occasionally soothed themselves with a pint of ice cream after a bad day. These were people, Gold told the conference attendees, whose lives were consumed by food, who kept eating and eating despite increasingly negative consequences to their physical and emotional health.

Many compulsive overeaters displayed strong willpower in other areas of their lives, but they were incapable of controlling their cravings for food. Gold wasn't sure what was going on in their brains, but he suspected that they were as powerless over food as many other Americans were over drugs.

Gold's timing could not have been worse. That year the tobacco industry—needing ammunition against ASAM, which was leading the fight to have the American Medical Association officially call nicotine addictive—claimed that ASAM was so loose in its scientific standards that it also believed that "food, sex, and surfing" could be addictive, recalled then-ASAM president David Smith. To protect ASAM's credibility, and to ensure that the tobacco industry didn't win, Smith argued against Gold's proposal.

"It wasn't that he didn't make a compelling argument," Smith told me. "I personally believed that food addiction was real, just as I do now. But for political reasons, we couldn't say that *then*. We made a purely political decision, and it was the right one. Had we included food addiction, we would have likely lost the much bigger battle we were fighting against the tobacco companies."

There were other forces working against Gold that year at ASAM. "The most traditional people in the addiction field, the people treating heroin addicts and alcoholics, rightly questioned whether calling obesity a substance abuse disorder, and food the substance of abuse, would trivialize their work," Gold says. "I remember one guy asking me, 'What's next? If we go down this road, couldn't sex be addicting?' Well, now it turns out that there's a field for that, too."

A decade later, Gold returned to an ASAM conference again to make his pitch that food could be a debilitating addiction. A lot had changed in ten years. For one thing, researchers at the U.S. Department of Energy's Brookhaven National Laboratory had built a brain-imaging table big enough to fit the morbidly obese. (Until that time, it had been impossible to peer into their brains, because they couldn't even fit on the table.)

"We now know that the messengers in the brain that anticipate food or drug rewards are the same," Gold says. "We also know that food and drugs compete in the brain for the same pleasure and reward signals." Train animals to self-administer drugs, and they'll do it most when they're hungry. Feed them, and they're less interested in getting high. "It also turns out that people who stop using drugs or alcohol tend to overeat," Gold explains. "It's like a seesaw. If drugs are on, food's off. If food's on, drugs are off."

Gold received a decidedly more positive reception in 2003 than he had a decade before. "Nearly everyone agreed that it was a verifiable addiction," he says, adding that the *Journal of Addictive Diseases* asked him to write an introduction to a special issue devoted to the topic.

But in the years since, Gold and other food addiction researchers have been surprised by how rarely food addiction is mentioned as a factor in this country's obesity epidemic. Americans are the fattest people in the world. Two-thirds are either overweight or obese, and between 2000 and 2005, the proportion of severely obese (one hundred or more pounds overweight) increased by 50 percent.

Still, many of those studying obesity have mostly ignored food addiction, Kelly Brownell, director of the Rudd Center for Food Policy and Obesity at Yale, told me.

"Our field has been amazingly reluctant to look at the possibility of food being addictive despite the fact that our patients often use the language of addiction to describe their problem," she says. "People are worried about what's going into food, but nobody is asking whether these things could be addictive for some people. There was a time when food had only one ingredient, and that was food. Lettuce was lettuce, an orange was an orange, and meat was meat. Now we concoct this chemical cocktail with many ingredients, and we don't know what they do to the brain of certain people."

We also don't know for certain what differentiates a food addict from a nonaddicted overweight person. As Dru Myers, Ellen's food addiction counselor says, "Not everyone who's overweight is a food addict, just as not everyone who gets a DUI is an alcoholic." Gene-Jack Wang, a senior scientist at the Brookhaven National Laboratory, concedes: "Right now the line between an overeater who isn't addicted and a food addict is very blurred. There are no studies that look at the difference. Obesity is a very, very complicated issue involving so many different factors."

One of the most important is genetics. Studies of adopted kids and twins raised in separate families show that nature matters far more than nurture when it comes to fat. Weight is more strongly inherited than breast cancer, heart disease, or mental illness. Still, overweight people are often blamed for their predicament, and Brownell and Gold argue that much of our reluctance to accept food addiction stems from our cultural bias against fat people.

"We'll only be able to help obese people if we can stop blaming them and start developing new hypotheses that can yield new treatments," Gold says.

One of the most popular obesity treatments is gastric bypass surgery, although it's unclear whether the procedure is helpful for food addicts. "The problem with gastric bypass is the same as with just plain diets," Myers says. "If food addicts ate just because they were hungry, the surgery, or the millions of diets out there, would work fine. But food addicts eat because we're hungry right between our ears, and/or we're addicted to sugar and white flour. There's no pill, no operation, no magic bullet that will stop *that*."

There's also evidence that some food addicts who've had the surgery start abusing alcohol or other drugs. "There are many cases where people who didn't abuse alcohol before the procedure turn into alcoholics after it," Gold says. "What does that tell us? It tells us two things. First, people switch addictions. Second, it's further evidence that food competes with alcohol and drugs for the same reward centers in the brain. When food addicts are overeating, most don't feel a need for alcohol. But make it so they can't eat compulsively, and they turn to alcohol to fill the void. Making a food addict's stomach small doesn't turn them into nonaddicts. They're just addicts who need to feed the compulsion in a different way."

17 SEAN

*Our physical appearance, our mannerisms,
the way we went about our careers or other
activities, many of the traits we thought of as
our identifying trademarks, as who we were,
had been designed to serve our sex and love
addiction. . . . Yet, whether we were aware of
it or not, our entire being had been molded by
our failure, or refusal, to solve from within the
problems of our real lives: insecurity, loneliness, and lack of any abiding sense of personal
worth or dignity. Through sex, charm, emotional appeal, or persuasive intellect, we had
used other people as "drugs," to avoid facing
our own personal inadequacy.*

—SEX AND LOVE ADDICTS ANONYMOUS

"IT'S NOT EVERY day that you get a break from treatment because of
a *hurricane*," Sean tells me as we drive to a Boston train station on a
warm Sunday to pick up Ann, a twenty-two-year-old escort.

Sean met her several weeks ago, the day before he flew to Hattiesburg, Mississippi, and checked into the Gentle Path sex-addiction program at Pine Grove Behavioral Health & Addiction Services. Sean should still be there (the Gentle Path program lasts six weeks), but it closed for two weeks after Hurricane Katrina damaged several of its buildings. "Man, they wouldn't be happy if they knew I was hanging out with an escort right now," Sean says with a nervous laugh.

He's not the only addict in treatment in Louisiana or Mississippi who has struggled to stay sober since Hurricane Katrina, when most rehab centers, methadone clinics, and Twelve Step meetings closed. But just as there's been a dearth of support, so, too, has there been a shortage of drugs and dealers, at least in New Orleans. There, Hurricane Katrina managed temporarily to do the impossible: It made the city a nearly drug-free zone.

It hasn't been a great few months for Sean, who started relapsing with porn and escorts soon after we returned from the Vermont retreat at the Wilson House. And as we drive to the train station, Sean seems anxious. He says he's not sure how he feels about hanging out with me and Ann at the same time.

"It's really a fucked-up situation," he says. "I'm a sex addict in treatment who's hanging out with an escort. But I really like spending time with her. We don't even really hook up anymore—we're just really affectionate with each other."

Sean asks me what I think, but I don't know what to tell him. Spending time with an escort is probably not the best idea for a sex addict trying to stop seeing escorts, but it's hopeful—even in this bizarre context—to hear of him actually bonding with a woman on a human level. She isn't charging Sean to hang out, and, as Sean tells it, they genuinely like each other.

"I know that meeting her was part of my addiction," he concedes, "but she has this really nurturing and motherly quality, and I can't get enough of it. I know it's a fucked-up situation, but when I'm with her I feel *so good*. It's like I'm high."

After picking up Ann at the train station, I can see why. She's pretty (tall and tan, with long blond hair), but she's also smart and whimsical, exuding a calming aura that serves as a stark contrast to Sean's social awkwardness. As we head to Boston's Public Garden, Ann quickly delves into introspection. "I don't know if I'm the worst thing or the best thing to happen to him," she tells me. "I know he's had a tough time lately."

Sean's recent relapse included sneaking on my computer one night and surfing escort Web sites and online communities where men describe and rate their experiences with specific high-end escorts. (I had agreed to let him stay on my couch when he said he didn't want to be alone because he was afraid he would hire a prostitute.) The next morning, he sheepishly confessed to going on my computer. "I feel like such an asshole," he told me at the time. "You trust me, and I go and do that."

A week later, Sean called an escort service to set up an appointment with a twenty-year-old who Sean said was pretty and had "good reviews." The woman who answered the phone said Sean could see the girl an hour later for $300. But how was he going to get that kind of money? He had purposely made it impossible for himself to withdraw hundreds of dollars from his bank's ATMs. But Sean tried his best, going from store to store ("Like a madman," he says) to get cash back, and then to a handful of ATMs, where he tried to get cash advances on his credit card. Finally, at a Bank of America ATM, he got the last $100 he needed.

The escort turned out to be as pretty in person as she was in her online pictures. She was originally from Paris, and she and Sean talked for a few minutes before he got on top of her on the bed and started kissing her. "I was trying to be all romantic, kissing her like she was my girlfriend or something," Sean told me, but she wouldn't

French kiss him. They had protected vaginal sex, and then she performed oral sex on him (again using a condom).

"So I started to get more aggressive while she was doing that," Sean said. "And I guess it hurt her, because she jumped up and was like, 'What the fuck are you doing? I'm *human!* You pay me, but I'm not a *machine!*' I didn't mean to hurt her, but I see that shit in porn all the time. I was scared. Was she going to tell her boss? Would they hurt me? So then I was real nice, and she was like, 'Okay, it's okay, don't worry about it.' But I was still mad inside. Even when I pay a woman, she yells at me and cuts me down."

On his way home from that debacle, Sean called his sponsor, Dave, and they both agreed that Sean needed to go to treatment. In an unusual move for a sponsor, Dave, who is wealthy, agreed to pay Sean's way. But on the day before leaving for treatment, Sean broke down and called another escort service. They told him to meet Ann, whom Sean had read favorable reviews about, at a nearby hotel.

Ann did a double take when she opened the door to her room and saw Sean standing there. "I usually don't get cute twenty-year-olds paying to have sex with me," she tells me at the Public Garden, leaning back on her elbows in the grass. "At first, I thought maybe it was some kid staying at the hotel with his family who had just knocked on the wrong door."

Sean and Ann spent the rest of the hour talking, French kissing, and having sex. As they lounged naked on the hotel bed, Ann asked him why he was paying for sex. Sean felt so comfortable with her that he blurted it out. "I'm a sex addict," he told her.

That was a first for Ann, but his honesty only made her like him more. "He's so cute and vulnerable," she remembers thinking. When their hour was up, they agreed to meet later that night, for free. In many ways, it was Sean's ultimate fantasy. He had hired ten escorts in his life, but he had always dreamed of one actually liking him enough to become his girlfriend.

The next day, Sean was off to treatment at Pine Grove, where he spent most of the first week crying. "I just wanted to go home," Sean recalled. "It was hard being out of my environment, in this place with all these rules."

On his fourth day there, Sean broke down and called Ann. Patients are allowed one phone call during their first two weeks (unless they have young children at home, in which case they're encouraged to call home every night). Most use their call to let family members know they've made it there safely. But Sean still hadn't told his mom or his grandparents about his addiction, so instead he called Ann. Another patient heard him on the phone and confronted him, and later that day Sean copped to the call in group therapy.

"Everyone was really disappointed," Sean told me. "Treatment is a lot different than regular Twelve Step meetings, because people in treatment call you on your bullshit. One guy said that my calling her was like 'bringing a crack pipe into a room full of crack addicts.' In my mind, I was like, 'Dude, way to fucking exaggerate to make your point.'"

At the Public Garden, Ann and I both notice that Sean seems on edge. "Why are you nervous?" she asks him, scooting closer to him and taking his pale hand in hers.

"I don't know," he says.

"Take a deep breath," she tells him. "It really helps."

"It does?"

"Yeah, trust me," she says, a tender smile on her face.

He takes a long, ponderous breath. "I need to meditate," he says. "I haven't meditated in a couple of weeks." He looks at me and laughs. "And it's all *your* fault! Ever since I taught you Transcendental Meditation, I haven't been able to get in a good trance. It's like I jinxed myself. I knew I should have listened when they said never to teach it to anyone."

A few minutes later, I bring up the topic of Sean's addiction. We had talked about it briefly on the car ride over, but I was curious to hear what Ann thought. As an escort, I figured she saw her fair share of sex addicts. But before meeting Sean, she says she had never heard of sex addiction.

"Now, I'm trying to figure out which of my clients are sex addicts," she tells me. "I have this one guy who I see every week. His nickname is 'Reliable Richard.' He's pretty much seen all the girls. He has this one routine he likes, and every time I see him, it's the *exact* same thing. I think he might be a sex addict, but I don't know. It's hard to know what's going on in their head when they come in and when they leave. It's weird, because I don't want to be anyone's *drug*."

"I usually feel horribly guilty when I leave after seeing an escort," Sean says. "I didn't with you, but usually I do."

"Maybe I'm in denial, but I like to think I make a positive difference in the lives of many of my clients," Ann says.

"How do you mean?" I ask.

"You totally think I'm in denial, don't you?" she says with a giggle. "Well, a lot of times there's a real connection that's made, in addition to the sex. Guys talk to me and tell me their secrets. But sometimes I feel kind of like a therapist, and that can be weird. A lot want this kind of emotional support, and sometimes I'm like, 'Why are you coming to me for *that*?'"

Ann explains that she's escorting to pay her way through community college. "This is definitely not what I plan to do for long," she says. Ann briefly attended a prestigious East Coast university, but she says she left because of a serious depression. "I'm starting to burn out on escorting," she continues. "I need to take a step back. Part of the reason I want to stop is because, when I'm doing this, I really just detach myself emotionally from what's happening, and I don't think that's very healthy."

"That's sort of what sex addicts do, too," Sean tells her. "It's like we're there, having sex, but we're somewhere else. We're totally detached."

"Really?" Ann asks. "You do that, too?"

"Yeah, sometimes I don't even feel like I'm in my body when it's happening."

"Part of the way I keep doing this work is by not talking about it," Ann says, looking at me. "This is really hard now, talking about it with you. It took a lot of therapy sessions for me to admit that I'm a prostitute."

By the end of our conversation at the park, Ann seems to have convinced herself to stop escorting. This clearly delights Sean, who told me earlier that he would love to date her. But that seems unlikely. Soon, Sean will be heading back to Pine Grove, where the counselors will surely try to end this unusual relationship. "I'm going to have to tell the group that I saw Ann," he says. "I'm sure that's gonna go over *real* well."

————

When I call Pine Grove two weeks later to see if I can visit Sean in treatment, a counselor denies my request. But I had visited the program in August of 2004, during only its second month of operation.

Patrick Carnes, one of the leading experts about sex addiction in America, founded it after spending eight years treating sex addicts at The Meadows, a treatment center in Wickenburg, Arizona.

There are a handful of respected inpatient sex addiction treatment centers in this country, but they are expensive, ranging from about $11,000 to more than $40,000 for four to six weeks. They're also rarely covered by insurance, making inpatient treatment for sex addiction mostly a luxury of the upper classes. For my own recovery, I've been to two of the least expensive inpatient treatment centers that treat sex addicts.

At the first, I was one of a handful of sex addicts among twenty or so drug addicts, alcoholics, and food addicts. I was deeply ashamed to be there (had I really made this big a mess of my life?), and I wanted to rip my head off during what I felt was an endless display of hysterics and vulnerability in group therapy.

I also wasn't used to the confrontation, or, as one counselor put it, *care*frontation. In most Twelve Step meetings, there isn't feedback— you're not supposed to comment on what another person says. At this rehab, though, as at most, confronting the denial of fellow addicts is considered integral to treatment.

There was a good amount of sexual intrigue among some of us there, although ironically the sex addicts were the least involved. In withdrawal from their substances of choice, many of the drug addicts and alcoholics turned into raging sex and romance junkies, sneaking around the grounds late at night to hook up or pledge their eternal love.

As a sex addict, I wasn't even supposed to masturbate while I was there. I had signed a celibacy contract upon my arrival, which is standard for inpatient centers that treat sex addicts. While I don't have a problem with compulsive masturbation, a counselor said he didn't want me using masturbation to squelch the torrent of feelings that would inevitably hit me during my stay there.

I assured him that I never used masturbation as a "coping mechanism," but a week later, after a particularly brutal group therapy session where I was taken to task for my lack of empathy for those I had hurt emotionally through my sexual behavior, I ran to my room and proved the counselor right.

The staff wanted me to stay longer than thirty days. They worried that while I was progressing in my recovery, I hadn't fully accepted the extent of my powerlessness over the addiction. I was also apparently too clever for my own good.

"The problem with smart addicts," a counselor told me, "is that you're really good at rationalization, at convincing yourself through all kinds of intellectual bullshit why you don't need to do the basic things every addict needs to do every day to stay sober. You're always up in your head. You need to get down to your *heart*. If you think too much, you're not going to *get* recovery."

I thanked him, assuring him that I wasn't nearly as smart as he thought I was. And I was sure that I had all the information I needed to make good sexual decisions in the future, as if having *information* is enough to fight addiction. I left there convinced I was essentially cured.

A week later, I relapsed. I spent the next five years struggling to get back on track—a few weeks of sobriety, then a slip, and so on— before deciding to give treatment a second chance. This time I went to a highly respected inpatient center for sex addicts that focuses heavily on healing childhood trauma and helping addicts learn to take responsibility for their sexual behavior.

If the staff's philosophy can be summed up briefly, it's this: *You are not responsible for your addiction (it was likely caused by childhood trauma, which we will help you begin to face and heal from), but you are responsible for your recovery.* (In a 1998 interview with Bill Moyers, neuroscientist Steven Hyman likened an addict's responsibility to recover to that of someone with heart disease. "We don't blame [heart patients] for having heart disease, but we ask them to follow a certain diet, to exercise, to comply with medication regimes. So it is with the addicted person—we shouldn't blame them for the disease, but we should treat them as having responsibility for their recovery.")

Thoroughly convinced of my powerlessness and increasingly able to "feel my feelings," I arrived at the center eager to do whatever the counselors suggested. There was a diverse cast of sex addicts during my five weeks there, including a friend from college I hadn't talked to in years (college buddies in treatment together was a first, according to the staff), an affable husband and father arrested for soliciting a minor over the Internet (the "minor" was actually a cop), a sexually abused and deeply traumatized gay man who had started cruising parks for public sex when he was eleven and now spent most of his days in X-rated bookstores, a shy college student who was caught stalking girls on his campus, a married corporate executive who had cheated countless times on his wife (with both men and women), a minister who was fired from two colleges for accessing pornography at work, and a cantankerous retired community college professor addicted to pornography and prostitutes.

We nicknamed one of the most intense group therapy sessions "Crime & Punishment." It seemed to us that the goal of Crime & Punishment was to make us feel so rotten for what we had done that we wouldn't dare do it again. But as the staff explained it, the real purpose was to make us take responsibility for our actions, to honestly face the damage we had done in our addiction and to build empathy for those we had hurt.

In that pursuit, men who had repeatedly cheated on their wives had to write "empathy letters" to them, which would never be sent but were read in group and usually criticized for not being nearly empathetic enough. The wives, meanwhile, wrote painful "cost letters"—detailing how the addiction had affected them—that were read to their husbands for the first time in group by another group member. Family therapy was also an important part of treatment for the men there, many of whom were on the brink of breakup or divorce.

We also had to write a "Victims List," in which we named everyone we had hurt in our active addiction and imagined how our actions made them feel—or *would* have made them feel, had they known about them. It was a painful exercise; reading mine to the group was one of the most humbling and difficult things I've ever done.

Another group therapy session, which focused on grief and childhood trauma, was equally intense. Those who had been sexually abused as children (about half) and those who had been neglected or suffered emotional abuse (pretty much all of us) worked on facing the trauma and grieving over the loss.

Those of us who were gay—including myself—were encouraged to look at the homophobia and emotional abuse we had suffered growing up gay, and how it had fueled our self-destructive behavior. One counselor echoed what Brian McNaught wrote in his book *Now That I'm Out, What Do I Do?*

"Most gay people have been enormously, if not consciously, traumatized by the social pressure they felt to identify and behave as a heterosexual, even though such pressure is not classified as sexual abuse by experts in the field," McNaught wrote. "Imagine how today's society would respond if heterosexual thirteen- to nineteen-year-olds were forced to date someone of the same sex. What would the reaction be if they were expected to hold the hand of, slow dance with, hug, kiss and say 'I love you' to someone to whom they were not and could not be sexually attracted? The public would be outraged! . . . Years of therapy would be prescribed for the innocent victims of such abuse. Volumes would be written about the long-term effects of such abhorrent socialization. . . . Yet, that's part of the everyday life of gay teenagers. And there's no comparable public concern, much less outcry, about the traumatizing effects on *their* sexuality."

As at the vast majority of addiction treatment centers in America, the staff at the program I attended believed in the Twelve Steps, and every night we either ran a Twelve Step meeting at the center or attended one in the nearby community. Before graduating from the program, we also had to complete the Step One exercises in Patrick Carnes's book *A Gentle Path Through the Twelve Steps*, including listing thirty examples of how our addiction had caused unmanage-

ability in our lives, and thirty examples of our powerlessness over
the addiction.

I had read so many of Carnes's books in the course of my recovery
that I was a little awestruck when I sat down with him in a conference room on the main campus of Pine Grove Behavioral Health &
Addiction Services, which is nestled among twenty-two acres of pine
trees and is also home to treatment programs for chemical dependency and eating disorders.

A tall, friendly man with a long forehead, thinning gray hair, and
a Minnesota accent, Carnes listened patiently as I told him about
Sean, whom I was considering following for this book. Carnes wasn't
surprised by Sean's story; he said more and more teens are fitting the
criteria for sex addiction.

"We know, by talking to adult sex addicts about their experiences growing up, that their addiction often starts manifesting itself
in adolescence," Carnes said. "But the Internet has only exacerbated
the problem. I'm getting calls every week from parents of nine-, ten-,
eleven-year-olds who are shocked to discover that their kids are
watching thirty or forty hours of pornography online a week. Even
when confronted about it over and over again, the kids can't stop."

But while adolescents between the ages of twelve and seventeen
are some of the most frequent consumers of Internet porn, those
hoping to bring attention to sex and pornography addiction among
young people are often dismissed as paranoid reactionaries. Take the
case of Eric Griffin-Shelley, who in 1994—a few years before many
teens were regular Internet users—wrote a book, *Adolescent Sex
and Love Addicts*. Griffin-Shelley wrote that "teenagers are suffering every day with sexual behaviors and relationship dependencies
that they cannot control," and that "it is time that a diagnosis for
adolescents be recognized by the therapeutic community."

Griffin-Shelley's book hardly made a ripple. "People just can't wrap their heads around the idea that it's possible to be a teenage sex addict," he told me. "They say that *all* teens are obsessed with sex, and that these kids will grow out of it. It's the same thing most people believed forty years ago about drugs and alcohol—that teens were just being teens, and that they couldn't be *real* drug addicts or alcoholics. Now we know that's wrong."

Still, it's hard to argue that teens can be addicted to sex or pornography when there isn't even an official sex addiction diagnosis for adults. Nowhere in the American Psychiatric Association's Diagnostic and Statistical Manual of Mental Disorders (DSM-IV, published in 1994), considered the Bible of the mental health field, is there a diagnostic criteria for sexual addiction or sexual compulsion.

There is "no scientific data to support a concept of sexual behavior that can be considered addictive," Chester Schmidt, chair of the DSM-IV Sexual Disorder Work Group, wrote at the time. Schmidt told me that what is called sex addiction is more likely a symptom of other psychological problems like depression, obsessive-compulsive disorder, or bipolar disorder.

But believers in a sex addiction diagnosis point out that for many years, doctors and psychiatrists similarly dismissed alcoholism, refusing to accept that it was a serious problem in itself, not merely a symptom of something else. The psychoanalytic view of addiction in the first half of the twentieth century was that "alcoholic drinking and addictive drug use were not primary disease entities, but symptoms of neurotic conflict or underlying psychosis, or manifestations of a disordered personality," William White points out in *Slaying the Dragon*. Treat the underlying psychosis, the theory went, and the addiction will go away.

Psychoanalysts at the time linked alcoholism to a plethora of psychological problems, including "primary maternal identification," "fear of castration," and "latent homosexuality." "Every drinking-bout is tinged with homosexuality," announced one psychoanalyst.

Remarkably, this belief had currency into the second half of the twentieth century.

According to Harry Tiebout, one of the first psychiatrists to see addiction as an illness in its own right, the biggest problem with relying on psychoanalysis alone was that the patient rarely stopped drinking long enough for any of the deeper therapeutic work to happen.

"In rather doctrinaire fashion," he wrote, "we persisted in treating the alcoholism as a symptom which would be cured or arrested if its causes could be favorably altered. The drinking was something to be put up with as best as one could while more fundamental matters were being studied. The result of this procedure was that very few alcoholics were helped."

As William White put it, Tiebout believed that alcoholism was "a symptom that had itself become a life-threatening, primary illness." Most believers in a sex addiction diagnosis now believe the same thing about compulsive sexuality. Fueled by an unwavering belief in their cause, and confident that large-scale studies of sex addicts—including brain scans—will prove that sex addiction is real, they hope to get some version of the disorder into the DSM-V (due out in 2012).

To do that, they know they'll need to convince both the psychiatric community and the general public that sex addiction is more than just a metaphor, a pop psychology diagnosis, or an attempt to explain away recklessness and perversion.

Advances in neuroscience may help in that endeavor. Five or ten years ago, Dr. Peter Martin, a psychiatrist and the director of the Division of Addiction Medicine at Vanderbilt University, would have dismissed any comparison between sexual compulsivity and alcoholism or drug addiction. Drugs and alcohol are foreign substances. Sex is natural—a basic biological drive critical to our survival as a species. Clearly, Martin thought, a case of apples and oranges.

But using MRI technology, Martin began studying how people's brains react to sexually arousing images. What he found has radically changed his perspective on addictions. Now he believes that "there are many behaviors, including sex, that appear to be driven by the same brain mechanisms that drive addictions to drugs like cocaine and heroin." University of Pennsylvania psychologist Anna Rose Childress agrees, telling the journal *Science* that sex addicts resemble cocaine addicts and probably share a problem with brain "inhibitory circuitry."

Still, the science of sex addiction is in its infancy, and those hoping to further study the brains of sex addicts struggle to get the funding they need. "People don't exactly throw money at you when you say you want to study sex addiction," says Patrick Carnes. "And in the end, getting sex addiction in the DSM is not going to just be about science and empirical evidence. The concept of sex addiction makes so many people uncomfortable, so it's really going to take a public relations and education effort to get it seen as a serious disorder. Because if we as a culture really accept the idea of sex addiction, then we're going to have to look at a lot of things we don't want to. We'll have to talk openly about what constitutes healthy sexuality, which will invariably bring morality and religion into play. We'll have to look at gender roles, at how we treat women, at childhood sexual abuse and trauma, at how we use sex and relationships to make ourselves feel worthy and lovable, and at the way anonymous sex has been normalized in gay culture. Sex addiction really has something to offend everyone."

Among the most offended are some sexologists who see sex addiction as a moralistic construct that portrays human sexuality as something dirty and shameful. Some addiction treatment professionals, meanwhile, worry that equating sex addiction and drug addiction will detract from their efforts to have alcoholism and drug addiction fully accepted as *diseases*. And some feminists and victims rights advocates worry that an official sex addiction disorder could be used by sex offenders or philandering men to claim that they didn't have control over their actions.

It's unclear if a "sex addiction made me do it" defense has ever actually worked, except on an episode of ABC's *Boston Legal*. There, Shelley Long played a self-described nymphomaniac who compulsively hired male escorts, got arrested, claimed to be powerless over her thundering libido, flirted shamelessly with the judge, and was acquitted.

So was Shelley Long's character really addicted to sex, or did she just have a creative legal team? Pathological and addictive sexuality is, it seems, very much in the eye of the beholder. In a 1995 study published in *The American Journal of Family Therapy*, highly religious male therapists were much more likely to see patients as sexually addicted than were nonreligious therapists.

For many people, honestly assessing their own sexual behavior is difficult. How many one-night stands are too many? How many hours on the Internet masturbating to pornography or looking for sex are a sign of addiction? Is a man who has sex with fifteen people in a two-week period engaging in normal behavior? Probably not, but does his behavior necessarily make him an *addict*?

What if he has sex with five different people a week for a month? Six months? A year? And what if he slows down, or stops having sex altogether for months or years with little difficulty? Was he a sex addict before but isn't anymore? Was his sex addiction a phase he outgrew, or will it reappear in a year or two? And is how he views his sexual behavior relevant, or is the behavior enough to call him addicted?

There are few easy answers. "The guy who sees a woman standing on a street corner, suspects she might be a police decoy because he sees the cop car down the block, but says to himself, 'I need this so badly that I'll go pay her to have sex with me anyway,' that person clearly has a problem and has lost the ability to control his sexual behavior," Carnes says. "But often the behaviors are in a gray area. One clear way to figure out if someone is addicted is to look at negative consequences."

Bill Clinton—who some sex addiction experts believe is a sex addict—certainly suffered negative consequences because of his sexual behavior. While he's never admitted to being addicted to sex, Clinton allegedly broke down in tears when Dolly Kyle Browning, who testified that she had a long-running affair with him, asked him a series of questions for self-diagnosis that she learned in her own sexual addiction treatment (Clinton denied sleeping with Browning). So is Clinton a sex addict, or is he simply someone with a high sex drive who made staggeringly poor choices?

Further complicating the concept of sex addiction is this: Should the criteria for sex addiction differ among groups or communities with different sexual norms? Does a gay sex addict look anything like a straight sex addict?

"It's much harder to be a straight sex addict," joked sex addiction therapist and author Robert Weiss at the 2006 Society for the Advancement of Sexual Health conference in San Francisco. "Straight guys usually have to either talk to the woman or pay the woman. Gay men will do it for free, and they often skip the talking."

In a 2004 study of nearly two hundred sexually compulsive gay men in New York City, sex researcher Jeffrey Parsons found three main types of sex addicts: The first group regularly engaged in sex to alleviate negative feelings, anxiety, and stress. The second group was addicted as much to the chase as to the actual sex—for them, it was about the thrill and excitement of the newest catch. The third group, which Parsons called "relationship obsessed," had sex with many men in hopes of landing "Mr. Right," who would, as the fantasy goes, make everything okay. (I see a bit of myself in all three groups, although I relate the most to the first.)

Parsons also found men in all three groups who blamed their sexual compulsivity on New York City. "We had a lot of guys who said things like 'New York made me this way! I moved here from Kansas, and there are so many hot men here, how can you not want to fuck them all?'"

Gender, too, certainly influences how we view sexual excess. At Gentle Path, I spoke to a woman who said she began picking up men at bars and having sex with them after her marriage ended. Although she soon labeled the behavior problematic and addictive ("It wasn't what I wanted to be doing," she told me, "and I was using sex to medicate my feelings"), that same behavior in a man might be seen—by both himself and his friends—as an understandable way to deal with being dumped.

Still, for the two dozen actors, politicians, businessmen, lawyers, and other high-profile types who gather four times a year at an undisclosed hotel in Arizona for an invitation-only gathering called "Leadership Weekend," their sex addiction is not in doubt. They come to Arizona to read books like *The Four Agreements* and *The Spirituality of Imperfection* and to find support among other men who know what it's like to have compulsive sexual behavior rule their lives. Some couldn't stay away from prostitutes. Others had five affairs going at once. A few spent half their waking hours masturbating to Internet pornography.

Why travel to Arizona four times a year to talk about it in secret? Because while a public stint in alcohol or drug rehab is par for the celebrity course, being known as a sex addict is still not considered a wise career move. Actor David Duchovny and Hall of Fame baseball player Wade Boggs are two of the few celebrities who have admitted to being sex addicts.

Charlie Walker, a sex addiction expert and former facilitator of the Leadership Weekends, hopes for the day when a celebrity with long-term sobriety will "come out" as a sex addict. "Thirty years ago, no one could stand up in Congress and admit to being a recovering alcoholic," Walker says. "Now it's almost passé. Wouldn't it be great if we got to the point where admitting to sex addiction was passé? But that would probably mean that we had come to a point where we could talk honestly and openly and sanely about sex in our culture. And as much as we're obsessed with sex in America, we aren't there yet."

18 KATE

*In my own life, as well as in the lives of count-
less others, there exists an unseen history of
trauma. More often than not it passes unrecog-
nized, unacknowledged, or denied. The fossil
remains of traumatic events are intellectually
discussed: "I had a difficult childhood." "My
father was an alcoholic." "My mother tried to
kill herself." "I was molested." All true statements,
but rarely with an emotional reality. The real
legacy of childhood trauma knocks at the door
in disguise—as alcoholism and other substance
abuse, unmanageable emotional outburst,
chronic resentment, debilitating fear and depression. It manifests in the feelings of fragmenta-
tion and fraud which pervade one's day-to-day
existence; in the disconnect from creativity and
an authentic self. Perhaps, in the saddest manifestation of all, we tell the story of our trauma
without words by perpetrating our own devas-
tating experiences as children onto others.*

—HOLISTIC HEALER MICHAEL GROHALL

THE SCENE OF many of Kate's shoplifting crimes is an unremarkable shopping center in a small town near the modest one-story white house where she lives with her husband and son. As we pull into the center's half-empty parking lot on this sunny afternoon (Patrick is at kindergarten, and her husband is working), I ask her how many times she's shoplifted from these stores—Sears, Mervyns, Target, Hallmark, and a large craft store.

She looks at me as if I had three heads. "You think I keep track?" she says. "I really have no clue. It's safe to say, *a lot*." Here is what Kate can remember: She's swiped clothes and picture frames from Sears, sneakers and sweaters from Mervyns, food and air freshener from Target, greeting cards and teddy bears from Hallmark, and just about everything she could grab (yarn, pins, stickers, stamps) from the craft store.

Sometimes she planned to shoplift, but more often she saw something she wanted but didn't want to pay for, or only wanted to pay half price for. One of her primary shoplifting methods is to switch price tags, usually on clothing. She'll also pocket small items from her cart while waiting in the checkout line.

"It's almost like I say to myself, 'Well I'm obviously not going to pay for *everything*, so what can I take that's going to get me in the least amount of trouble if I get caught?'" Kate tells me. "My shoplifting isn't about saving money, because if it was, I would try to steal expensive things. But it's like my mind tells me that I *have* to shoplift something every time I shop."

Kate is tall and slender and is dressed today in her usual understated, slapdash style: old tennis shoes, jeans, and a baggy sweatshirt. She has an athlete's physique, but she seems determined not to show it off. She never wears makeup, and her movements are sluggish and uninspired, as if she would rather be at home on the couch with the blinds drawn. Her face is round and youthful (with striking hazel eyes), but she rarely smiles or laughs, and she wears the wan look of a woman who long ago gave up on enjoying life.

As we meander through the Sears store, she says it's one of the easiest stores to shoplift from. She points out the ceiling-mounted security cameras, but she seems more interested in showing me the four sets of doors located in different corners of the store. "Anyplace that has this many entrances and exits is easy for shoplifters," Kate explains. "That's a lot of places for people to come in and go out, and at Sears they don't monitor them well. I have to avoid those places like the plague."

Next door, the Target store has one entrance and one exit. It has also recently implemented new technology—including closed-circuit television systems, video analytics, and electronic article surveillance—that makes shoplifting difficult. But that's never stopped Kate. "When I went into a store and they had new security technology, to me that was a challenge," she says. "Basically the store was saying, 'Now you can't shoplift.' I was like, 'Oh, really? Watch me.'"

In Target, Kate and I walk by a petulant, candy-wielding boy demanding that his mother buy him the bag of candy he's squeezing proudly in his right hand. "Mom, if you don't, I'm going to steal it!" he says. "If you try to steal *anything*," she huffs, snatching the bag from his little hand, "you won't be watching TV for a month!"

Kate smiles. "My son stole a plastic bead from this huge bead store a few weeks ago," she tells me. "And boy, did I make a big deal about it when we got home and he showed it to me. I said, 'You're going to put it by the telephone, you're not going to touch it, and every time you walk by, I am going to remind you that you took the bead without paying for it.'"

When they went back to the store a week later, Kate made Patrick return the bead. "So he gave it to the lady," Kate continues, "and she was like, 'Oh, thank you sweetheart.' I said, 'Noooooo, you don't understand, last time he was here he put this in his pocket and *did not pay for it*.' She got that I wanted her to make a big deal about it, so she was like, 'OHHHHH, you know that it's not okay to take something without paying for it, so don't ever do that again.' I wanted to scare him a little bit. One shoplifter in this family is enough."

As we're leaving the store, Kate brings up Claude Allen, George Bush's former domestic policy adviser, who resigned after he was caught repeatedly shoplifting from a Hecht's and a Target in Maryland. Allen reportedly bought hundreds of dollars' worth of goods, returned to the store with the receipt, shopped for the same items, wheeled them to the customer service desk, handed an employee the receipt, and announced that he wanted to return the merchandise.

"Basically," Kate says, "he was taking the merchandise home and then getting refunded for it." Kate has never done that, but she has shoplifted goods and then returned them for store credit (some stores don't require a receipt).

Kate isn't surprised by Allen's arrest. "There's a woman in our online group who's always e-mailing us stories of high-profile people who get caught," she tells me. "She sent us one about a school board member, another about a judge. One guy was a police officer who got caught stealing aftershave at a grocery store, and he tried to get away by flashing his badge and running."

Outside, I ask Kate if we can go in the craft store, but she shakes her head. Both the craft store and Hallmark are way too tempting. "When I'm in the craft store, everything looks really good," she explains. "I don't need any of it, but I want *all* of it. It's a big store, and half the time I can walk up to the register and there isn't anyone in sight, and I'll think, 'I can take everything in my cart and wheel it out the front door, and no one would know any different!'"

Hallmark is challenging for a different reason. "I always feel so guilty when I go in there," she says. "They were so nice to me, and

I would talk to them like I was their friend, at the same time that I was stealing from them. It felt like we were in this relationship based on a lie."

Kate hasn't shoplifted anything in a year, although she has had some close calls. The first was two months ago at Target, where Kate sensed she was in danger even before entering the store. The previous day, a stray dog had wandered over to her house. She called the phone number on his tag, but it was disconnected. She even drove to the owners' house, but a neighbor said they had moved to California and left the dog.

In a posting to the CASA site, Kate detailed what happened next:

> Normally I would not have identified my rage (at the dog owners) as a trigger for shoplifting, however this day I did. I KNEW I was at risk. I was hesitant about going in & my awareness was on heightened alert the whole time. I got what I needed & I got out. I talked to my husband about the experiences of that day when he got home from work. He said he was glad I didn't shoplift, but more than that I was glad I had told him instead of holding it all in like I would have before.

Then, during a trip with her husband to Las Vegas, Kate lost a fiber-optic, color-changing rock necklace she bought for Patrick. Convinced that someone swiped it when she wasn't looking, Kate was angry and wanted to go back to the store and shoplift a replacement. She posted the following:

> I felt lousy and irresponsible. In a shoplifter's state of mind, where we carry these thoughts of being unworthy, overcharged or taken advantage of, and feeling a need to get back, get even, get something for nothing, this was a total nightmare. My husband kept reassuring me it wasn't a big deal and not to worry about it, asking me if I'd be okay. He even stopped gambling so he could hang out with me. When we flew out of Vegas I was relieved I made

it out safely but still sad about the necklace at the same time. Even today, almost 3 weeks later, I am still sad about losing it. Is it also a shoplifter's commonality to have great difficulty just letting things go? I could not count for you how many times I have heard, Just let it go.

But Kate's most powerful recent urge to shoplift happened the day her oldest son, who was stillborn, would have turned six. She posted this to the board after her trip to the cemetery on his birthday:

It was an emotional day to say the least. I had to make a couple store stops which, luckily, were uneventful. Don't get me wrong. Oh, I thought about it! How I could just slip the left-over holiday merchandise the stores could really care less about in my jacket, and what would it matter?

I also thought about how THAT was the very last conversation I wanted to have. Would it be with store security or with my husband when I got home? I decided neither would be best for me. It helped that I called my husband before I went into the grocery to buy roses for my angel and I called him again when I was leaving the cemetery. He said he was concerned and wanted me to be safe, especially knowing the significance of the day.

I read a lot of books on grief and loss. I once read that God does not give us anything we cannot handle. Being as neutral as anyone could be with regard to religion, I choose to remember that statement. Fitting that I would recall it yesterday amid my emotional rollercoaster ride. I'd like to think it was my little angel watching over me. Keeping me safe. Hey! We all believe what we want to believe to keep us going in even the worst of times.

———

Long before actress Winona Ryder's famous 2001 Saks Fifth Avenue shoplifting spree (store employees said she claimed, rather unconvincingly, that she was practicing for a film role), people have been trying to understand why otherwise law-abiding citizens would risk humiliation and incarceration to shoplift something they have the money to pay for.

One of the first shoplifters to gain unwanted notoriety was Jane Austen's wealthy aunt, who in 1799 was arrested for pocketing a piece of lace. Some seventy years later, wealthy feminist and New York City philanthropist Elizabeth Phelps was arrested at Macy's for stealing a small package of candy. The press had a field day with the story, and by 1880 newspapers routinely reported the "shocking" shoplifting arrests of respected middle- and upper-class Victorian women.

In her book *When Ladies Go A-Thieving*, historian Elaine Abelson argues that shoplifting first permeated the nation's consciousness with the introduction of the department store in the second half of the nineteenth century. Women were expected to venture out into a novel setting that not only presented commodities in polished form, but also celebrated the shopping experience and enticed women with temptation and sensory stimulation.

"It is not that we need so much more, or that our requirements are so increased," one Victorian-era woman said at the time, "but we are not able to stand against the overwhelming temptations to buy which besiege us at every turn."

In 1898, the *New York Times* wrote about two women, both described by the *Times* as "well-dressed," "dutiful," and of "unblemished reputation," who were charged with stealing a bottle of perfume and an umbrella from a Sixth Avenue department store. One culprit, the wife of a minister, allegedly hid the umbrella in the folds of her skirt "when one of the clerks was not looking," the store security manager testified. The women were arraigned but released by the court when the store dropped the charges.

A 1901 study titled "Les Voleuses des Grand Magasins" (The Department Store Thieves) published by Paul Dubuisson, likened the department store to a sexual experience where women could act out fantasies that were otherwise unobtainable in their daily lives. "Temptation is so strong, surging desire so powerful, so impervious, so irresistible that the act is accomplished before reason has time to plead its cause," Dubuisson found. "Afterward, all the considerations of honor, reputation, and security will attack the unhappy spirit and bring forth remorse, but for the moment pleasure is everything."

The increase in shoplifting at the time even inspired an English ballad, titled "When Ladies Go A-Thieving":

> *Oh, don't we live in curious times,*
> *You scarce could be believing,*
> *When Frenchmen fight and Emperors die*
> *And ladies go a-thieving.*
>
> *A beauty of the West End went,*
> *Around a shop she lingers,*
> *And there upon some handkerchiefs*
> *She clapped her pretty fingers.*
>
> *Into the shop she gently popped;*
> *The world is quite deceiving*
> *When ladies have a notion got*
> *To ramble out a-thieving.*

Physicians were quick to brand this new social phenomenon of shoplifting a physical and mental illness. Many of the women in question were labeled kleptomaniacs, while others were deemed irrational, further proof of the innate inferiority of the female gender.

In 1967, *Life* magazine published an article headlined, "One Out of Sixty Is a Shoplifter," and offered a new explanation for why people steal. Kleptomania was not to blame. Rather, it was the adrenaline rush—the shadowy dance with danger, "a desire for the thrill of getting something for nothing," as one criminologist interviewed for the article put it—that made shoplifting so hard to resist.

Today, that dance with danger isn't any easier for some to resist. Richard Hollinger, a professor of criminology at the University of Florida, regularly tells his students that if they want to study crime, they should head to the mall. "Retailers are sitting ducks because they don't want to turn the retail environment into a Draconian environment," he told me. "You add up automobile theft, bank robberies, embezzlement, and straight property crime, and they don't add up to shoplifting alone."

Retailers lose about $13 billion a year to shoplifters (and an additional $19 billion to employee theft). Some shoplifters are professional thieves or drug addicts who sell the stolen goods for money. Others are thrill seekers or occasional shoplifters who usually grow out of it or quit for good if they're caught. But many are compulsive and longtime shoplifters who can't seem to help themselves. About two-thirds of this group are women, says Terry Shulman, the founder of Kate's online recovery community and the author of the book *Something for Nothing: Shoplifting Addiction and Recovery*. While some balk at calling the latter group addicts, Shulman argues that some shoplifters fit the criteria for addiction.

"If it walks like a duck and quacks like a duck, it might, in fact, be a duck," he told me. "An addiction is something a person has difficulty stopping on his or her own, one where there's an escalation of the out-of-control behavior, and where there are feelings of withdrawal or preoccupation when not engaging in it. That fits drug addicts, and it fits thousands of shoplifting addicts I've talked to."

But as with other behavioral compulsions, there are powerful forces lobbying against understanding shoplifting as a true addiction. Retailers, for one, don't want people who steal from their stores to be thought of as addicts who are powerless over their actions.

"What really worries the retail industry is that if the corporation is not seen as a legitimate victim and the shoplifter is viewed as sick, then it's going to be a hell of a time getting the cases prosecuted, particularly if they go before a jury," Hollinger told me. "The shoplifters aren't the victim. The *store* is the victim. But it's kind of hard for people to see a place like Wal-Mart as a victim. We call it the medicalization of deviance. Anytime you have a problem you don't want to deal with, you cry helplessness and addiction."

Those cries generally don't hold up in court. When Shulman—who is often asked to appear as an expert witness in shoplifting cases—testifies that shoplifting is a real addiction, he sometimes gets shouted down.

"A lot of judges just can't understand," Shulman said. "Others get upset when I try to explain that most compulsive shoplifters are unconsciously dealing with a real or perceived unfair loss in their lives, and that they become addicted to getting relief that way. I'm actually in favor of prosecuting shoplifters, because if you're caught and let go, which happened to me a few times, for a moment you're really relieved and say you'll never do it again, but the next day you're back at it. But even mentioning addiction and shoplifting in the same sentence sends some judges over the edge."

In one case, Shulman testified for a woman who had shoplifted shortly after suffering a miscarriage. The judge became apoplectic at the suggestion that the woman was suffering from an addictive compulsion. "My wife had four miscarriages, and she doesn't go and shoplift!" the judge fumed, according to Shulman. "And it's because of people like *you* that the shirt on my back costs so much!"

Jon Grant, a shoplifting and gambling researcher at the University of Minnesota, studies the judicial system's ambivalence regarding addiction. "With all addictions," he told me, "a person's free will is greatly impaired, but the law doesn't want to entertain that. I find that fascinating. The law entertains it with other mental illnesses, but it draws the line at addiction. I always hear, 'Aren't you just trying to excuse bad behavior?' That knee-jerk reaction really goes to show that addiction is still not seen as a real or serious illness. Why shouldn't someone's addiction be considered as a mitigating factor, especially in sentencing?"

Shulman believes that the common denominator among shoplifting addicts is a sense of victimization, of having been unfairly taken from in their lives. Shoplifting from a store is an attempt to regain their lost power, to get even for a lifetime of unjust deprivation. Shulman has found a handful of commonly held beliefs among the thousands of compulsive shoplifters he has met or counseled over the years: "Life is unfair." "The world is an unsafe place." "Nobody will be there to take care of me." "I'm entitled to something extra for my suffering." "Nice people finish last."

Will Cupchik, a psychologist and the author of *Why Honest People Shoplift or Commit Other Acts of Theft*, agrees that many shoplifters are subconsciously trying to "get back at the world." In his research, Cupchik discovered a link between shoplifting and the recent onset of a serious illness like cancer. In one study, Cupchik found that nearly one-third of shoplifters had, or knew someone close to them who had, a major illness at about the same time that they stole.

"Cancer can be viewed as an invasion of the host body and the stealing away of what belongs to that body," Cupchik said. "Like cancer, shoplifting is an invasion of the host body and the stealing away of what belongs to it."

Cupchik says that many of his shoplifting patients don't understand why they steal. In one case, Cupchik treated a lawyer who marched into his office and announced that he wouldn't accept "any psychobabble excuse" for why he shoplifted toothpaste from Sears. "I don't know why I did it," the lawyer told Cupchik. "It makes no sense."

When Cupchik asked the lawyer what was going on in his life at the time of the theft, he said that his son was undergoing chemotherapy for cancer the very morning the shoplifting occurred. "I see this over and over again in my practice," Cupchik told me. "There's a perceived unfair personally meaningful loss, which causes a person to go out and try to make someone else, namely a department store, experience a loss."

For longtime compulsive shoplifters like Kate, the unfair loss often occurred during childhood. But like many shoplifters, Kate was adamant about one thing the first time we spoke: She wasn't going to "blame" anyone from her past for her shoplifting problem.

"I'm not here to blame my parents," she told me at the time. "Yes, I had a crappy childhood. Yes, I was sexually abused by a family member. But I just don't see how that's connected to my shoplifting. I shoplifted because I thought I could get away with it. I read stories all the time about people who have crappy childhoods, but they don't all drink and they don't all gamble and they don't all steal. If they can avoid doing that stuff, why can't I?"

Kate's question struck me as a red herring, one that many addicts use to avoid having to face the pain of childhood abuse. After all, if the trauma in Kate's past has little or no relevance to her adult dysfunction, then she has a perfect rationale for never having to face the abuse. And that, Kate told me one of the first times we spoke, is exactly what she intended to do.

"I don't like talking about what happened to me," she said. "I don't see how it's going to change what happened, nor am I convinced it will help me stop shoplifting."

Still, Kate had one advantage over many addicts in early recovery: She didn't deny that her childhood was a nightmare. As Kate opened up to me about it, I pictured her in a kind of domestic war zone, alone in combat on a seemingly endless tour of duty.

A relative of Kate's began sexually abusing her in the third grade. He first exposed himself to her when they were alone and then progressed to sliding his fingers into the front of her bathing suit at the local public swimming pool. Next, he offered her money to pose nude. Initially she said no, but he persisted, and eventually she relented. He would give her $50 in exchange for sexual acts, and in high school he also plied her with alcohol for sex.

Kate's father had left before she was born. Her mother, who Kate says was cruel and physically abusive, seemed more concerned with her own romantic relationships than with raising her kids (she married three times before Kate went to college). Kate never remembered being happy in her mother's house. There were only two places in the world she felt safe: the art room at her high school, and the home of an elderly neighbor whom all the local kids trusted.

Still, Kate never told the neighbor about her sexual abuse. It never occurred to her to tell anyone, especially her mom. "I knew from experience that she wouldn't believe me," Kate says. "My brother and I had tried to tell her difficult things in the past, and she would just blame us and say we didn't know what we were talking about. In high school I actually hinted to the wife of the man who abused me about what he had done, but she wouldn't listen. She said, 'There's never an opportunity for him to do anything like that to you. Stop making things up.'"

Kate started shoplifting around the time the sexual abuse began, and it didn't take long before she was caught. With her younger half-brother as an accomplice, Kate tried to swipe candy from a corner store near their school. The store's owner saw them do it, and he called the police. An officer said he would drive Kate and her brother to their nearby home.

Frightened, Kate lied and pointed the officer to a friend's house who lived two blocks away. Kate thought she was being clever, but she hadn't planned on the policeman walking them to the house, ringing the bell, and waiting.

"Ma'am," the officer said when their friend's mother opened the door, "I have your kids here."

"Um, no you don't," she said.

"I don't?"

"Those aren't mine. They live down the street."

The officer drove Kate and her brother to their house and explained to their mother that they had a) stolen candy from a store, and b) pretended to live two blocks away. Kate's mom was doubly upset. She scolded Kate and her half-brother and told them that it was wrong to steal and lie.

But Kate's mom, it turned out, was a hypocrite. A few years later, Kate says she watched her mother switch price tags on a pair of jeans in a department store. When Kate asked why, her mother sent her and her brother to the car. Soon after, Kate switched tags on a ballpoint pen in a grocery store. A clerk caught her and called the police station across the street, which sent over an officer. "Why did you do that?" the policeman wanted to know. "I don't know," Kate told him. "But my mom does it, too."

Kate, who was thirteen at the time, had to attend a shoplifting diversion class for that offense, but soon she was stealing again. She tried desperately to project an "I've got it together" facade, but Kate couldn't understand why she did a lot of what she did. In high school, she tried to make herself feel better by sleeping with as many boys as possible, but she usually felt worse after.

"Guys would have sex with me, but it was always on the hush-hush," she told me. "For me it wasn't that the sex made me feel good. It was that these boys wanted to spend time with me."

When she was sixteen and still being abused, Kate tried to commit suicide using her mother's many pain medications. She woke up in a hospital. "After it happened, my mom never talked about it with me," she says. "We never cried on each other's shoulders and had a big hug. I can't tell you a time before I graduated from high school that my mom ever put her arms around me."

Kate's mom did send her to see a therapist, but Kate didn't have her driver's license, so the relative volunteered to drive her to therapy. He molested her to and from each session.

After high school, Kate attended community college and worked at a J.C. Penney. She stole from the store and had a series of short-lived relationships before meeting her husband, Eric, in 1993. Kate shoplifted regularly early in their marriage, and she battled anger and depression; it wasn't uncommon for her to sleep fourteen hours a day. When Kate was awake, she usually stayed at home by herself. When she went out, she shoplifted.

After getting caught with the Dora the Explorer DVD at Costco, Kate went to see a psychologist. Kate didn't initially reveal the sexual abuse, but she did open up about her depression and shoplifting. "When the psychologist asked me why I was there," she recalls, "I told her that I didn't want to be a mean mom. I was depressed and angry and I would snap at Patrick when he didn't deserve it. It scared me to see me acting in ways that my mom acted toward me."

Kate started taking the antidepressant medication Wellbutrin, and she finally told her husband about her arrest and the countless times she had shoplifted during their marriage. Eric had suspected that something was amiss, but he couldn't believe what he was hearing.

"Honestly, when she told me that, I wasn't sure our marriage could survive this," Eric said. "I don't do lies. I don't do deception. It's just not what I want in a marriage. I was in shock—there's no other way to describe it. My entire foundation had been ripped out from underneath me. I just went into defense mode and thought about all the deception that had gone along with this, all the trust she hadn't shown in me over the years by not telling me, and I thought I needed to do whatever I could to protect our son. Her behavior put us at risk. She could go to jail, or she could get a huge fine that would hurt us financially."

Eric insisted that she go to counseling, and they even saw a therapist together for a while. It all seemed to be working. "For most of our marriage, she was reclusive, and she would have these severe depressions and mood swings," Eric told me. "But when she started the counseling and the Wellbutrin and pretty much stopped the shoplifting, her moods got better, and the little things that used to set her off didn't so much."

Still, Kate was often listless and emotionally withdrawn. Her therapist urged her to face and begin healing from her childhood abuse, which she suspected would help Kate stop shoplifting. Intellectually, Kate said she understood that her shoplifting might be a symptom of unresolved trauma. But changing a lifelong pattern of blaming herself—"And pretending her childhood didn't happen," according to Eric—wasn't proving to be easy.

"I guess it's just been ingrained in me since I was little to beat myself up for everything," Kate says. "I suppose it would be a relief to accept that this hasn't all happened because I'm a bad or weak person. But I feel stupid blaming my childhood for my shoplifting. I'm not sure what the hurdle is I have to jump over before I'm ready to deal with what happened. All I know is that here I am, twenty-five years from when the abuse started, and I still don't want to talk about it."

Kate was surprised by how often I wanted to talk about it. I suggested she read books about sexual abuse. I regularly asked her how therapy was going—and when she told me that she didn't feel like she needed to go anymore, I didn't hide my disagreement. I expressed surprise when she said she hadn't told her husband much about her childhood. (When I asked Eric what he knew about her trauma, he said, "I don't push the subject—she's told you more about the abuse than she's told me.")

But the more I pressed, the more I worried that I was overstepping my bounds. I was writing about her recovery, not dictating it. "Your instincts are right—to live a full and healthy life, she's going to need to heal from what happened to her," Wendy Maltz, an expert on child sexual abuse and the author of *The Sexual Healing Journey*, told me after I described Kate's situation to her. "But it's not productive for people to look at it until they're ready, and she doesn't sound quite ready. Like other victims, Kate needs to realize that it wasn't her fault. Her perpetrator was responsible. It's his shame, not hers."

For those, like Kate, who are abused over many years by a relative, Maltz said that facing the abuse can be particularly agonizing. "In many ways, it's easier to recover from an isolated molestation by someone a child doesn't know," Maltz explained. "When the abuse happens over many years from a family member, someone who is supposed to be there for the child, it can create a lifelong confusion around safety and intimacy. The victim may have difficulty trusting or feeling okay anywhere. Her relative had essentially constant access to her, he groomed her slowly, and he took advantage of the fact that her needs were seriously neglected by her parents. The neglect and emotional abuse is the first trauma, because that's what created conditions for the sexual abuse to happen. As disturbing as the sexual abuse was, Kate may have participated due to a normal need for adult attention. If this was the case—as it often is with incest—it would have further confused Kate about what was going on and who was to blame."

Maltz added that she wasn't surprised Kate chose shoplifting as her coping method: "She's spent years taking things that weren't hers, much like her abuser spent years stealing from her what wasn't his to take."

19 ELLEN

Acknowledging the existence of something
larger than our own towering ego does seem
to be asking a lot. . . . Trying to do what our
Higher Power wants us to do—relinquish our
will—shouldn't be as hard as this but it is, isn't
it? Ask anybody. It's about as easy as qualify-
ing for sainthood. . . . At this point we're about
ready to give up the whole idea. But something's
tugging at our shirtsleeves. A tiny voice asks,
"What if? What if it were really possible?"

—HOMER P., *TURNING IT OVER*

ELLEN, THE FOOD addict, sits behind a large, wraparound desk in her office at the radio group where she works, a forgettable one-story brick structure on the south side of town. The room is decorated with plants, a lava lamp, and Christmas lights, and the walls are adorned with gold and platinum records from artists like Dido, David Gray, and Fleetwood Mac, and pictures of Ellen with Lyle Lovett, Toby Keith, Josh Groban, and Billy Joel.

Except when she's at home (where she wears oversized flannels and comfortable cargo pants), Ellen can be counted on to look stylish and eclectic. Today is no different. She's sporting designer jeans, snakeskin boots, a tight V-neck red sweater with multicolored hearts and embroidered graffiti, and colorful handmade hoop earrings from a craft fair. "I dressed the same way when I was fat," she told me once. "If I was going to be fat, I was at least going to be a fat person with style!"

As Ellen sips on a decaf, nonfat, sugar-free vanilla ice mocha (otherwise known as the *Why Bother?*) from Starbucks, she launches into a story about Billy Joel. "About two years ago, he was dating a girl who lived around here, and he spent a lot of time in town," Ellen tells me. "So one day I'm sitting in my office and the receptionist calls and says, 'Ellen, Billy Joel is here.' I'm like, 'Yeah, yeah, very funny.' But she says, 'Noooooo, you don't understand, it's *really* Billy Joel.' And it was! He told me that he listens a lot to the station and appreciates that we play his music. So we hung out for a while, and he came on the air with me and sang a song. It was unbelievable. Nothing like that had ever happened in my career."

Life at work hasn't been nearly as agreeable for Ellen lately. The station—which has long been known for its diverse classic hits sensibility—recently changed its format to appeal to a younger demographic. Now the station plays more contemporary songs, and Ellen had to move her midday show to the oldies station, which is also owned by the same radio group.

Ellen supported the changes because the ratings were slipping, but that doesn't mean she's not mad as hell about them. "I feel like my baby is gone," she says, looking like she might cry. "I've had so many feelings come up around this. I'm sad. And I'm so mad!"

"Who are you mad at?" I ask her.

"I'm mad at all the morons who don't understand what a quality radio station is," she says. "They forced us to change because they want this lowest common denominator stuff." And she's not sure how she feels about her midday show being moved to the oldies station. "I guess the cool thing is that I can act my age and relate to people from my era," she tells me, "but it also feels like where old DJs go to die. It kind of feels like I'm being put out to pasture."

Not surprisingly, Ellen has been craving food constantly and sometimes overeating during the format change, although she's quick to downplay it. She insists she's not in "full relapse," but she has gained seven pounds in two months, and the only thing giving her comfort lately is food.

"I'm grateful I didn't go up fifty pounds," she says. "I was just having an extra bite here or there, or grazing the cupboard and eating half a bag of potato chips." Still, she concedes that it's "not very sober behavior for me. I'm doing anything I can to stuff my feelings over all of this."

Ellen recently came clean to her sponsor, Marianna, about her overeating. "So Marianna said to me, 'Well, it seems like you've really said Fuck You to God,'" recalls Ellen. "In my head I was like, 'Do we really have to talk about *God* right now?' But she was right. I was trying to control everything, hold on to everything, and I was just in self-will run riot. I couldn't accept that the station was changing. Basically, I couldn't accept that life changes. Marianna told me that my homework was to feel all these feelings that I was trying to avoid by stuffing my face with food."

In the last week, Ellen has stopped overeating and is "sitting" with her feelings. "So guess what I'm doing now?" she says. "I'm crying *all the time*."

The next morning, I follow Ellen to a nearby Starbucks, where she meets with Marianna most Saturdays before an OA meeting. A tall forty-six-year-old with curly brown hair, Marianna has been sober for sixteen years in AA and abstinent on her OA food plan (no sugar, white flour, or dairy) for five. For Marianna, a deeply spiritual person, one of the keys to her longtime recovery is her willingness to work Step Eleven: *Sought through prayer and meditation to improve our conscious contact with God as we understood Him, praying only for knowledge of His will for us and the power to carry that out.*

At Starbucks, Ellen and Marianna sit near a window, drink tea, and talk.

Ellen: Marianna, I can't stop crying. I'm not sure I want to be feeling my feelings this much.

Marianna: Oh, I'm so proud of you for feeling your feelings. But I relate to the fear that you'll never stop crying. I have this dramatic fear that once I start, that's it, I'm going to get totally overwhelmed and soon I'll be owning stock in Kleenex for the rest of my life! But that's not the truth. The thing is, feelings pass. Good and bad feelings. They come, and they pass. The beauty of sobriety is that, for once, we actually *feel* our feelings. We're not using food to constantly numb ourselves.

Ellen: You know me, I so live in my head. I don't like feelings, except maybe anger. Anger can be fun! Lately I've had to think when I could feel myself starting to cry, "Is this an appropriate place to cry?" I was at my daughter's therapist, just me and the therapist talking, and I started to cry. And I thought that was reasonable, because if you can't cry in a therapist's office, then where *can* you cry? I think the reason I have such a hard time with crying in front of people is because of my mom. My mom just cried about everything, everywhere, all the time. For me it's like, I'm not going to let people see me cry, because I don't want to be like my mom.

Marianna: When I see someone who's capable of just being in their emotions, I used to label them as weak. I didn't want anything to do with that crap. But what I'm really doing when I do that is shutting down that function in myself, because I don't want anyone to think whatever they're going to think about me. Yesterday, I was talking to a friend who has cared enough about me recently to recognize my struggles. In the midst of saying a sentence, I just broke into tears. And it was really interesting, because I didn't have that filter of self-judgment we're talking about. I've lost that filter. I think I lost it at the end of the Fifth Step. But I thought, Isn't this fabulous? I don't really have control about when I might feel a feeling or start to cry, and it doesn't matter, it's not in my control anymore, and I'm actually quite happy about that. I never thought that would come out of my mouth, but there's been this realignment in me around a much more appropriate connection to emotion. It's a humbling thing. But you know what? The Twelve Steps are about ego reduction at its best. Kudos to you for just crying everywhere. I encourage that. Go team!

Ellen: And I've been really angry, too. Really angry. And I've been trying to figure out who I'm angry at.

Marianna: It doesn't matter. Who cares? You don't need a target. It's just anger. You can pick it apart and analyze it to death, but it doesn't matter. It all comes down to, Are we angry with God or aren't we?

Ellen: Well, I know I've been angry at God for putting a bunch of idiots on this earth. I've been angry with God for not having things go the way I think they should.

Marianna: Yeah, we always think we have a better plan.

Ellen: I don't even know what my better plan is. It's just not the one that's actually happening! I have to trust that God's plan is the right one, but it's really hard.

Marianna: I can relate to that. I don't want to be open to the unknown a lot of times, too. But I realize that this is such old stuff. Control issues. Wanting some guarantee about the future. I want to avoid all that and just get to the good stuff. The good stuff being all the addictive behaviors. It doesn't work that way, of course, but that's the way our brains think. But it's not appropriate for us to want to skip that stuff, because we're losing out on all the growth. This is the good stuff, believe it or not. You know, being able to cry means I'm free. I'm no longer numbed out by my addiction. But how else can I get free if I don't do the behaviors that terrify me?

Ellen: What's kept me abstinent is when I think about taking a compulsive bite, I know it's just going to make things worse. I just need to get through it. But part of me is always thinking, "Why don't I just eat for *one* day?"

Marianna: I know what it's like: It's okay to have this *one* thing, I'm not going to eat *that* much, I'll just have *one* extra bite, I feel fine, I look fine, my clothes fit, all those justifications, and then twenty pounds later we're wondering what happened. Because, again, it's not about the food. It's about the *thinking*. It's the faulty thinking that gives us permission. In Al-Anon they say, "My mind is a dangerous neighborhood, I can't go there alone." And some days, that's really quite true. It is about justification. It isn't that we're maniacs.

Ellen: Sometimes I feel like one.

Marianna: As addicts, we have so much practice splitting ourselves in half and living in a different reality. I can convince myself of anything in the moment if it gets me to the good stuff. If I can eat over it, beautiful, I'm all over it! I've never been on crack cocaine, so I don't know what the high is like or the time frame, but with ingesting food it's moments, and then it's gone. And so when I think about all the carbs I consumed, those were the shortcuts to numbing out. Because I could get in a carb coma, like many of us have, and we could then be numbed out for hours, we'd be feeling full and sick, but that would distract us from whatever else was going on. So I knew that if I ingested a certain amount of stuff, then I could just escape from that thinking for X amount of time. But it requires more and more food.

Ellen: Yeah, there's almost a double payoff. Now that I'm in recovery, if I eat too much, I get really miserable and unhappy about having gone there, and that obsession with what I just ate blocks out the other emotions I don't want to feel. So I just experience the safe unhappiness, the one I've known my whole life, feeling like I'm a failure, feeling like I'm unhappy because I used food, as opposed to sitting with and getting clarity about what's really bothering me, which is sadness and grief and fear and anger and all the emotions I avoided my whole life. My therapist, Dru, asked me, "What's it going to be like on the other side of this? What are you going to be like?" I said, "I don't know. I can't see that, I can't feel it." She said, "Good, that's great!" I didn't understand. She said that the normal way I would operate would be to say, "Okay, now it's time to feel these feelings. I'm going to feel these specific feelings, then they're going to be all done, and then I'm going to be in this place and this is what it's going to be like." She said that it gives me security to have all that figured out mentally. It's unusual for me to be riding the wave and say it's going to deposit me somewhere, and I don't know what that somewhere is going to look like.

Marianna: It's fabulous that we don't know what the future holds. We need to *not* know. I used to hear people talking about that in meetings, and I was always puzzled by how people could say things like, "Well, I'm being directed to do X, Y, and Z, so I'm going to have faith and do that." I just thought those people were crazy! And I wasn't sure I was in for *that* part of the program. It's difficult, because the bottom line is that what you're finally surrendering into is the reality that we don't control the world around us. All of our attachments, anything outside of ourselves, will create a false sense of security. And that includes our addiction. So everything about that has to be removed. We need to surrender to the idea that we aren't in control, and anything we use to deceive ourselves into thinking we are in control has to be removed. And that's a shock, because we just don't live that way in this society.

Ellen: I have a hard time wrapping my head around what you're saying right now. I mean, that's fine for Mother Teresa or someone who lives in a monastery, or maybe it's fine for you.

Marianna: Right, right, because I'm Mother Teresa and I happen to live in a monastery.

Ellen: No, but you live on a higher spiritual plane than I do. It sounds too New Agey or something.

Marianna: Yeah, where's my granola?

Ellen: I mean, I do think you're more evolved. Your role in my life is as a guide, a teacher. So I have this feeling that maybe I won't be that evolved in this life. But to embrace the concept that having attachments taken away will put me in a better place is hard for me. And then I think, "What's a *better* place? Happiness and joy, but that's still all about self." And so the thought that if I can get outside myself and not be self-centered and that's my job on earth, well I don't think I want that job. I want to be happy and be fulfilled in self.

Marianna: Well, what makes you think you can't be happy *and* live a spiritual life?

Ellen: Well, there's where I get confused. Seeking happiness feels like a self-centered goal.

Marianna: Accepting that happiness comes from the outside rather than the inside is the difference. I'm not going to be happy if I have a relationship that I think I want or deserve, if I have a great paying job, if I eat what I think will make me feel better, if I have everything materially that I've ever wanted. Those things won't create happiness. I may temporarily be in a *delusion* around it. When you were talking about not being a monk or Mother Teresa, I related to that. For many years I thought, "Let's not even bother doing this spiritual stuff, because I'm not a saint, I'm not willing to have my eyeballs removed, swords thrown at me, all that stuff I learned in Catholic school. None of that's appealing. If that's how you have to be a saint, I'm not that!" But what I was trying to do was make this condition so extreme that I wouldn't even bother to approach it. The key is integration. It's about living this life, having love, experiencing joy and happiness, but because of our connections with people, not because of *things*.

Ellen: I get you about the things. Things aren't going to bring me happiness. Food's not going to bring me happiness. But what I'm hearing you saying is that I need to detach from *everything*. Which means I need to detach from my job, or my identity around my job? I have such a hard time detaching from ego.

Marianna: Of course you do. We all do. But it doesn't matter what my ego has invested itself in—it's still not who I really am. This is what I know: Left to my own devices, I have a history that tells me that my thinking isn't very clear. Left to my own devices, I get very creative and destructive, and I turn to my addiction, and I don't want to do that again. So I need to have my thinking rearranged. I need to have my consciousness lifted radically, and that's exactly what's happening. And that has to do with loss after loss, because how can I get to the new thinking if I don't let go of the old?

Ellen: And that's where the fear comes up.

Marianna: Absolutely. It's fear, it's anxiety, it's loss, it's freaking out, it's whatever you want to call it. But it's inevitable. I have to experience loss, and be okay through it, and survive, before I come to a place, finally, of relative calm and faith, that I'll be okay. But that has to get beaten into me.

Ellen: I was just talking to a friend whose sister was diagnosed with cancer. And last summer, the sister's eighteen-year-old son was killed in a car accident. So my friend is watching her sister walk through this cancer cavalierly. And my friend is like, "How can you do that?" And her sister said, "I've had the worst thing happen to me that could ever happen to anyone in their life. This is not like that. So I just put one foot in front of the other. I've been through the worst. Now I have faith."

Marianna: What a power of example. She's shifted her thinking and sees this from that spiritual point of view. She's saying, "Okay, this is an experience that's happening, how can I walk through this in as alert a fashion as I can and with the willingness to be present?" There's no self-pity there. No *why me*? 'Cause, you know, why *not* me? Like, who else do I think this should happen to? I try to remember that when I get in that self-pity mode. Why shouldn't I be walking through this? Who am I to try to dictate the outcome of this experience before I even experience it? Over and over, I want to be assured that everything will be okay. Well, what's my definition of *okay*? It's probably not appropriate to begin with. So that whole thing has to be blown up, and then I can finally get to, "Oh, this is what was meant for me to be. This requires trust and faith." But that's so hard to do, so it makes sense that you would be kicking and screaming, but the ultimate outcome is an improvement. I mean, look how much you've changed.

Ellen: Definitely more peace, more serenity.

Marianna: Absolutely. If you look at the changes between when you walked in the door of OA and today, regardless of all this up-and-down stuff, think about how much more level of acceptance you have, how less resistance you have, how much more willing you are. There's so much growth there. It's funny, when I was coming home from Florida, I was in the airplane, and there was a woman sitting in front of me reading the addiction book *A Million Little Pieces*. This was before the news came out that he made a lot of it up. We were standing and waiting for people to leave the plane, and this other woman across the aisle said, "Oh, I see you're reading that book. Isn't it amazing?" The woman said, "Yes, my niece is an alcoholic. I'm trying to read this book and trying to understand her experience and see if I can help her. But I think she probably has to go to AA."

The woman shot back, "You know, it's a cult. They have to do the steps, and they have to go to meetings every day!" So I'm standing there wanting to jump into this conversation and say, "Hello, wait a minute. Who cares if she has to go to meetings? Who cares if she has to do the steps? Thank God she has a solution other than addiction and death!" But I didn't. It wasn't any of my damn business. It's funny, though. When I think of a cult, I think of brainwashing. AA and OA are so far from being cults, but I can also look at it another way. You know what? My brain needed a good washing. We can change our consciousness through a lot of stuff, but when we work the steps, we eventually find ourselves saying and doing things that were not possible before. So I don't give a rat's ass what I have to go through to get there, because what I've tasted so far is so much better. I'm not going to go back. I just can't, nor do I want to.

Ellen: I was thinking that. You can't go back, I can't go back. Things have changed. Things have shifted forever. I could go back to overeating, but my thinking will never be the same as it was when I was eating before. I've got too much recovery in my brain.

Marianna: Right, because if we do go back, it will be so much more of a painful experience, because now we know better.

Ellen: What time is it?

Marianna: Time to go to the meeting!

(They get up, put their jackets on, and walk out the door. Outside, Ellen turns to Marianna.)

Ellen: Benoit was telling me that some addicts want to have a Million Addict March on Washington. Do you think we'll ever have one?

Marianna: Wow, that would be so cool. What would we sing?

Ellen: While we march?

Marianna: No, on the bus. We'd have to sing cool songs on the bus ride there.

Ellen: Well, we wouldn't sing "A Hundred Bottles of Beer on the Wall."

Marianna: Marching for recovery would be so fun. Can you imagine a million of us marching our asses off for recovery? It would be fun. We'd be with our peeps!

20 BOBBY

*I know of no class of people who have been so
victimized by the quack as the inebriate.*

—LESLIE KEELEY, FOUNDER OF
THE KEELEY INSTITUTE

BOBBY SITS IN the passenger seat as his godmother, Margaret, drives
us through South Boston on our way to St. Elizabeth's Medical Center on this clear, frigid winter afternoon. We're a few days removed
from a massive northeaster, and in a post-storm Boston tradition,
the streets remain littered with traffic cones and garbage cans and
whatever else residents who shoveled out their cars can use to temporarily claim their parking spots.

Margaret called me yesterday with the good news. After nine
months of using heroin (and avoiding me), Bobby finally wants to
get sober. "Meet us tomorrow," she said. "We're going to get him
some Suboxone."

Approved by the FDA in 2002, Suboxone, like methadone, is essentially a substitution drug that mimics the effects of heroin, binding to opiate receptors in the brain and blocking other opiates from

having any effect. But Suboxone has two distinct advantages over methadone: It can be prescribed by a doctor (meaning no daily visits to the methadone clinic) and produces less of a high, limiting its potential for abuse and overdose. Suboxone is arguably the most effective anti-addiction medication on the market.

"I'll be on them like a week or two," Bobby says, turning around in his seat to face me. He's wearing baggy gray sweatpants and a black Adidas track jacket, and his short hair is still wet from the shower he just took. He has a black burn on his thumb from smoking crack (which he sometimes defaults to if he can't get heroin), and his middle finger is fractured from punching a friend who Bobby thought, in a paranoid rage, was trying to "poison" his drugs.

"The Suboxone will help me detox, help me get my shit together," Bobby tells us. "It's better than going off heroin cold turkey. But then again, sometimes I think going cold turkey might be better. If I'm going to be sober, I want to *really* be sober. I hate having to depend on medications."

"A week or two?" Margaret says with skepticism. "I don't want you to fool yourself, Bobby. This is not a short-term thing. You could be on Suboxone for more than a year. It will depend on what the doctor thinks. Are you ready for that?"

"Yeah, I'm ready today," he says, fidgeting with the radio dial in search of a station he likes.

"Well, you didn't sound very ready with what you just said," Margaret tells him.

After a long silence, during which Bobby gives up his station search and turns off the radio in frustration, I speak up. "Is Suboxone enough to stay clean?" I ask Bobby.

"I know I'll have to go to meetings," he says, giving lip service to my question. It's not the answer I was hoping for. Like many addicts in Southie, Bobby is as hooked on the junkie lifestyle (scheming, robbing, manipulating) as he is on heroin, and while Suboxone is a highly effective medication, it won't erase the decades' worth of addictive thinking and behavior that have made Bobby a chronic relapser.

One recovering heroin addict I spoke to who tried Suboxone (but got sober without it) said the medication can lull an addict into a false sense of security. "It's not recovery—it's a crutch," he told me. "The government would rather have heroin addicts on Suboxone than on heroin out robbing little old ladies. For society, it's great. For addicts, it's bullshit. It gives you a false sense of recovery, and you forget that what's really going to keep you sober is radically changing your life."

Bobby has already been taking Suboxone for three days; he got some pills from a friend who has a doctor's prescription. "Margaret, I'm starting to feel better already," he says, staring out the passenger-side window. "A couple more days, a couple more weeks, and I'll feel good."

"But what are you going to do in a couple of weeks when maybe things aren't going your way?" Margaret inquires. "That's a critical time. What are your goals? How are you going to make this time different than the other times?"

"I know," he says. "I have a plan all written out."

"Could you let me in on it?" Margaret wants to know.

"First, I'm going out looking for work."

"That's good," she says, "but how will you deal with the disappointment of not getting the job you want right away?"

"I don't care what kind of job I get," Bobby tells her, "as long as I'm making enough to get by and see the kids and take care of the kids."

"So how much would that be?" she asks, her voice becoming more patronizing with each question.

"I dunno, about $400 a week. I'll do anything. I'll work in demolition taking houses apart. There's plenty of that stuff around."

"I know there is," Margaret says, "but you know how those jobs go. A lot of those guys are using."

"Well, what the fuck am I supposed to do, then?" Bobby says, losing his patience. "What do you want me to do?"

"Hey, don't get all jumpy with me," she tells him sternly, shaking her head. She's used to Bobby's reaction to her nagging, and she doesn't back down. "I'm just trying to help you plan for the future. A lot of those guys are using, and that's probably not the best place for you to be."

I ask Bobby why he's choosing to get clean now. "I'm just sick of all the bullshit," he says. "The heroin around here lately has been terrible. You do a hit of it, you get the rush, and it's over in like a second. It's just like you're giving away your money to these dealers. The shit they're selling now—those fuckers should be shot. No wonder everyone is trying to get clean now. The heroin sucks. So it's a good time to get sober. I mean, it was a good time two years ago, but the heroin now doesn't even work."

Again, it's not the answer I was hoping for. I thought he might mention his kids, or his health, or the likelihood that he'll end up in jail again if he keeps using, but his reasoning seems more practical: The drugs aren't working anymore.

"I need some coffee," he says. Margaret pulls the car over in front of a coffee shop, and Bobby runs inside.

"I might seem mean," Margaret tells me, turning in her seat to face me. "But I have to stay on him. I know all his tricks, all the ways he sets himself up for relapse."

"In his mind, does he think it's the last time he'll ever use?" I ask.

"Oh, yes. Every time he tries to stop, he's convinced that this will be the time it works. He's not bullshitting us. In his mind, he's getting clean today. And even when I'm not convinced, and part of me doesn't think he's ready to stop today, I'll do whatever I can to help.

But I'll tell you, it's a good sign that he wants to get on Suboxone, even if he thinks he's just going to use it a few weeks. I've been trying to get him on Suboxone for almost two years."

Since he last agreed to see me nine months ago, Bobby has been using between $40 and $100 of heroin nearly every day. On the days he couldn't find heroin, he bought methadone on the street for $10. "I'm pretty resourceful when it comes to avoiding going through withdrawals," he says when he's back in the car. "I'll do whatever I have to do."

Recently, that included robbing a heroin dealer of his stash. Bobby says he was starting to shake and "freeze up" from impending withdrawal when a friend called with some good news: He had found a dealer they could rob. The friend drove the dealer over to Bobby's house in a snowstorm, and Bobby jumped in the back seat and put the dealer, who was in the passenger's seat, in a headlock.

"I said, 'Listen, kid, it's not about the money. It's about the drugs,'" Bobby recalls saying. The dealer had thirteen bags of heroin on him, which Bobby took even though he knew they would probably turn out to be "crap." Bobby's friend took the dealer's money (he was carrying more than a thousand dollars), but Bobby says he made him give most of it back.

"For some reason, I felt bad for the kid, started worrying that he might starve or something," Bobby tells us. "He was this young Spanish dealer, and he looked like a nice kid. Lately my conscience just kicks in. The next day, I was like, 'Fuck, I should have taken the money!'"

"Bobby, you're a *good* person," Margaret says, energized by Bobby's apparent random act of kindness. It reminded her of the Bobby she knew years ago—the pre-drug Bobby who thought about other people's feelings. "Your instincts are to do good. The real you is the person who worries about other people, who cares about other people."

"Yeah, I'm getting all emotional lately, caring too much about stuff," he says. "The other day I was watching *Braveheart,* and I started crying my eyes out. Over *Braveheart*!"

"That's good!" she tells him. "It's good to feel feelings." Margaret makes eye contact with me in the rearview mirror. "When Bobby was a kid, he wasn't allowed to have feelings or show his feelings," she says. "A lot of kids in South Boston aren't allowed to show their feelings. He always had to be this big strong tough guy, even in his own family." She turns to face Bobby. "The fact that you're starting to feel and cry, that's really good!"

"I can't believe I didn't take the money," Bobby says again, shaking his head. "He had so many twenties."

"No, you did the right thing," Margaret insists.

"When things get real bad, like when I was in the shower, I'll do crazy things to get drugs," Bobby says, turning in his seat again to face me.

Margaret nods. "Like rob your father."

"Yeah, I've taken checks off my mother and father. I've probably written like $2,000 worth of bad checks from my parents. When it gets bad, I have no shame. I'll steal from my own family."

"That's how low addiction takes people," Margaret says as we pull into the hospital parking lot, where she will drop us off before heading back to work. "Now, Bobby, just listen to whatever the doctor tells you," she tells him as he pushes open the passenger-side door and lifts his body out of the front seat.

In the doctor's waiting room, Bobby passes the time by skimming through an issue of *Health* magazine. "You wouldn't think it, but I'm a total health freak," he says. "When I'm sober, I get up every morning real early, I work out, and I'm obsessed with eating right."

After urging Bobby to go to therapy and Twelve Step meetings, the doctor writes him a prescription for a two-week supply. "This is the first time I'm seeing him," the doctor tells me, "so I don't want to give him a month's worth of Suboxone and say, 'See you later.'"

"How often do you get patients who don't show up for their second visit?" I ask.

"Most people show up. If they don't show up, they don't get any more from me. And there are only two hundred doctors right now in the state who can prescribe this, so it's not always easy to find another doctor right away if you screw up with the doctor you have."

His prescription in hand, Bobby and I head back toward Southie. After taking a crowded bus to Kenmore Square near Fenway Park, we have to take the first of two underground trains, after which we'll hop on a bus to Bobby's house. We both pay $1.50 for an entry coin, but when it comes time to drop his in the turnstile, Bobby pockets it and tries to sneak through an open gate where people are rushing to exit the station. The employee who handed us our coins sees the whole thing, and she's not pleased.

"Sir, put the coin in," she demands.

"Damn, it's like I stole her paycheck or something!" Bobby tells me. A minute later, he has a realization. "It's like I'm addicted to pulling things over on people," he says, shaking his head in disbelief. "I've gotta change all my habits."

The more I hang out with Bobby, the less surprised I become by these occasional moments of clarity and introspection. They usually arrive unsolicited. He will do something or say something that stops him in his tracks, surprising even him and temporarily breaking through his denial. The revelation usually prompts an earnest pledge to change the behavior, but minutes or hours later he's back to his old ways.

The turnstile incident is no different. After his epiphany about changing his habits, I try to engage him in a conversation about whether he can realistically do that in Southie. I've known several addicts from the neighborhood who had to move away for months or years to get clean, and many addicts who routinely relapse choose to move to what are essentially recovery enclaves on the Florida coast. One Boston heroin addict who knows Bobby, and who escaped to West Palm Beach and Jody's sober living community to get sober and never moved back, told me that he hoped Bobby would also move away.

"In recovery they say that you need to stay away from people, places, and things that remind you of using," he said. "In Southie, *everything* is going to remind Bobby of using. For someone like him, I think the only way he'll have a chance is if you take him out of his environment and keep him away from his boys that he uses with. Once he moves, he won't have to play the bad-ass role that he's been playing for years in Southie."

But as we wait for the subway train, Bobby seems uninterested in talking about change—especially if it means moving from Southie for a few months or a year. "I've seen people get sober there," he says dismissively, as if that means it's necessarily the right decision for *him*, who has failed so many times to get clean there. "Besides," he continues, "I don't want to move away from my kids."

I decide to take a risk. "But are you much good to them as a dad if you're a junkie?"

The question lingers in the hot, stale subway air. "Man, you go right for the jugular," he says finally. "I don't know. I don't know how good I am to them as a dad."

Later, on our bus ride through Southie, Bobby points out two teenage boys hurriedly walking down a main street. The younger of the two is skinny, with baggy jeans and a baseball cap pulled low over an acne-covered face. The other is bigger, with black sweatpants and curly blond hair. "They're both hard-core addicts," Bobby tells me. "They're known as neighborhood fuck-ups."

"Does it bother you that some people look at you the same way?" I ask him.

"You know, I was just thinking that," he says with a laugh. "Right after I opened my mouth, I realized that it's sort of hypocritical of me to say that. I know that people look at me the same way, and that sucks. But if I'm doing the right thing and trying to get clean, I don't care what people think."

The bus turns a corner, offering us a spectacular view of the Boston harbor. "I am so over doing drugs," Bobby says, his hands gripping the bar on the seat in front of us. "I can't do it anymore. I'm done. The party's over. The last year has really, really sucked. I'm really lucky I'm not dead. I need to be a dad to my kids. I need to start taking care of myself again. I've been sober before. But then I'll get complacent, and soon I'm rationalizing that since things are going so well, I can get high *just once*. But there's no *just once* for me. That's the problem. I get high, and the next day I sleep in all day, I have a hangover, and the next thing I want to do is to get high again. And then there I go, losing another year of my life. I'll tell you one thing. I'm done with drugs. I'm done with this fucked-up lifestyle. The party's over."

We agree to meet the next night at his house to talk more. He never shows up.

———

A few months later (with still no word from Bobby), I fly to San Diego for the American Society of Addiction Medicine (ASAM) conference, where a half-dozen pharmaceutical companies—including Reckitt Benckiser, the maker of Suboxone—hawk their anti-addiction medications alongside traditional treatment centers like Hazelden and Betty Ford.

It's a strange scene, but one that perfectly illustrates the new ways we're beginning to understand addiction and recovery in this country. In the conference's main exhibition hall, the treatment centers promote their usual message of serenity, spirituality, and a Twelve Step–based form of recovery that has long existed outside the reach and understanding of mainstream medicine.

Next to them, the pharmaceutical companies—armed with charts, graphs, clinical study results, and eager young marketing and sales teams—talk a lot about "shifting the paradigm" and doing for addiction what the industry did for depression: medicalizing it, and destigmatizing it in the process.

The pharmaceutical companies tell me they came to the conference to put the *medicine* in addiction medicine. They don't discount the importance of environment in inducing addictive behavior or therapy and Twelve Step treatment as part of the recovery process, but they argue that addiction is a chronic and recurring disease like diabetes or hypertension—and no one, they say, tells a diabetic to "tough it out" without his insulin. (The National Institute on Drug Abuse and the National Institute on Alcohol Abuse and Alcoholism agree. They're studying hundreds of addiction medications.)

In the ASAM exhibition hall, the prime booth location near the entrance belongs to Alkermes and Cephalon, two pharmaceutical companies producing and marketing Vivitrol, an injectable form of the medication naltrexone. Studies have found that naltrexone can help some alcoholics abstain from or cut down on their drinking. Alkermes and Cephalon hope Vivitrol will sidestep a huge challenge facing those seeking pharmacological solutions for addiction: unless they're getting high from it, most addicts aren't compliant medicine takers. (Vivitrol requires a monthly shot from a doctor.)

Alkermes and Cephalon are initially focusing on doctors who specialize in addiction, but they plan eventually to market the drug directly to primary care physicians, most of whom are used to outsourcing their addicted patients to treatment centers and Twelve Step groups.

"It would require a complete paradigm shift," Doug Neale, a product director at Cephalon, tells me over lunch at the conference, "but we'd like to see the day when a patient who is struggling with alcoholism can walk into their primary care doctor's office, say, 'Doc,

I'm drinking too much and can't seem to stop,' and the doctor will have a handful of options for medications that he could prescribe."

After lunch I bump into Dr. David Smith, the founder of the Haight Ashbury Free Clinic in San Francisco and the former president of ASAM. Smith calls himself a "rare two-hatter" in the addiction field, meaning he believes in both the power of the Twelve Steps and the aggressive pursuit of pharmacology.

"In medicine, if something isn't working, you try something new," he tells me. "In addiction, if someone goes to treatment and fails, for years we've just sent them back again and again and expected different results. That's insanity. And we're starting to realize that. The field of addiction treatment is changing right before our eyes, and it's only going to continue to change. Advances in neuroscience and pharmacology will change everything."

They're certainly changing expectations, prompting people like Matthew Torrington, a young addiction medicine doctor in Los Angeles, to say: "With the scientific advances we're making in understanding how the human brain works, there's no reason we can't eradicate addiction in the next twenty or thirty years."

Eradicate addiction? "But in order to do that," I ask him at the conference, "wouldn't we first need to eradicate pleasure seeking in human beings? And do we really want to go *there*?"

Torrington, who has a rugby player's build and red hair, leans forward in his chair. "We can eradicate addiction by fixing the part of the brain that turns on you during drug addiction and encourages you to kill yourself against your will," he says. "People are always going to drink and always going to try drugs, but do they need to become crack addicts? Do they have to take meth to the point where they lose their teeth and ditch their kids? Is that really *necessary*? I think addiction is the most beatable of all the major problems we face. And I think we will."

When I later tell Torrington's mentor, neurologist Walter Ling, what his pupil said about eradicating addiction, he nearly falls out of his seat laughing. "That's kind of like predicting world peace, isn't it?" he says, holding his belly. "Oh, Matthew is still young. Give him time, and he'll get pessimistic like the rest of us! Do I think we're making tremendous progress? Yes. But I don't think we'll ever make addiction go away. The problem with addiction is that it's very, very complicated."

But Torrington isn't alone in his boundless optimism. When some of the top scientists in Britain were asked to forecast how new technologies and scientific advances could be used to influence society in twenty years, they made some remarkable projections: That the brains of addicts could be "reprogrammed" to counter the effects of long-term addiction; that neural imaging could allow us to "identify former, current, and potential addicts"; and that anti-addiction vaccines could be used to immunize children deemed at risk of becoming addicted. (Vaccines for nicotine, cocaine, and meth are already in development. They work by producing antibodies to a specific drug, binding to it when it enters the bloodstream, and keeping it from entering the brain.)

Any addiction vaccine will likely come booby-trapped with contentious ethical questions. Should we force addicts, especially those who commit crimes (or those, like Bobby, who repeatedly fail at taxpayer-funded treatment programs), to be vaccinated? And should children deemed "genetically predisposed" to addiction be vaccinated, even though they might never grow up to abuse drugs?

In their fifty-two-page report, entitled "Ethical Aspects of Developments in Neuroscience and Drug Addiction," the British scientists hinted that we might even consider a mandatory national vaccination. "If it is not justifiable to vaccinate the entire nation," the scientists wrote, "it could be feasible, and more affordable, to target certain groups within it. While there may be legitimate reasons to screen a certain population . . . groups could be selected on more dubious arguments."

It wouldn't be the first time we proposed radical solutions to deal with incorrigible addicts. In the early 1900s, some doctors called for the sterilization of drug abusers, and the state of Indiana passed a law banning marriages between "habitual drunkards." These extreme measures came only after countless miracle medications and cures—including an anti-alcohol vaccine extracted from horse's blood and a bottled sixty-nine-cent cure for morphine and opium addiction advertised in the Sears, Roebuck & Company catalogue— turned out to be useless. (Others were laced with the very drugs they were supposed to be "curing." One study found that nineteen of the twenty opium cures at the time contained opium.)

In *Slaying the Dragon*, White recounts other failed treatments for addicts in the nineteenth century and first half of the twentieth: shock therapy, prefrontal lobotomy surgery, spinal puncture, colonic irrigation therapy, and "the exposure of alcoholics to hot-air boxes and light boxes that mimicked the climatic conditions of the equator, where alcoholism was rare."

Science, it seems, has always been *just about* to save us from addiction. "But it has never lived up to its promise," argues Bruce Alexander, professor emeritus of psychology at Simon Fraser University in Vancouver. "Addiction doesn't demand a scientific solution." Alexander is among a vocal minority of addiction researchers who believe that focusing on a pill to treat addicts fails to address the primary cause of becoming and staying hooked: our unhappy, disconnected lives.

In 1981, Alexander and his team of researchers set out to study the role of our environment in addictive behavior. Like most addiction researchers at the time, they planned to use rats. But they went about it differently. Until then, most scientists studying addiction had simply put rats in small, individual cages and watched as they eagerly guzzled drug-laced solutions and ignored water and food, sometimes dying in the process. This phenomenon was regarded— first by researchers, then drug czars, then parents trying to keep their kids off drugs—as proof of the inherently addictive quality of drugs and of the inevitable addiction of any human who used them repeatedly. (This was false, of course. Most people who try drugs don't become addicted to them.)

So, what made all those lab rats lose their minds? Bruce Alexander and his research team had a simple hypothesis: The rats had awful lives. They were stressed, lonely, bored, and looking to self-medicate. To prove it, Alexander created a lab rat dream house he called "Rat Park Heaven." The two-hundred-square-foot residence featured bright balls and tin cans to play with, painted creeks and trees to look at, and plenty of room for mating and socializing.

Alexander took sixteen lucky rats and plopped them in Rat Park Heaven, where they were offered water or a sweet, morphine-based cocktail (rats love sweets). Alexander offered the same two drinks to the sixteen rats he isolated in cages. The results? The Rat-Parkers were apparently having too much fun to bother with artificial highs because they hardly touched the morphine solution, no matter how sweet Alexander and his colleagues made it. The isolated and stressed rats, on the other hand, eagerly got high, drinking sixteen times the amount of the morphine solution as the rats in rodent paradise.

When I spoke with Alexander, he predicted that unless we undergo nothing short of a "cultural renaissance" and all start living in a human version of his Rat Park (which he conceded isn't likely), we won't be eradicating addiction anytime soon.

While National Institute on Drug Abuse director Nora Volkow doesn't agree with Alexander that developing addiction medications is a fruitless enterprise, she does believe that a positive and nurturing environment, particularly during childhood and adolescence, is a strong protector against addiction. Volkow says that addicts are more likely to have been unnecessarily stressed during childhood (from neglect; emotional, physical, or sexual abuse; or poverty), and that they're less able to deal with stress as adults.

Studies show that animals stressed during early development are more likely to self-administer drugs later in life, and that living in an enriched environment—one with a minimal amount of strain and anxiety, like Rat Park Heaven—appears to protect animals from developing addictive behavior.

"We know from human twin and family studies that about 50 percent of a person's vulnerability to addiction is genetic," says Volkow, who in addition to being one of the leading thinkers in America about addiction, also happens to be the great-granddaughter of Leon Trotsky. "But if you're never exposed to illegal drugs, or if you grow up and live in an environment without trauma and too many stressors, you probably won't become addicted."

A few weeks after the ASAM conference I travel to Cambridge, where the Picower Institute for Learning and Memory at MIT hosts a one-day conference about addiction and memory for a small, invitation-only crowd of clinicians, public policy makers, and scientists (including Volkow). Addiction conferences are usually sober affairs, but MIT offers up a lavish cocktail reception—with an open bar, no less.

Neuroscientist Steven Hyman leads off the day by proposing that addiction is a form of "pathological learning" and "extreme memory." The problem with the addicted brain, Hyman believes, is that it remembers the good feelings that come from drug use but forgets the pain, suffering, and demoralization that inevitably come after them. This dysfunction is critical to the addictive process, because long after the drug has left the body or the addictive behavior has been stopped, the powerful memories associated with them remain. These hardwired memories can cause intense craving when triggered, leading to a rush of dopamine (the brain expects the reward) that can overwhelm the brain's frontal cortex, which is responsible for planning and decision making.

What is happening in the brain, Hyman wonders aloud during his lecture, "so that passing an alley where you used to shoot up can, after all kinds of trouble and treatment and Lord knows what else, reinitiate a set of addictive behaviors? As we understand learning and memory, something essentially permanent, some remodeling of synapses has occurred in this survival pathway related to reward. The question is, can we reverse it, or find some countervailing method?"

Volkow is intrigued by the prospect of developing medications that can dampen or eliminate cue- and stress-related craving. After presenting her stump lecture, "Addiction: The Neurobiology of Free Will Gone Awry," in her usual intense and rapid-fire speaking style, Volkow takes me aside.

"When you're an addicted person and get exposed to cues," she explains, "you liberate dopamine in the brain. Could we develop medications that interfere with that release of dopamine when you see a conditioned cue? Or could we come up with a pill that someone puts under their tongue when they start to get a craving, just like someone does if they start to get chest pains?"

For much of the past two decades, Volkow and other researchers exploring the physiological basis of addiction have focused on dopamine, which was originally thought to serve as a kind of pleasure signal in the brain, telling us when something feels good or rewarding. But scientists now believe that dopamine is more a predictor of salience—it tells us, and then helps us to remember, what we should focus on. When you see a person you're strongly attracted to, for example, scientists will see a spike of dopamine in your brain. If you're hungry and smell a food you like, dopamine also increases.

Drugs, particularly cocaine and meth, cause a large increase in the amount of dopamine secreted and pooled between brain cells, leading to feelings of euphoria. But with regular and repeated drug use, the brain eventually responds by reducing its normal release of dopamine. That, in turn, makes the brain's reward system less likely to respond to behaviors (a good meal, the company of friends) that produce a normal dopamine surge. The addicted brain essentially becomes pathologically selective, dependent on bigger and bigger blasts of a specific reward to feel satiated.

Studies in both animals and humans have indicated that those with low levels of dopamine D2 receptors, which regulate the release of dopamine in the brain, are more likely to find the experience of taking drugs pleasurable. Volkow also found that obese subjects have lower levels of D2 receptors than those who eat normally (there have been no such studies on gamblers or sex addicts). Volkow believes that people with fewer receptors experience a less intense reward signal, causing them to overindulge in order to feel satisfied.

In one experiment, Volkow increased the level of dopamine D2 receptors in rats that had low levels. After the increase, the rats significantly curtailed their intake of alcohol, which they had eagerly gulped down before. Unfortunately, we don't yet know how to safely increase the number of dopamine D2 receptors in humans.

Studies of people with Parkinson's, a disease characterized by insufficient dopamine in the brain, have shown that a significant number develop compulsive disorders (gambling, hypersexuality, excessive shopping) when given a dopamine agonist, which mimics the effect of dopamine and activates their dopamine receptors. Take them off the medication, and the compulsive behaviors stop.

There is also some evidence suggesting that environment can affect the number of dopamine D2 receptors in an animal's brain. In 2003, researchers at the Wake Forest School of Medicine measured the levels of receptors of twenty macaque monkeys while they were housed in isolation. They then assigned the monkeys to social groups of four monkeys each, letting natural social hierarchies develop. Three months later, they tested the levels of D2 receptors again. The dominant monkeys—who, the theory goes, were less stressed and anxious than the subordinate ones—had 20 percent higher D2 receptor function, while the submissive ones were unchanged. The monkeys were then taught how to self-administer cocaine by pressing a lever, with researchers finding that the dominant monkeys took significantly less cocaine than did the subordinate ones.

But when the animals that seemed to be protected from addiction were given cocaine repeatedly, the number of their D2 receptors eventually decreased, and they then became addicted. The lesson of the monkey story, Volkow says, is that environment—if good or bad enough—can sometimes trump genetics and biology.

Still, while it appears that dopamine plays a primary role in many types of addictions, studies of the neurotransmitter haven't led to any effective medications, the ultimate goal of many researchers. "The field has wasted a lot of time on dopamine," argues George Koob, the director of the Division of Psychopharmacology at the Scripps Research Institute.

Because addiction seems to disrupt so many different brain regions, neuroscientists are now casting a wider net in their pursuit of effective pharmacology. For some, the new frontier involves the brain's two major "workhorse" neurotransmitters: GABA (gamma-aminobutyric acid) and glutamate. GABA is the brain's major inhibitory transmitter, and its role, in essence, is to keep glutamate, the main excitatory transmitter, from overwhelming us. In the extreme, too much glutamate can cause a seizure and too much GABA can put us in a coma. Researchers are particularly interested in the brain's critical balance of GABA and glutamate—some hypothesize that addictive craving is the result of too much glutamate or too little GABA.

And it might be, but it also might not. Walter Ling, the neurologist, cautions that we still have many hurdles to overcome before we truly understand what's going on inside the addicted brain. And that means we're likely years away from highly effective addiction medications. Other than Suboxone for heroin, arguably the most effective addiction medication on the market—Antabuse—is also one of the oldest. (Developed in 1948, Antabuse makes people violently ill if they drink alcohol.)

So while addiction neuroscientists eagerly peer inside the addicted brain in search of a medical solution that they believe is in there somewhere, most of those on the front line of addiction treatment aren't holding their breath.

"We're open to medications that will actually work, but the fact is that today Twelve Step treatment is still the best treatment there is—nothing even comes close," says Betty Ford Center president John Schwarzlose, adding that millions of addicts have recovered without the help of pharmacology. "The best addiction treatment is still a spiritual one, and whether you get your spiritual connection by going to church or by climbing mountains doesn't really matter. In the age of neuroscience, the best antidote to addiction hasn't changed."

21   JODY

Gambling is the son of avarice and the father of despair.

—FRENCH PROVERB

IT IS 6 A.M. on a Saturday, hours before Jody, the addiction counselor, would prefer to be conscious, and as we begin our trek across southern Florida to a Gamblers Anonymous conference in Sarasota, Jody demands that we stop at Dunkin' Donuts to indulge his caffeine addiction.

Iced coffee in hand, Jody lights a cigarette. He's disappointed that he still smokes, but he's never actually tried to quit. "I'm just not willing," he tells me. "I've given up so many addictions in my life. I'd just like to have one or two that I don't have to let go of."

As we drive through sleepy West Palm Beach, Jody can't stop talking about James Frey, the author of *A Million Little Pieces*. "You wouldn't believe how much resistance I was getting from families based on that book before Oprah finally laid the smack-down on him," he tells me. "I mean, what's the message of that book? *The Twelve Steps are for pussies. Fight everybody. Hold on. Get better on your own. Don't do anything the treatment center says. Get in a re-lationship right away. Go in the crack houses and save people. Fight the fury.* Basically, all the messages that our addictions want us to believe so we stay addicted. If you know anything about addiction, you know that he's this typical grandiose, un-recovered, wannabe bad-ass. Typical addict shit."

Jody is particularly upset by the book's criticism of the Twelve Steps. "I'm not saying that working them is the only way to recover," he says, "but if you've got melanoma, I'm not going to send you to the beach, either. It would be irresponsible for me to recommend anything other than the Twelve Steps. And man, there's so much fucking irony in him saying that you just need to really *want* to get better, and that you don't need to work the steps. Because if you had to explain recovery through the Twelve Steps in one word, what word would that be?"

I hazard a guess. "Honesty?"

"Exactly. Rigorous, painful, gut-wrenching *honesty.* And he couldn't even be honest about his recovery. What a fucking coward. I just wish people understood a little more about recovery so they could really get the irony."

We're driving to the GA conference—where Jody will lead a workshop on "relapse prevention"—as a favor to Rick Benson, a gambling addiction specialist and the founder of Algamus, a gambling addiction treatment program with residential facilities in Florida and Arizona. Benson recently partnered with C.A.R.E. and chose Jody as the main counselor to implement C.A.R.E.'s gambling addiction program.

About three million Americans, or one percent of the population, fit the criteria for pathological gambling. Another few million are called "problem gamblers"—they aren't as severely addicted, but they still gamble excessively and suffer negative consequences.

Problem and pathological gamblers tend to come in two varieties,

Jody says: The first, an "escape seeker," is typically a middle-aged or older woman addicted to slot machines. But the more common gambling addict who shows up at C.A.R.E. is an "action seeker," usually a young or middle-aged man addicted to card games or sports betting.

Action seekers are a challenge to treat. "They're so highly functioning," Jody tells me, "so you've got to be on your game as a counselor. You can't just tell them to 'settle down' and do 'the next right thing' and talk all spiritual to them, because they ain't feeling that *at all*. They come in here all grandiose, plotting and scheming, asking tough questions, lying their asses off, thinking they know everything. You can see them gambling in their head during group therapy. 'If I divulge this much, I'll get this in return,' crazy manipulative shit. More than drug addicts, gamblers won't open up to you until you stand up to them and earn their respect."

To do that, Jody throws out his conventional treatment approach. With substance abusers, Jody tries to keep them moving and busy their first week, because all they want to do is sleep or isolate in their rooms. With gamblers, he does the opposite.

"Most are truly addicted to the *action*, so when they come in, we slam the brakes on them," he explains. "They don't like that at all— they feel like they're losing their mind. That's their withdrawal. They think they're getting nothing done, and they get real nasty." But if they get through that, soon they're crying like babies. "They start to see how crazy and unmanageable their life was, how they weren't living at a human pace. Once they're feeling some feelings, then you can treat 'em."

One of Jody's recent gamblers was a young professional poker player named Ron. On a typical weekend, Ron would play poker all afternoon and evening at the Bellagio Casino in Las Vegas and then retire to his room, where he went online to play for another few hours (and he wasn't the only one—he was often competing against the same guys from earlier in the casino). But while Ron was a great poker player, he couldn't stay away from the casino's black-jack table. And that was a problem, because Ron wasn't very good at blackjack.

"He's a professional poker player," Jody says, "and he's over at the blackjack table being a chump." Ron eventually lost all his money, and his family sent him to treatment. "They're like, 'Okay, time to come out of the casino now!'"

But gambling addiction professionals are treating an increasing number of gamblers who rarely set foot in casinos. Instead, they spend hours each day on the Internet, feeding the $15 billion-a-year online gambling industry. Americans account for 60 percent of the industry's revenue. Internet poker, in particular, is staggeringly popu-lar among young men, some of whom are quickly finding themselves broke—and addicted. (Simon Noble, who co-founded one of the first online sports betting sites, may have put it best: "Gambling is the fu-ture of the Internet. You can only look at so many dirty pictures.")

Many gambling addicts turn to crime—usually nonviolent of-fenses like forgery, larceny, tax evasion, and embezzlement—to pay off debts or get money to place bets. In two extreme cases, a Lehigh University sophomore from an affluent family robbed a Wachovia bank of $2,800 to finance his addiction to sites like Pokerstars.com and Sportsbetting.com, and a Long Island bookkeeper and mother of three embezzled $2.3 million from her job to support her $6,000-a-day addiction to lottery tickets.

One of Jody's most brazen patients was a charming, fast-talking swindler who committed mail fraud, stole hundreds of thousands of dollars from bank accounts, and even sold his parents' house (with-out their knowledge) for $1.6 million. "He hired a couple to come in and pretend like they were his parents," Jody says. "The old guy was sitting in a rocking chair, and the old lady was doing dishes, acting like she was deaf. And he sold the fucking house!"

Many gambling addicts are also hooked on alcohol and drugs. A 1997 study of Minnesota's problem gambling treatment centers found that one-third of the patients had received prior treatment for either chemical dependency or mental health problems, and a national survey found that problem and pathological gamblers were significantly more likely than the general population to have been dependent on substances at some point in their lives.

A few months before my visit, a twenty-year-old gambler in Jody's program left after only three days. "His urine came back positive for cocaine," Jody explains, "and when I suggested we might also want to think about addressing that, he bolted."

At C.A.R.E., gamblers and drug addicts are sometimes in group therapy together, making for a steady diet of conflict. "The gamblers will sometimes throw around attitude, like they're better than the drug addicts," Jody tells me. "They just can't wrap their head around sticking a needle in their arm."

Gamblers do differ from drug addicts in one important way, Jody says. Many drug addicts who want to quit realize that heroin or cocaine is the problem, but they don't usually see it as the *solution*. Gamblers tend to see gambling as both the problem and the solution. They get in such a big financial hole that they see gambling as the only way out.

But Jody says that when gamblers leave treatment, they tend to stay abstinent longer than drug addicts and alcoholics. (For gamblers, abstinence means no gambling of any kind, including directly investing in the stock market.) Their success is partly due to the strength of the Gamblers Anonymous fellowship, which was established in 1957.

"Maybe it's because so many gamblers are numbers- and business-oriented, but they're tremendous networkers in their recovery," he says. "GA is probably the strongest fellowship I've seen. The guys there are all about meetings and phone lists and staying connected so they don't gamble again. It's very difficult to slip through the cracks of GA."

As we pull into the parking lot of the Sarasota church where the conference is being held, Jody flashes me an evil grin. "This is probably totally inappropriate for a gambling addiction counselor to say," he tells me, "but I have the coolest idea for a television show. You know how they always have those poker tournaments on ESPN and ESPN2 with those ugly guys with wacky hats and sunglasses so no one can see their eyes? I had this idea of getting *Playboy* or *Hustler* to do a pay-per-view strip poker tournament with a bunch of hot models sitting at a table. No one wants to see fat guys playing poker. But girls taking their clothes off—now that's your fucking show."

Jody's panel isn't until later in the day, so in the meantime I seek out Arnie Wexler, the former executive director of the New Jersey Council on Compulsive Gambling and one of the leading experts on gambling in America. I want to talk to him about gambling addiction, but I make the mistake of telling him that I'm in recovery from sex addiction.

"Now answer me this question," he says, "because I've never been able to understand how you sex addicts do it. How do you not hit on each other during Twelve Step meetings? How do you focus and get anything done? Isn't it distracting to basically have your drug— *other people*—sitting around you in the room? It's like if I went to a GA meeting, and there was a roulette table in the corner!"

I assure him that while attractive people in meetings can be a distraction, sex addiction recovery fellowships tend to be the least flirtatious of all Twelve Step groups, because everyone is there to work on precisely that issue. He's unconvinced.

"I don't know," he says. "You're telling me that people aren't relapsing with each other all the time in meetings?"

"Yes, that's what I'm telling you," I say.

"Hmmm," Wexler says.

I eventually excuse myself to speak with Rick Benson, the Algamus founder. A talkative fifty-nine-year-old (as a general rule, male
gambling addicts love to talk) who's been sober from drugs and
gambling since 1991, Benson tells me that it took only an hour of
watching Jody work to decide he was the right person to treat gamblers at C.A.R.E.

"He's an exceptionally smart guy," Benson says. "And you need
to be smart to keep up with gamblers, who have higher IQs than the
average person. Jody also has the ability to confront someone if it's
needed, combined with a real empathy and understanding for what
they're going through. Maybe most importantly, he's not the kind of
guy who's going to get conned by gambling addicts, who are some
of the best liars in the world."

While many drug addicts lie to "protect use" or "prolong supply,"
Benson says that compulsive gamblers lie because they're riding a
power rush that "gives them a right to lie" and to get over on people.
"One of the things I hear over and over again from employers and
family members of gambling addicts is, 'It was so complicated and
intricate, it couldn't possibly have been a lie,'" he tells me.

Benson believes that while problem gamblers share many of the
characteristics of other addicts, there are enough differences to warrant separate inpatient treatment centers for them. But there are few
around the country financed with state money.

"Many states are as addicted to gambling revenue as some gamblers are to gambling," he says, adding that most states receive
money from some form of legalized betting. "I don't want to close
casinos any more than I want to close bars and liquor stores because
there happen to be alcoholics in this country. But, here's the distinction: I don't know any state that sells crack cocaine on billboards,
but I know lots of states that sell gambling on billboards in the form
of the state lottery. When you become the purveyor of gambling, I
think it raises the ethical, moral, and social responsibility to return

some percentage of those gambling profit dollars for the purpose of information, education, and treatment. Right now, most states don't do nearly enough of that."

Benson joins me later for Jody's panel, which takes place in a church classroom that doubles as the main meeting room for a local Boy Scout troop. I sit next to Dickie, a friendly sixty-nine-year-old gambling addict with a big nose and preposterously thick eyebrows. Dickie lives in Jody's sober living community, and I've spent the last two nights sleeping in an empty bed in the apartment Dickie shares with a twenty-two-year-old drug addict. They make an odd pair, but they had quickly become close friends. They stay in most nights to chain-smoke and watch movies together, and then get up early to meditate before heading off to work.

Dickie told me his life story late one night as he smoked a cigar. He was raised in a community very similar to the one depicted in the movie *A Bronx Tale*, and in his early teens he started running money for a local don. Dickie placed his first bet when he was sixteen, winning $600 on a horse race. "Suddenly I had all the girls, and I was the king of the kids in the neighborhood," he said. "I've been chasing after that first high my whole life."

A successful businessman as an adult, Dickie eventually lost it all to gambling. At one of his lowest points, he stole $20,000 from a Gamblers Anonymous international conference fund and flew to Atlantic City, losing the money in two hours. (He embezzled a total of $36,000 from the fund, which he has since paid back.)

"All right, let's get started," Jody tells the group of a dozen gamblers, mostly middle-aged and elderly men and women. "So the conference organizers called me yesterday to say that they had some bad news. They said they needed to switch me from leading a workshop about sponsorship to leading this one, about relapse prevention. They were very apologetic. I told them that I would have been upset, too, if I had actually prepared!"

This opening gets Jody a few chuckles, although not as many as I suspect he was hoping for. "So let's talk about relapse prevention," he continues, sounding more serious now. "To me, the fact that we even have panels and workshops about relapse prevention is a little silly. I mean, isn't everything we do in recovery about preventing relapse? Don't we do all the hard work in recovery to prevent ourselves from going out and gambling? I understand that recovery is about growth, and that it's not just about *not* gambling, or *not* using drugs. But in order for any of that growth to happen, in order for us to have a spiritual awakening, we can't relapse. We have to stay in recovery.

"One of the classic relapse prevention exercises is to make a list of triggers. Anyone here ever made a trigger list?" A few hands shoot up. "Okay, so the point of a trigger list is to write down all the places or situations or people that might want to make us use, to relapse. I get the idea, but I don't know how practical it is. I don't know how it was for you all, but my main trigger was when my alarm clock went off in the morning. *That* was a trigger. If I was awake, I was liable to gamble or use drugs. I was like, 'Oh, it's a shitty day? Well, then I might as well gamble.' 'It's a beautiful day? Perfect day to gamble!'" Dickie can relate to that—he laughs and nods his head in agreement.

"For me," Jody continues, "the key to relapse prevention, to not using, is getting to a point where I don't *want* to use anymore. I'm not that strong or disciplined a person. If I wake up every day and I want to gamble or use drugs, eventually I'm going to do it. So for me, the challenge of relapse prevention is to get to the point where I no longer desire gambling or using. For me, that started happening around Steps Eight and Nine.

"The problem is that I have a built-in forgetter, and I can't really remember the pain my active addiction puts me in. I can't go back and truly recall, *truly* feel the discomfort, the anxiety, the pain, the shame. My mind plays tricks on me. I can remember some of the pain, but not really. There's a distance there. I can't reexperience that. Many of us, addicts or not, aren't very good at remembering pain. Any of you have older brothers or sisters?" Again, a few hands shoot up. "Well, if we could really reexperience pain, you wouldn't be here, because your mom would have thought better about having you." This earns Jody some heartfelt laughs, which seem to energize him.

"You know how people in recovery, or an addiction counselor, will remind you to 'play the tape through' before using or gambling," he continues. "The point is that we're supposed to stop and try to remember what happens when we relapse. We're supposed to try and remember the pain it causes us, the unmanageability it causes in our lives. And for some people that is helpful, but for me, the fear of pain doesn't keep me sober. It was helpful when I was first getting sober, but the further away I get from my last relapse, the less pain-motivated I become.

"Since I can't play the tape all the way through, since the VCR in my head is broken, relapse prevention puts a lot of freaking pressure on me. I have to be a vigilant observer of my thoughts, because my distorted thinking is what will make me relapse. I can't control the thoughts that come into my head, but I can choose to believe them or not. I can choose whether to act on them.

"So what is relapse prevention? For me, it's establishing a relationship with a power greater than myself, going to meetings when I don't want to, and driving four hours to a conference like this on a Saturday morning. The truth is that I've been coming to Twelve Step meetings since I was seventeen, and I haven't heard anything new since the first thirty days. It's not like they discovered this whole *honesty thing* a couple of years ago. I don't go to meetings today to hear new discoveries. I go to be reminded of the things that my addict brain tries to make me forget. The fact that you all came to this conference, even though some of you haven't gambled for ten or fifteen years, is really what relapse prevention is about. You all don't need to be in here wasting your time listening to me talk about how to prevent relapse. You already know how, because you're here."

The irony of Jody being asked to lead a discussion about relapse prevention was not lost on him. "I am the king of fucking relapse," Jody tells me after the workshop. "Preventing relapse? Not so much. But relapsing? Yeah, I've been pretty good at that in my life."

Jody first got sober at twenty-four. He was dead-set on getting rich and retiring by thirty-five, and it looked like he was well on his way after starting a successful roofing business. He had no idea how to roof, but he was good with numbers, and he subcontracted everything. Before long he owned two more businesses, a fast car, and a big boat.

Convinced he had his addiction under control, Jody did what many addicts do: He stopped going to Twelve Step meetings. Before long, he was using drugs again. A year later, broke and hopeless, he sought treatment at the Caron Foundation, a nationally respected substance abuse center in Pennsylvania. When he completed the program, counselors there suggested he move into a halfway house in West Palm Beach.

"So I hadn't been in town two hours," Jody recalls, "before I went to a local AA meeting, raised my hand and said, 'My name is Jody, and I'm an alcoholic and an addict. I just got out of treatment. I'm blind. I've never been here. I don't know anyone. I've never stayed sober. I'm scared to death. I need help. Ya'll are supposed to help me. *Please* help me.'" After the meeting, a man in his sixties who ran a halfway house gave Jody his card. A month later, when Jody was kicked out of another halfway house for sneaking a girl in, he called the man and moved in.

The man traveled a lot for work, so Jody enforced the house

rules and collected rent checks. A year of sobriety later, Jody—fascinated by addiction, and convinced he could help other addicts—cofounded his own sober living community, which he called C.A.R.E. (Comprehensive Addiction Rehabilitation Education). But Jody liked starting sober living communities more than he liked running them, and soon he left C.A.R.E. to start another one. He also founded an addiction treatment consulting business.

"What I envisioned was, You've got your daughter blowing some dude for coke, or you've got your son in the backyard getting stoned all day, or you've got your alcoholic husband making an ass of himself at family functions, or you've got your wife gambling away all the money," Jody says. "But you're not in the loop. You have no idea what to do, or how to go about getting help, or how to figure out what treatment centers are good. So you would call me, give me all your info, what your insurance was, if you had insurance, if you've been to treatment before. I had a whole series of questions designed to help you figure out the best place to get help. And it wouldn't cost you a penny to call me and have me do all the arrangements, because I was getting paid on the back end."

At the second treatment center he founded, many of his patients were referred to him by an addiction psychiatrist in Virginia. The psychiatrist urged Jody to address his longtime ADD, but as a recovering drug addict, Jody was wary of taking medications that might be addictive. "He told me about this new miracle ADD drug, Adderall XR," Jody recalls. "He's like, 'Jody, you can't abuse this stuff. It's not habit-forming.'"

Until that point, Jody had begun each morning on the beach, meditating and praying before working out at a local gym and then heading to work. But the first week he started taking Adderall Jody quit the morning routine and stopped going to AA and NA meetings. He thought he had found the wonder drug. (So do many college students without ADD who get Adderall from friends and use it to stay up all night studying. In a study of 3,639 college students, about one-fifth admitted to taking prescription drugs to get high.)

"Before Adderall, my thoughts were always so scattered," he says. "I thought in fragments and run-on sentences, and I needed meditating and Twelve Step meetings to calm my mind. On Adderall, my thinking totally changed. I thought in complete fucking paragraphs. Man, I was so organized. I was getting shit done in like half the time it took me before. I was like, 'Damn, I can do whatever I want on this stuff.' Suddenly I understood how other people lived."

Jody was more productive than he had ever been, and his treatment center became wildly successful. To reward himself, he bought a convertible BMW and hired a beautiful assistant to drive him around. He was getting rich, and he was doing it in shorts and flip-flops.

The psychiatrist saw his success as further proof that Adderall was a miracle drug. "The doctor believed, as many do, that Adderall stimulates the same part of the brain as opiates, and that the reason opiate addicts are opiate addicts is because they have untreated ADD," Jody says. "So if you prescribe the right medication, the theory goes, they'll no longer have the need to self-medicate. It makes sense on paper, but it suggests that the reason you do heroin isn't because you suffer from the disease of addiction, but because you suffer from the disease of attention deficit disorder."

Jody started needing more and more Adderall to function, and he began taking Valium and Xanax to take the edge off. To get enough pills to feed his addiction, he swiped medications intended for his patients. He didn't feel guilty—he didn't even accept that what he was doing was wrong. Jody had never felt denial quite that strong, even as he lost forty pounds and could barely sleep.

Jody's patients suspected he was using drugs, and one night ten of them confronted him. Jody denied it. He "flipped the script" on them and had them second-guessing each other in no time. "I raised hell, kicked a couple guys out, said something like, 'If you don't trust me, then you don't need to be here,'" Jody recalls. He escaped that intervention, but soon his staff confronted him. Finally, he copped to everything. "I went back to the community and said, 'You know, this place is kind of like the Hair Club for Men. I'm not only the president—I'm also a *client*.'"

Jody stopped taking Adderall, but two weeks later he took off with an ex-girlfriend to Virginia, where they spent four months in an abandoned building shooting heroin and smoking crack. No one knew where Jody was, and he wasn't about to answer his cell phone, which quickly filled up with irate messages from staff members, clients, doctors, and lawyers.

Eventually the landlord evicted Jody's patients, and his staff quit. After four months, Jody ran out of money. "I knew I had really messed up good this time," Jody says. "So I finally called the psychiatrist. His first words were, 'Jody, where the FUCK have you been?'"

Jody couldn't afford inpatient treatment, but he did have connections at many rehab centers, and one agreed to waive its fee. When Jody returned to West Palm Beach after completing the program, there was no homecoming party.

"No one would talk to me," he says. "It was awful. We're not supposed to shoot the wounded, but I had done so much damage and hurt so many people with what I had done, and a lot of people resented me. I didn't just have egg on my face. I had a fucking omelet."

Still, Jody went to meetings every day and worked the Twelve Steps harder than he ever had. He wasn't convinced he would get better, but he didn't see any other choice. "The only way I was going to have any kind of quality of life," he says, "was to be an AA story, an AA miracle."

When he was eight months sober and working Steps Eight and Nine, Jody told his sponsor that he wanted to make amends to his ex-girlfriends. "My motives weren't exactly the best," he concedes. "Basically, I wanted to show them how great I was doing so that I could get back in their lives."

His sponsor had a better idea—Jody should instead make amends to C.A.R.E. Jody didn't love that idea. He had burned many bridges there when he left to start his second sober living community. "I really screwed them over and affected their pocketbooks," Jody says. "They didn't like me at all. But I did what my sponsor said, and I went in and told them I was wrong. I was honest as I could be. I said, 'I'm scared of you all. I know I fucked up, but quite frankly, I'm trying to break this chain. I have a way of building things up and destroying them, and I have to stop doing it. I'm told that if I do these things and make amends, this may help me.'"

The amends weren't well received. "One guy was like, 'You know you'll never work here again,'" recalls Jody. "And I definitely knew that. I knew I had a better chance of winning the lottery than working there. And I didn't care to work here. That was not my intention. I said, 'This ain't about a job.'"

Two weeks later, though, they did offer Jody a job—as night manager at their inpatient center. It was the lowest job on the totem pole, but he wasn't about to complain. And two years of sobriety later, Jody says the greatest lessons he's learned are gratefulness and humility.

"I'm just another fucking addict trying to get better," he told me on our drive across Florida that morning. "I needed to be stripped of everything to learn how to appreciate life. And I've learned that I'm not what I *do*—I'm not how much money I make or how powerful I think I am or how many girls I can get to love me. I'm just Jody. But just being Jody isn't easy. There are so many times when I'm depressed, anxious, crawling out of my skin. If you look at my life, it's clear I'll do anything to not have to feel my feelings. I hate slowing down, because when I'm going a million miles a minute, I don't have time to actually think about what's going on or feel anything. That's my game. That's why I like gambling. That's why I like working like crazy. That's why I like drinking and drugging. That's why I like exercising. If you saw me in the gym boxing, you'd think I was a maniac. I'm in there like I'm training for fucking Rocky. And I'm blind! I'm not going to beat anybody up. But as long as I'm moving all the time, I don't have to feel shit.

"But what I've learned is the solution is the last thing I would ever consider. For me it's go inside, turn off the TV, turn off the cell phone, turn off the radio, and get quiet and feel my feelings. And I swear to God with my hand on the Bible, I am happier than I've ever been in my life. I don't know if this is *normal* happy, because I don't know what that is, but I actually feel pretty good about myself for the first time in my life."

22   JANICE

*I once had a dad who would pick me up, put
me on his shoulders, and I was his pride and
joy. One day he put me down and found a new
joy, a new toy: It was called crack. But wait,
dad, I'm your boy.*

—POEM BY DARRYL BOYCE,
THE SON OF A CRACK DEALER

"**JANICE, BABY, YOU'RE** a miracle. A walking miracle!"

Janice and I are standing on the corner of 146th Street and Adam
Clayton Powell Jr. Boulevard in Harlem on a sunny and unseason-
ably warm Saturday. She's on a twenty-four-hour pass from Odyssey
House, and before taking me to the Bronx to meet her children and
grandkids, she wants to show me the neighborhood where she lived
and used drugs for most of her adult life.

Janice told me we might run into "a few people" she knew during
our walk. If by "a few people" she means virtually the entire neighborhood, most of it adoring and reverential, then yes, we do run into
a few people Janice knows. In these few square blocks of Harlem,

Janice is a kind of a grandmotherly rock star, and our stroll through the area feels like her reunion tour.

In front of a small grocery store, a former professional basketball player in black pants and a Yankees jacket—he played a few seasons of pro ball in Europe before coming home and getting addicted to crack, Janice says—gives her a bear hug and calls Janice a "walking miracle."

"I got my food handler's license!" she tells him proudly, over-dressed for this weather in a light green rain jacket draped over a white sweater. "When I finish the program, I'm going to get a nice job."

"That's good!" he says, gripping a six-pack of beer in his right hand. "See how good life can be when you step outside the crack house? Don't come back this way. You're doing so good. You look so good! They're feeding you well down there."

Another man, whom Janice has known for thirty years, tells me that he can't believe how different Janice looks since she entered treatment at Odyssey House nineteen months ago. She's gained nearly one hundred pounds, ballooning to 245. She's overweight, to be sure, but everyone in the neighborhood seems to like Janice better this way.

"Baby, you're looking beautiful," he tells her on the corner. "The drugs had you too skinny. That wasn't you, girl. Now you're looking real healthy. I love it. I love it!"

"Thank you," Janice says with a big smile, showing off her dentures.

"How are your grandkids?" he asks her.

"They're good!" she says, before introducing me to the men and explaining that I'm following her for a book about addiction.

"Oh, well, you're definitely in the right spot," the former basketball player tells me. "This is addiction city."

"Yeah, Janice and I used to do our party thang together," the other man says with a hearty laugh. "I was *crazy* back then. I was one of those guys with my gun out all the time. When I was high, Janice would put me in a room by myself so I didn't hurt anybody if I got all paranoid."

"Bad shit started happening around here in the early 1980s—cocaine blew through this neighborhood like a hurricane," the basketball player says, slowly moving his extended arm across his body as if pushing heavy winds. "When cocaine hit New York City, it was over."

"Shoooot," Janice says. "People went crazy."

"You know what really did it?" the basketball player says. "That movie *Scarface* started an uproar, then all those movies like *New Jack City* glorified coke, like it was the poor man's dream. Everyone thought they could become a millionaire. Some did, but most didn't, and a lot of people got killed." (Many others went to jail. The U.S. prison population more than doubled during the crack scare of the 1980s. By 1990, roughly 25 percent of black men in their twenties in America were behind bars or on parole or probation. Today, while blacks and whites use drugs at about the same rate, black Americans are still ten times more likely to be jailed on drug charges.)

Janice wants to keep walking—she has more of the neighborhood to show me. "We'll be back!" she tells them. As we head up Adam Clayton Powell Jr. Boulevard, past a double-parked car blasting rap music and a bald, middle-aged man walking hand-in-hand with his young daughter, Janice stops briefly to say hello to a rail-thin woman in jeans and a black-hooded sweatshirt. Janice says she used to call the woman when guys she was getting high with wanted someone for sex.

"And she *always* came running," Janice tells me. "I used to tell her, 'Don't do it for drugs, do it for money. They're going to give you the drugs anyway."

Janice insists she was never a "crack whore," that she never had to sell her body for drugs or cash. "I was the girl the guys respected," Janice says. "I was their friend, and they trusted me. They trusted me to hold their money for them, and they knew I was a reliable person. My momma raised me right. Even when I was using, I was trustworthy. I knew right from wrong."

This is a recurring theme in Janice's narrative about her many years using drugs. The way she tells it, she was a crack addict with honesty and class—even as she sold drugs, eventually lost everything, and had to sleep in crack houses and homeless shelters. I don't doubt that she's telling the truth about never selling her body for drugs, but I'm skeptical that her using years were as dignified as she likes to remember them. As addicts, part of the denial many of us have to break through is that we're somehow different or better than other addicts—the ones who lie, manipulate, and cheat their way to their next high.

Further up the street, Janice and I run into a young, sharply dressed drug dealer in designer blue jeans and black shades. "Lady J., what's up, baby?" he says, smiling. (Lady J. is Janice's nickname around here.) "You're looking good."

"Yeah, those days are over," Janice tells him.

"That's good, that's good," he says, eyeing me warily.

Another young drug dealer, this one in a hooded sweatshirt and black jeans, saunters over to where we're standing. "Lady J., you got all big on me—like a house or something!" he says. "A big old house!"

"Shoooooot," Janice says. "I feel good."

"You look good!"

"You know I'm in a program now, right?"

"Yeah, I heard. You're looking real good, real healthy. Damn girl, you're like a big old house!"

As we walk away, I ask Janice if most of the drug dealers around here use the same crack they're selling. "The smart ones don't, but some of them put it in their reefer and smoke it and think they're better than the crack heads," she says. "Shoooot, I hate that word, *crack head.*"

After buying five scratch lottery tickets at a corner store ("Every week I say I'm going to stop," she tells me, "and every week I don't"), Janice stops in front of a five-story apartment building. She points to the fourth floor, where she lived in a three-bedroom apartment overlooking the street from 1971 to 1998.

"That's where I smoked crack for the first time," she tells me. The woman who convinced Janice to try it lived directly underneath her, and they soon developed an efficient system to pass crack back and forth. If the woman was too lazy to walk upstairs, Janice would put some crack in a can and lower it to her window on a string.

"Whatever happened to her?" I ask.

"Oh, she's dead now. She wouldn't give it up, and she died."

Janice shows me the police station on the corner of 148th Street and Frederick Douglass Boulevard, which has been there since 1998 and has made a serious dent in the area's drug trafficking, she says. That's hard to believe, considering how many dealers we've run into already. "Oh, no, they used to be on every corner, in the middle of the street, everywhere," she tells me. "Shoooot, there are a lot less now than there used to be."

Still, we keep meeting more on our walk. On 149th Street, Janice stops briefly to talk to a group of middle-aged and elderly men sitting on the front stoop of a brick building. When we're out of earshot, she tells me that they're the area's elder statesmen drug dealers.

"They've been around here since *before* I started getting high," Janice says. "Ain't nobody going to come on this block and take over their territory. Sometimes the cops will bust one or two of them, but they do their time and then come right back out and start selling."

Maybe it's because she also used to sell drugs, but Janice holds no ill will toward the drug dealers we bump into. She's also convinced (although I'm not sure I agree) that most wouldn't sell to her now that she's put so much work into getting clean. "The boy with the shades—I knew him when he was a little kid," she tells me. "He wouldn't sell to me now that he knows I've changed my life. Some of the others wouldn't, either."

I ask Janice if she would consider moving back to this neighborhood when she leaves Odyssey House. After all, she does seem loved here, even if much of the love comes from other dealers and active addicts. "Whaaaat?" she says, sounding hurt that I would even ask. "No way I'll be living here. I don't trust myself around here. If I move back into the Devil's Den, then I'm just asking for trouble."

"But was walking through here today okay? No temptation?"

"No, today was okay," she says with a smile. "I'm glad we came. I love being the center of attention."

As Janice and I head toward a nearby bus stop, we walk by three men huddled together on a corner talking. Janice makes eye contact and says a quick hello to one, a bald man in a gray sweatshirt, but she apparently doesn't think enough of him to stop and talk, as she did with virtually everyone else.

"Who was that?" I ask.

"Oh, that's the dealer who told the police that I sold him the coke in the phone booth," she tells me. "That's what started all of this."

"You're not mad at him?"

"Whaaaat?" she says. "No way. He did me a favor. I didn't think so at the time, but now I'm glad it happened. Only good things have happened since then!"

While it's nice to hear Janice so upbeat, she hasn't always been singing that tune during her nineteen months at Odyssey House. Just two months ago, she called me from treatment with some bad news: She would be stuck there longer than expected. The court was requiring her to pass the GED (she badly failed it her first try) before letting her graduate the Drug Treatment Alternative-to-Prison Program (DTAP). That meant another three months of GED classes, followed by a few months of looking for an apartment and a job. "I'm so mad," Janice told me over the phone. "So mad! Sometimes it feels like I'll never get out of here."

James Waldron, who runs the Odyssey House elder care program, shared Janice's frustration with the court's decision. Soon after Janice arrived for treatment, Waldron and the other counselors determined she would be unlikely to pass her GED, so they opted to send her to vocational training.

"My guess is that it would take Janice nothing but a full year of concentration only on the GED for her to pass it," Waldron told me. "She has a very limited educational background, and it was many years ago. Sometimes the requirements can be unreasonable. Someone will be here fifteen months, and the court will say, 'Oh, now the person has to do this and stay six more months.'"

Unreasonable or not, Janice is back in GED classes five days a week, although Waldron doesn't expect her test results to increase significantly. The plan is for Janice to take a predictor test and then the regular GED, and, armed with those scores, Waldron will appeal to the court.

"Basically, we'll say, 'Listen, guys. This is the second time she's tried, and based on these results, it might not be possible for her to pass,'" Waldron said. "The frustrating thing is that Janice has done so well in most areas of her treatment, and she excelled in her vocational training."

I saw that for myself one morning when Janice and I took a crowded bus to a job training center where she worked in the cafeteria for three months and earned her food handler's license. Janice was in good spirits, and she looked unusually casual in a black jacket over a Mickey Mouse T-shirt.

"Are you a good cook?" I asked her on our way there. "Whaaaat?" she shot back. "I'm a great cook!"

Sporting a hair net and white apron, Janice worked dutifully in the kitchen alongside a handful of other men and women, most of them in recovery. Her manager at the cafeteria, Latasha Nelson, told me that Janice was one of her favorite employees. "There's no need to push her—she just does what she's supposed to do, and when she's done with that she asks what else she can do to help," Nelson said.

Janice's vocational counselor, Louise Munde, explained that with her food handler's license, Janice would likely end up working in airport catering, in a nursing home cafeteria, or in a restaurant as a cook's assistant. Munde told me that while some employers are leery of hiring addicts in recovery, they often make the best workers.

"Many people in recovery are more grateful for the opportunity," she said. "They've come so far and had to go through so much just to get the job, and they're not about to take it for granted."

Janice seemed happiest when she was out of Odyssey House and working in the kitchen. Stuck in the treatment center most evenings and two weekends a month, frustration sometimes got the best of her, and she was twice hospitalized with pain in her back and chest— likely caused by stress, doctors told her.

The first hospitalization happened a year into her treatment, the day before Family Day, a yearly Odyssey House event where the elder care patients get to show off their considerable talent (and sobriety) to their families, mostly their adult children and grandchildren. I was hoping to meet Janice's grown son and daughter there that day, but they didn't show.

Janice barely made it, having been discharged from the hospital only hours before the event. She hurried to her room, changed into a pink dress, and promised that we would talk after the talent show. Its theme was "Rockin' with the '50s and '60s," and except for one man in a *Don't Hate the Player—Hate the Game* shirt, most of the elder care patients were decked out in their snazziest dresses and suits. (Local charities donate clothes to Odyssey House.)

Never mind that it was mid-afternoon, or that we were all sitting

on plastic folding chairs under purple and white balloons in the Odyssey House cafeteria/meeting room. When one of the talent show
hosts announced, "We have a great show for you this evening!" the
room erupted in a round of hoots and hollers.

In the rousing opening act, a petite black woman in her mid-fifties
brought down the house with a flirtatious, butt-shaking rendition of
"My Guy." It was a tough act to follow, but Luis, a short and plump
Latino in his early sixties with green khakis pulled up high on his hips,
bravely belted out the words to "Que Sera, Sera." One of the hosts
made it clear how lucky we were to hear Luis sing. "This man has
performed around the world," he told the crowd. "He has appeared
in Europe, Scandinavia, the subcontinents, and right before coming to
Odyssey House, he was appearing in front of a grand jury!"

After two men in suits and ties gyrated wildly to Latin music, it
was time for a comedy routine. Ronald, a black man in his sixties
wearing suspenders, thick glasses, and a tie that was much too long,
delivered his jokes in a deadpan monotone:

"You know, I wanted my wife to attend, but she had a date with her *boyfriend*.
She said, 'You can come along,' and I said, 'Wouldn't that be awkward?' She
said, 'Oh, don't worry, we'll find a girl for *you*.'"

"My wife is a very skinny girl. How thin is she? She swallowed a lima bean
whole, and I thought she was *pregnant*."

"I tell you what. We go to my mother-in-law's house for dinner. You know,
eating with the in-laws and the *outlaws*. We sat down to dinner—there were
thirteen of us, but only four pork chops. I've never seen such a disgusting fight
over pork chops. It was terrible. But the two I got were good."

"So my wife says, 'Take me somewhere I've never been before.' I said, 'Okay,
let's go to the *kitchen*.'"

"She said, 'I want to go someplace really nice for our second honeymoon.' So we go to the same motel, same honeymoon suite, but this time I grab the bedpost and say, 'It's too big, it's too big!'"

"So one day I said, 'If you knew how to cook, I'd fire the maid.' She said, 'Yeah, and if you knew how to make love, I'd fire the chauffeur.'"

It took the elder care patients a good minute to stop laughing after Ronald's routine. When everyone settled down, it was Janice's turn to perform. She had planned to sing a song with two other elder care women, but she didn't feel up to it after spending the night in the hospital. Instead, she read "Autobiography in Five Short Chapters," a poem by Portia Nelson that many addicts can relate to.

"Hello, family," she said to the group. "My name is Janice, and I'm going to read an autobiography in five short chapters . . .

" 'Chapter 1: I walk down the street. There is a deep hole in the sidewalk. I fall in. I am lost. I am helpless. It isn't my fault. It takes forever to find a way out.

" 'Chapter 2: I walk down the same street. There is a deep hole in the sidewalk. I pretend I don't see it. I fall in again. I can't believe I'm in the same place. But it isn't my fault. It still takes a long time to get out.

" 'Chapter 3: I walk down the same street. There is a deep hole in the sidewalk. I see it is there. I still fall in. It's a habit. But my eyes are open. I know where I am. It is my fault. I get out immediately.

" 'Chapter 4: I walk down the same street. There is a deep hole in the sidewalk. I walk around it.

" 'Chapter 5: I walk down another street.'"

In her room after the show, I asked Janice if she knew what had caused the stress that landed her in the hospital. She wasn't sure, but she had an idea. A few weeks before, one of the elder care women had suffered a stroke and couldn't use her left hand, and Janice was charged with helping her get to doctor's appointments. But the more time she spent with her, the more Janice was reminded of the man she lived with for six years until he had a stroke and she put him in a nursing home.

"I was always too busy drugging to take care of him," she told me, crying suddenly. "When I smoked crack, he was off my mind. I feel so guilty now. I used his bank card for a long time after I put him in the home. He's been so good to me, and I put him in there more than two years ago and I've only seen him twice. Every time I have a day pass I say I'm going to see him, but then I don't."

Janice sat on the edge of her bed, her shoulders slumped and tears streaming down her face and onto her dress. She looked like a child. "See, I used to have drugs to block these feelings from coming up," she mumbled. "Now I just feel so ashamed, so guilty, and sometimes it's too much. I really have to go see him, but after all this time? I don't know what I'll say. He might be gone. He might be dead. I hope he's still alive. Do you think he's still alive?"

After the reunion tour through her old Harlem neighborhood, Janice and I take a long subway ride to the Bronx, to the cramped four-bedroom apartment where her daughter, Elisa, lives with her husband, Kevin, and their ten children ranging in age from three to twenty. (Kevin is the biological father of the last eight.)

Janice gets two twenty-four-hour weekend passes each month, and much to her Odyssey House counselor's chagrin, she spends most of them baby-sitting her grandchildren. "It feels to me like her daughter's using her," Robert Harven told me. "Her family probably cares for her, and she cares for her grandkids, but that's not going to be enough to keep her from relapsing when she gets out. Janice needs to get a support network of other women in recovery. She needs to go to AA or NA meetings and find activities she can do for herself. But so many women like Janice end up being full-time babysitters for their grandkids, and they end up feeling stuck and useless, and eventually they relapse."

On the subway ride, Janice insists that won't happen to her. "No way I'm going to baby-sit all the time," she tells me. "Shoooot, I know my daughter wants me around all the time to help, but I'm going to have my own life, too."

Still, Janice has spent a lot of time lately worrying about Elisa and the grandchildren. A few months ago, when Janice was stuck in Odyssey House and powerless to help, Elisa and her kids spent three nights in a shelter after getting evicted from their old apartment. Then came the news that Kevin had gotten another woman pregnant. "If I wasn't in Odyssey House when I heard about *that*," Janice says, "I would have beaten his ass."

When we arrive at the ground-floor apartment near the Bronx Zoo, Kevin is lounging on the black leather couch in the main room, which doubles as the entertainment center (there are huge black speakers everywhere). Kevin is forty-three, but he looks like a teenager in droopy jeans and an oversized white T-shirt that hangs down to his knees.

"I don't know why she married him," Janice tells me once he leaves the room, never to return during the few hours I spend there. "He's been in and out of jail for selling reefer. He doesn't do a single productive thing all day long."

Janice gives me a quick tour of the small, dark apartment. The family is still waiting for the kids' beds to be delivered, so until then they have to sleep on the floor. In the hallway, two of Janice's young grandchildren cling to her legs, and we're nearly all bowled over by two of Janice's teenage grandsons.

"Hey, now, slow down!" Janice screams as they lunge toward the front door.

"Sorry, Grandma!" one says, flinging open the door and preparing to bolt.

"Don't you move," Janice tells them, her voice more menacing than I've ever heard it. "Where are you going?"

"Uh, down the block," one says unconvincingly.

"Down the block where?"

"To the park?" he says.

"What park?"

"You know, the park."

"Shoooot, ya'll are the worst liars I know."

"Come on," the other boy tries. "We'll be right back."

"You bet you will," Janice tells them. "Y'all better be back in fifteen minutes."

Elisa, who works as a nurse in a nursing home, doesn't say much to me at first, and when she does it's to apologize for the state of the apartment or the behavior of her kids. "We only moved in like a month ago," she says, "so things aren't really settled." As for her kids, all she can do is shake her head. "You'd think they might make an effort when they saw you here," she tells me. "But nope. They act just as stupid as ever."

I'm amazed she can keep track of them all. They zigzag in and out of the apartment at breathtaking speeds, congregating on the front steps or meandering down the block, only to reappear minutes later and disappear into one of the cluttered bedrooms.

"Big families run in the family—I've got eyes in the back of my head," Elisa says. "I definitely didn't expect to have this many kids, but they kept popping up, and I wouldn't get rid of them. But let me tell you—you know how they say that birth control works like 99 percent of the time? There's no way that's true. No matter what I used, it didn't work."

Janice seems accustomed to the chaos, although she loses her cool when her seven-year-old grandson threatens to punch her. Sitting next to me on the couch in the main room, Janice asks him for a clarification. "*What* did you say?"

"I'm going to punch you, Grandma," he says again, flailing his arms about and jumping up and down.

Janice looks at me and laughs. "Okay, who has a belt?" she says, lifting herself off the couch. While she rummages around the apartment looking for a belt, her grandson scurries to a bedroom and hides in a closet. Janice eventually finds him pleading for his life. "I'm sorry! I'm sorry!" he yelps as she tries to swat him, although the angle of the closet makes reaching him with the belt difficult. Some other grandchildren hover around the scene, pointing and laughing.

"You can't hide in there forever," Janice tells him.

"Help! Help!" he screams, half afraid for his life, and half amused that she can't reach him.

Meanwhile, back in the living room, Janice's son, Mark, arrives with a friend in tow. Mark is twenty-nine and works as a security guard. I ask Elisa and Mark what it was like as kids to watch Janice use drugs.

"Basically, I had to take care of Mark myself," Elisa explains. "I was fourteen, but people thought he was my child. I was more of the adult growing up than my mom was sometimes. She would have parties, and I would give everyone the evil eye. People called me a nerd because I stayed in the house and read or did my homework, but someone had to be responsible."

Mark says he was too young to notice if Janice was high. Besides, he doesn't want to dwell on the past. "Now that she's clean," he tells me, "I could see her going far. I really can. When I heard she got her food handler's license, I was so happy. She talks about opening up a restaurant someday, and I could see her doing it. One of my friends that knows Janice, he told me he had a dream that she was going to win the Lotto, open a restaurant, and be a millionaire. I could see it happening. I really could. I could see Janice sipping a glass of wine on a beach somewhere, living the good life."

23 TODD

Being confronted with the thinking of an alco-holic, or someone with another addiction, can be as frustrating as dealing with the schizo-phrenic. . . . The addict may not always be as willfully conniving as others think. . . . Often addicts are taken in by their own thinking, actually deceiving themselves.

—ABRAHAM TWERSKI, *ADDICTIVE THINKING*

ON A CLEAR, crisp night, I visit Todd and his wife, Julie, in their new two-bedroom apartment overlooking a large lake in a gated com-munity. They moved here a few months ago, Todd explains, because "of all the crazy people who like to stalk and threaten and send nasty notes and follow me around."

It's one of the perils of being as public an escort as he is. "You come into contact with some unstable people," he tells me. The final straw came when Julie found their car's tires slashed outside their old apartment. "That really scared her," Todd says. "We moved here where there's security. There haven't been any problems since."

Todd and I are standing in front of a half-packed suitcase in his apartment's guest bedroom, which doubles as his office. (Todd always seems to be packing when I'm around. Tomorrow morning, he's off to Chicago for ten days to meet some thirty escorting clients.) Todd occasionally meets a client in this room, but mostly he uses it to organize his work trips. There are two books on his desk: The first, *Why Do Men Fall Asleep After Sex?*, is a gift from Julie, he says with a chuckle. The second, *The Leatherman's Handbook*, he calls "research material."

"I'm really trying to understand the leather and S&M world for my clients who I have to spit on, beat, whip, and so on," he explains. "I'm trying to understand what it means to be a *master*. Because I'm bigger and sometimes older, a lot of them want me to play that role. So I need to get into their heads to really make their fantasies come alive." (In that pursuit, Todd plans to drop by the Leather Archives and Museum in Chicago.)

Todd and Julie's apartment is a homage to bodybuilding and nutrition. In the main living area, which looks out over the lake and serves as Julie's de facto office, the carpet is hard to find under piles of nutrition books with titles like *Gender Differences in Metabolism, Nutrition and the Strength Athlete, The Health Professional's Guide to Dietary Supplements, Exercise, Nutrition, and Weight Control* and stacks of printed research articles about the "Effect of Creatine Loading on Neuromuscular Fatigue Threshold" and how "Vitamin D2 Is Much Less Effective than Vitamin D3 in Humans."

Julie hates to sit down, so she spends practically my entire visit today standing barefoot and working on her laptop, writing a nutrition article for a foreign fitness magazine and tinkering with her Web site, where she posts pictures of herself flexing and posing and advertises her Web cam shows (users can pay $4 a minute to watch her flex and pose).

"It's all G-rated—my clothes stay on," she tells me, her eyes glued to her computer. Still, her everyday wardrobe doesn't leave much to the imagination, and today is no different—she wears a green tank top and short, glutes-gripping black shorts. There's also a bandage on her left foot where one of her toes recently got infected.

"I keep telling her to *sit down* when she works," Todd says, resting on the couch next to me in a black Old Navy T-shirt and gray athletic shorts. "A foot can only take so much."

"Problem is, if I sit down, I fall asleep," Julie says.

Julie appears considerably bigger than when I first met her more than a year ago. Her thighs, which were already huge, now look as though tree trunks have been implanted in them. In fact, her whole body—especially her gut—looks bloated. In the guest bedroom, I ask Todd if Julie is using steroids. "Let's not talk about that," he says, one of the only times he deflected a question of mine.

Julie says she hopes to start competing in bodybuilding competitions in a year or two. In her late teens she participated in fitness competitions, but now she's eager to become a full-fledged bodybuilder. "People tell me now that I have the mass I need," she says, still staring at her laptop. "I'm 167 pounds right now. I want to trim down to about 135, and then I'll be ready."

Todd has mixed feelings about Julie's bodybuilding aspirations. He says he understands the pull of wanting to compete, but he's not sure he wants to see her body get much bigger.

"It definitely takes some getting used to seeing her body change this much," he says. "It's scary, because most female bodybuilders I've encountered don't look very good after a while. Julie's young, and she can get away with it—now. But I always have a fear that things will change too fast, and she'll be like those other girls who end up looking like men in the face, the body, and everywhere. I'm like, 'Ugh, I've been there and done *that*.'"

Julie laughs, turning away from the computer screen to face us. It's the first time her body language registers a willingness to be part of our conversation, and it occurs to me that this might be my only chance to ask her about Todd's work and his sexuality. Does she mind that he escorts for men? Does she think he's gay, bisexual, straight? Todd has told me many times that she's convinced he's straight, and that no matter how many times he tells her that he's likely bisexual, Julie dismisses it.

"Do you mind what Todd does for a living?" I ask her.

She mulls over the question for a few seconds—not because she doesn't know the answer, I suspect, but because she isn't sure she wants to go down this road. I got the sense early on from Julie that she would tolerate my occasional presence in Todd's life, but that she had no plans to let me into hers.

"At first, I thought the escorting thing was kind of peculiar," she says finally. "But then I got used to it, and I'm fine with it as long as he's safe. And as long as he escorts with men, that's okay. I wouldn't let him do it with women, for obvious reasons."

"Obvious reasons?" I ask. Both Todd and Julie have a maddening way of assuming that their logic makes sense to everyone, but I'm not sure what she means. Most women wouldn't marry a man who escorts for anyone, male or female.

"Two men together is a big joke for me," she says. "They have nothing I have. It's not a threat."

Todd chortles. "Honey, you're funny," he says. He looks at me. "She thinks gay sex is amusing."

"I know him so well—I know he's a straight man," she continues. "From what I've heard about his experiences with men, I can just tell that he's not really gay. I'm not worried about that."

"That's how *she* feels about it," Todd tells me. "I don't know. How can I say I'm straight when for years I had sex with men, and I can still look at a guy today and this part or that part of him turns me on? But it's not all there. I can connect on some levels with men, but I can't make all the connections."

"That's because you're not gay!" she interjects.

"See," Todd says, throwing up his hands in mock exasperation. "She's very opinionated about this."

"What do you mean by 'all the connections'?" I ask him.

Todd says he can't put the "love and sex together" with a man. "I've tried," he tells me. "I can't do it. Take my ex-boyfriend. I loved him, but the thought of sex with him, it wasn't appealing. We even tried doing it when we were high, but it didn't work. I don't really like to have a man put his arms around me. Cuddling is very limited. I'd rather caress and envelop the other guy than have him hold me." He scratches his head. "I really can't explain it. I don't know for sure what I am. I don't know how to define what I am."

The closest Todd came to putting it all together with a man was with Christian, the fitness coach from Boston. He tells me that being with Christian "almost" felt right, although he was never truly comfortable being sexual with him. "Christian is big and is taller than me, and when we were fooling around, it didn't really click," he says. "There were things I was intrigued with about his body and his personality, but not all the wires met."

Christian tells a different story, saying that Todd was more emotionally invested in their connection than he likes to let on and even discussed moving up to Boston to be with him. Christian remembers being intrigued by Todd and enjoying the sexual flirtation between them, but he never took the possibility of a relationship seriously.

"I could not date a prostitute," Christian told me.

Todd's steroid abuse would likely have been a problem, too. "And I don't think I would have stopped taking them for him," Todd says. "I wasn't ready. Now, I'm ready."

I nearly fall off the couch. "You're what?"

"I'm taking a break," he says. "For two months, at least. And maybe longer. We'll see how it goes."

I can't help feeling skeptical. Todd hasn't been off steroids for four years, and when I last saw him in Boston, he seemed more dependent on them than ever. He was injecting himself three or four days a week instead of the two times a week his cycle dictated. He had lost the ability to "control" a drug that he never believed could cause him to lose control.

Todd's body started revolting soon after the Boston trip. In addition to the steroids, he was taking ephedra every day, and he wasn't sleeping enough or eating right. Before he knew it, he came down with a case of shingles.

"After a certain point, reality sets in, and you can only go for so long and push so hard before the body just gets overwhelmed," Todd tells me. "My body really needs a break. I made a deal with Julie and my doctor to go on two medications that will help me restart my body's own natural testosterone production, and then to go off steroids. The goal is two months."

Julie says she supports his decision. "We both love muscle and training hard, but health is the most important thing," she says. "Truthfully, as long as he's healthy and happy, I don't care how big or small he is."

I'm not sure I believe her. Their marriage strikes me as an outlandish experiment in the mutual enabling of body dysmorphia. They encourage—or at least tacitly approve of—each other's dysfunction, and Julie seems like an ideal match for Todd's rationalized form of "recovery." She doesn't question his use of steroids or ephedra, both of which are negatively impacting his emotional and physical health. She turns a blind eye to his escorting, and she seems comfortably in denial about his sexuality.

What a perfect deal for Todd, who, as I see it, had two options when he wanted to stop taking meth. He could do what most gay or bisexual men trapped in the world of meth and anonymous sex do: Go to treatment and/or Narcotics Anonymous or Crystal Meth Anonymous meetings, working hard to uncover—and heal from—

whatever emotional and psychological problems he was medicating away with drugs. Or he could do what he did: Leave the "gay world" behind (except in the highly controlled context of his work, where his alter ego, Billy, is regularly admired and fetishized), marry a woman as obsessed with muscle as he is, and abuse drugs—steroids and ephedra—that suppress whatever pain and insecurity he doesn't want to face.

Todd says his plan is to be steroid-free for a few months and then start them again two months before a competition this summer. "That would give me eight weeks of getting back on a cycle, and that would be tremendous," he says. "I'd be able to do a show. I have so much size that I'd be able to do a show even if I wasn't on steroids, but it's scary to me to go into a show natural. I could. That's the funny thing—I *could*. But I don't want to. I want to have more poundage. I would look good natural, but that's not good enough for me."

As for ephedra, Todd doesn't see himself giving it up anytime soon. While he says taking meth isn't an option, ephedra is a safer alternative that he's unwilling to go without.

"It's hard for me to operate if I don't have a stimulant when I wake up," he tells me. "I feel like I have to have one just to get moving and thinking. Sometimes I can force myself to stop taking it for two or three days, and then some sense of normalcy will return, but then something will trigger me, whether it's a bad day or I just don't feel good, and then I'm like, 'Oh, I know what will make me feel good!'"

Julie also takes ephedra, but she reacts to it differently, she says. "I get the hyperness when I take it, but when I'm off it I don't get depressed like Todd does. For him, it's like the world is ending."

24 SEAN

Relapse is not a failure of treatment. Relapse is part of the disorder.

—ANNA ROSE CHILDRESS, ADDICTION RESEARCHER

I PUSH OPEN the unlocked door to Sean's apartment in Prescott, a city of forty thousand in the Bradshaw Mountains of central Arizona. To my right, curled up in his boxers on a stained brown couch, is Ryan, a boyish heroin addict in his mid-twenties who Sean (the sex addict) warned me would probably be asleep on the couch when I arrived. Ryan isn't using heroin anymore, but he does spend most of his days drinking.

"Sometimes my roommate and I lock him out," Sean told me on the phone before my visit, "but he keeps showing up and sleeping on our couch. The first night he stayed here he gave us $50 and bought us food, so we were like, 'Sweet!' But since then all he does is mooch off us and bring girls over that he fucks on the couch."

The second-floor apartment—Sean officially shares it with Jack, a twenty-one-year-old gambling addict he went to treatment with—has potential, but much of it is buried deep under stacks of dirty dishes, empty cigarette packs and beer cans, and Papa John's pizza containers. In Sean's room, where clothes and soda cans cover virtually every square foot of the beige carpet, I find him asleep under a sheet on his bed, a small fan knocked on its side blowing air into his face.

"Sean," I say a few times, trying to rouse him from his slumber. When that doesn't work, I pick up a stained pillow off the floor and drop it on his head. He groans. "What the fuck?" he mumbles, opening his left eye and looking at me.

"Good morning," I say with a smile.

It has been more than six months since I last visited Sean in Arizona, during his second month at Prescott House, an extended care addiction treatment center. Sean came to Prescott House a month after graduating from Gentle Path, the sex addiction treatment center in Mississippi. Before leaving there, Sean's counselors recommended that he go to Prescott House, where addicts usually stay for six months or more, at a cost of $4,900 per month.

While most of Prescott House's patients are hooked on drugs and alcohol, some are addicted to gambling or sex, and sex addiction treatment centers around the country sometimes refer patients who need extended care to Prescott.

Sean hadn't wanted to go at first, but in the end he grudgingly agreed (his uncle said he would pay). And if Sean needed any more reason to follow Gentle Path's recommendation, he got it at the Jackson, Mississippi, airport on his way back to Boston, where he was going to put his belongings in storage before flying to Arizona. At an airport newsstand, Sean bought a *Playboy* and took it to a bathroom stall, where he looked at the pictures and nearly masturbated.

"Something stopped me from actually doing that," he told me soon after it happened. "I was like, 'I'm not that much of a sicko that I'm going to do this the same day I'm out of treatment.'"

Back in Boston, Sean was hoping to hang out with Ann, who had stopped escorting, but she told him that she couldn't see him any longer (her therapist suggested that their relationship was un-healthy). Depressed, Sean went on a porn binge and spent weeks holed up in his studio apartment. He barely saw the sun. He slept all day and watched porn and played video games all night.

Finally, Sean flew to Arizona and moved into Prescott House, and on a cool December night during his fifth week of treatment, I sat down with him at an old green picnic table at the center's entrance. Down the block I could hear teenage boys laughing loudly at a skate park. Behind us, on the wooden porch of one of Prescott's small three-bedroom suites (each sleeps two to a room), a young man strummed a guitar.

Sean, who had turned twenty-one the week before my visit, seemed ecstatic to see a friendly face. "It's so cool you came!" he said, shivering in the evening breeze.

Sean said he wasn't allowed visitors yet, so my visit had a clandestine feel to it. He hoped no one would come by as we talked, because in five weeks he had already earned a reputation as a troublemaker and slacker, he said. That didn't surprise me. Sean can come off as indolent and uninterested even when he's motivated.

Sean's biggest problem was that he couldn't seem to get up each morning at 4:30, which would give him enough time to walk more than a mile to the mandatory 6 A.M. AA meeting across town. Counselors even put him "on suitcases" once, he said, meaning that he had to pack his bags and be ready to leave the center if he woke up late again.

"This place is pretty hard-core," Sean told me. "There's a lot less freedom than I thought there would be, and I can't seem to do anything right, so I'm on all kinds of contracts. I can't play pool. I can't watch TV. I can't say 'yeah,' because my counselor says that I say it too much and that it sounds patronizing when I say it. He's like, 'I don't like it when you say that word.' In my mind I'm like, 'Hey, buddy, that's *your* issue.'"

Sean said the staff also wouldn't let him get a haircut, which might explain why his hair was thick and scraggly, standing straight up and lending him the look of a mad scientist who'd been wandering aimlessly for weeks in the woods. Fortunately, there were no girls at Prescott House for Sean to try to impress. The only women Sean saw were at the supermarket (addicts at Prescott House cook their own meals) or at the thrift store and a center for the blind, where Sean volunteered until he found a part-time job as a cashier at Staples. (Prescott House requires its patients to work in the community.)

"Having no girls around is really hard for a lot of the guys here, not just the sex addicts," he said. "Before I got here, three guys snuck into a treatment center nearby that's only for girls, and they ended up having sex with three of them. They got in big trouble for that."

For his part, Sean told me that he hadn't had many sexual urges since coming to Arizona. "It's like my sex addiction has vanished or something," he said. "I haven't wanted to look at porn or have sex. The first two weeks I was here I had some vivid sex dreams, just like drug addicts have dreams about using drugs. But since then, nothing. I think that for me, my addiction really hits me when I'm isolated. In Boston, I hardly knew anyone my age. I would feel connected with people at SLAA meetings, but that was only an hour a day. Here I feel plugged in, and I'm making a lot of friends my age." (Most of the addicts at Prescott are in their twenties.)

But while Sean felt like he had his sex addiction under control, two months after my visit he called me from Prescott House to say he was relapsing. At the blind center where he volunteered, Sean had gone on one of its computers and looked for escorts in Prescott, but he didn't find any. Then, on a Saturday night, Sean went to a video store to buy pornographic DVDs and then to Target, where he bought a portable DVD player. To get there, he had to walk perilously close to a busy highway in the dark. His pornography in hand, Sean then hurried back to Prescott House and masturbated most of the night.

Disgusted with himself, the next day he returned the DVDs and threw away the DVD player. Sean decided to tell his counselors that he'd had a slip with masturbation, but he left out the part about the pornography. "I wanted the help without the consequences," he told me. "I thought they would throw me out if I was completely honest. I saw so many people leave or get kicked out while I was there."

Sean said he lived in perpetual fear of being booted from the program, but it never happened. Instead, the staff kept challenging him—sometimes in ways he didn't understand or appreciate—to take his recovery more seriously.

"One day I got called into the director's office," Sean recalled. "He was sitting there gnawing on a chew stick, and the first thing he says to me is, 'Have you ever been raped?' I'm like, 'No, I haven't been raped.' So he says, 'You might want to get a jump-start on therapy for that, because the way your sex addiction is going, you'll eventually end up in jail, and the guys in jail are going to *love* you.'"

Sean was in shock—he didn't know what to say. "Your behavior is telling me that you're not really interested in being here," the director continued, according to Sean. "You don't seem interested in your recovery."

In many ways, Prescott House's treatment approach is the antithesis of the new wave of luxury rehab centers—with names like Beau Monde, Passages, and Harmony Place—that pamper addicts with pedicures, surfing lessons, or whale watching, and that would never challenge an addict in that way.

But while Prescott House is known for its tough love approach, it's also respected for its trauma and family-of-origin work, where counselors help clients heal from the abuse and trauma the staff believes is at the core of the addiction. Sean had mixed feelings about his treatment there.

"I saw them go too far a few times with the way they pushed people and scared them," he told me. "But for the most part I respect what they're trying to do. They just hold you accountable and try to take away all the coping mechanisms you use to avoid feeling your feelings."

(The Prescott House staff declined to speak to me about Sean or their treatment philosophy.)

Sean finally rolls out of bed, throwing on a pair of jeans and a T-shirt from his floor before we drive to a pool hall near the center of town (we take my rental car—Sean only has a bike). Sean spends most of his time lately playing pool; the pool hall's owner lets him play for free as long as he cleans the tables three times a week.

"I swear, pool is my new addiction," he says. "I'm reading all these books about it. I think about it all the time. I want to be a professional pool player all of a sudden. It's crazy."

Jack, Sean's gambling addict roommate, has also turned him on to poker and blackjack. When they're not playing poker with the heroin addict at their apartment, Sean and Jack are competing in free poker tournaments or hanging out at a local casino. On their first trip to the casino, Sean lent Jack $50 to play a game of Texas Holdem.

"Five minutes later he came over and was like, 'I need more,'" recalls Sean. Jack started winning later in the night, but soon he was losing again. "He just went nuts," Sean says. "You could see the addiction in his eyes. It was like he was on crack. Thank God I kept $10 for a cab, or we would have had to walk home."

Sean finally grew tired of enabling Jack's addiction and stopped going to the casino with him. Still, he could relate to Jack's powerlessness. Before going to treatment, Jack sometimes spent eight hours a day playing online poker. "I was the same way online," Sean says, "except I was looking at porn." At Prescott House, they bonded over being two of the few addicts there who weren't addicted to drugs. And in their apartment, they agreed not to have Internet access. "That would be like living with an alligator in the house for both of us," Sean says.

On our drive to the pool hall, Sean tells me that his sex addiction has cropped up only a few times in the two months he's been out of Prescott House. The first time, he had stayed up until 5 A.M. looking at porn on the computer of a friend he met at the pool hall. A week later, Sean was walking home from the hall late at night when he bumped into a girl he used to work with at Staples. She told him her boyfriend was out of town and invited him inside her apartment, where the floor was covered with empty liquor bottles and old French fries. Sean had a weird feeling about her, but that didn't stop him from accepting her offer to have sex. Sean said she would mumble things to herself while they were doing it, and at one point he heard her say, "I have a blade—I'll cut your throat."

That scared Sean, who told himself never to hang out with her again. But two weeks later, he was back in her apartment. While she performed oral sex on him, Sean told me she mumbled that she wanted to kill him. That *really* scared Sean, and he hasn't seen her since.

The more time I spend with Sean in Prescott, the less sure I am of what to make of his life after nine months of treatment. While he's acting out sexually less frequently than he did in Boston, in some ways he seems more lost than ever. He has no job, surviving instead on the $500 his grandparents send him each month. He lives in a filthy apartment with Ryan and Jack, two other addicts in relapse. He's not seeing a therapist, he doesn't have a sponsor, and he rarely goes to sex addiction meetings.

When I ask him what he hopes to be doing in a year, his answer is telling. "Honestly, I just want to play pool."

"What about college? What about music?"

"I don't know," he tells me at a sushi restaurant, his eyes watering from the wasabi. "Sometimes I think about going back to Boston and going to school, but part of me likes it down here more. I walk down the street here and people *know* me. That feels good. I don't feel alone and empty here, and I think that's why I don't want to act out as much."

There's likely some truth to that, but there may be a more practical reason why Sean isn't acting out as often. His addiction has lost its two favorite outlets—the Internet and escorts. He doesn't have access to online porn, and he says the nearest escorts are nearly two hours away in Phoenix. It also seems that Sean has channeled his sex addiction into his two new obsessions: playing pool and poker.

When I tell him that I'm worried about him, at first he seems surprised. "Really?" he says. The next day, though, as we drive to Sedona for a day trip, he's more open to introspection. "I was thinking about what you said," he tells me. "I think I am kind of floating out here, but I don't really feel like doing anything about it. I guess I wish I was more motivated to do music or go back to school, but I'm just not."

"What do you think you got out of all the treatment you've had?" I ask him.

He laughs nervously. "That's a good question," he says. "I think I definitely learned how to relate to people more, because I used to be so shy and isolated. I also learned that I shouldn't keep my feelings or anger bottled up inside. At Prescott House, they had me wail with this foam thing all the time on this big rectangular block because they said I needed to get in touch with my anger."

"And are you in touch with it?"

"Yup," he says with a smile, launching into a story about his mom's unexpected recent visit to Prescott. "I was just walking down the street minding my own business, and I heard someone say, 'Sean,' and it was my mom. I was so pissed that she just showed up, and she was doing her usual thing where she pretends to be all spiritual, but she won't even look at the fact that she's an alcoholic. So we went to

Sedona for the day, and I hated being around her. Just the sound of her voice drove me crazy. Finally I told her, 'When I'm around you for any period of time, I feel like jumping out of my skin.' So I left. I took a cab all the way back to Prescott."

"How much did that cost?"

"A hundred dollars. But how is *that* for getting in touch with my anger?"

25 MARVIN

Remember that we deal with alcohol—cunning, baffling, powerful! Without help it is too much for us.

—ALCOHOLICS ANONYMOUS

MARVIN, THE ELDERLY alcoholic, gazes longingly toward the putting green and shuffleboard court as we drive slowly through his sleepy retirement community on our way to a noon AA meeting on a warm weekday in Florida.

"I used to be shuffleboard champ, putting champ, *multiple years*," he tells me with pride. "I miss all that. Now I'm too old. And I got *lots* of problems. I got problems with my bone marrow, so I'm freezing no matter where I go. My feet hurt—I can barely walk. Not sure if it's a bone spur, but it hurts just sitting here talking to you. I have a heart condition, and my legs are killing me. I got bowel problems—I have to take a softener. I take eight pills in the morning and seven at night. Oh, and I can't hear anything."

"Do you wear a hearing aid?" I ask.

"Pardon me?"

"Do you wear a *hearing aid*?"

"A hearing aid? No, no, I can't wear one. It hurts my ears."

"So can you hear anything at AA meetings?"

"Nope. I still go to meetings, but I don't hear a thing," he says, sounding resigned. "No one speaks up, so what am I supposed to do? They're trying to be humble, I guess, but I want to yell, 'For crying out loud, speak up!' Sometimes I try to read lips, but mostly I just sit there and read the steps, or I read this book I have called *Practice These Principles*. But I keep coming, and I'm still sober. I guess that's the most important thing."

It's been nearly a year since I last visited Marvin in Florida. I checked in with him regularly by phone, but he rarely had much news to report and didn't seem interested in having me visit. "Things are good—same old, same old," he would say, hurrying me off the line as I tried to get him to open up more or commit to spending time with me. Still, he seems genuinely pleased to see me on this trip. "It's good for me to have company," he explains, seated in the passenger seat and wearing a dark blue-collared golf shirt and light khaki pants. "Gets me out of my routine."

After the AA meeting, which Marvin spends with his nose buried in *Practice These Principles*, he points the way to the ocean off Jupiter Island, where he wants to show me where he said his Fifth Step to his sponsor (*Admitted to God, to ourselves, and to another human being the exact nature of our wrongs*).

When we arrive, Marvin bundles himself in a V-neck sweater even though it's nearly eighty degrees outside. Seagulls fly overhead, a pelican rests on a nearby rock, and next to us a father teaches his young daughter how to fly a kite.

"It's a shame," Marvin says, pointing to the crystal blue water. "Four years in the Navy, and I can't swim."

"You can't swim?"

"What are you, deaf?" he says with a chuckle.

We sit on a bench—the same one, Marvin tells me, where he said his Fifth Step. "This is one of the most peaceful places I know in the world," he says. "Whenever I need to clear my head, I come out here."

It's been a difficult week for Marvin, who's spent most of his time worrying about a close friend he met in treatment at the Hanley Center. The man had recently relapsed, and Marvin couldn't get ahold of him. "I sent him a card saying that he wasn't alone, that a lot of people really care about him," Marvin says. "He's very wealthy, and he used to tell me, 'Marvin, I can buy anything I want, but I can't *buy* my sobriety.'"

Marvin doesn't hold out much hope of tracking down his friend. "He used to joke that if he ever relapsed, I could chase him, but I wouldn't catch him," Marvin tells me. "So I just hope he comes back to meeting on his own. He knows what to do. Before relapsing the last time, he was sober for eleven years."

Marvin has nearly four years of sobriety, and he keeps busy with six or seven AA meetings a week, doctor's appointments, and errands to the bank and the post office. Every Monday afternoon, he also plays poker with seven other residents of the retirement community. He usually loses ("They're *sharpies*," he says with mock bitterness), but he never wagers more than $25.

Marvin used to watch a lot of television, but his hearing problems preclude him from doing much of that these days. "And even if I do want to watch something, my wife will have idiot stuff on there," he complains. "I like to watch sports, either golf or baseball. She keeps saying, 'Buy your own TV,' but I'm too cheap to buy one. I'm a Depression kid—I grew up in the 1930s."

"You can get a TV pretty cheap these days," I tell him.

"Yeah, maybe you're right," he says. "One of these days I'll buy my own damn TV."

I ask him how things are going with his wife. On my last visit, he had complained about their relationship, especially that she seemed jealous of his AA recovery. And as Marvin tells it, the situation hasn't improved much.

"Yeah, things still aren't great with me and the *boss lady*," he says with a chuckle. "My memory is really shot, and she doesn't understand that I can't remember things, so she'll get upset when I forget stuff. And she always has to get the last word in! We'll get in these arguments, and I'll keep asking my higher power to help me keep my mouth shut, because if I open my trap, things just get worse. But I'm not very good at shutting up. I'm an egomaniac with an inferiority complex, you know, so all that pride and resentment and anger comes up."

"Have you considered couples therapy?" I ask, half joking. You'd have a better chance, I knew, of getting Marvin to cannonball off the nearby pier.

"Oh, please," he says dismissively. "We're too set in our ways."

Marvin gets up slowly from the bench and walks closer to the ocean, where a majestic white sailboat drifts past.

"Isn't this beautiful?" he says, pointing toward the water. "One of the best things about being sober is that I can enjoy stuff like this. I can enjoy beautiful things. If I'm drinking, I miss out on this stuff. If I'm sober, I get to really live and experience life, even if it's hard."

What a perfect description of sobriety. Life doesn't stop being hard, but it does start being *real*. As I stand next to Marvin, a man I can't claim to know nearly as well as the other men and women I followed for this book, it still occurs to me what a miracle he is. Four years ago, he lay in a hospital bed in an alcohol-induced coma. Today, he's sober. And while his sobriety hasn't made him a perfect man, healed a long-broken marriage, or cured his plethora of physical ailments, it has undoubtedly prolonged his life—and made it worth living.

I tell him what I'm thinking, but he doesn't hear me. I tell him again, louder this time.

"What?" he says. "Are you talking to me?"

"Who else would I be talking to?" I say with a laugh.

"Listen, kid," he says. "I'm an old man with a lot of problems. You've got to speak up to compete with the voices in my head."

"I was just thinking what a miracle it is that you're standing here, nearly four years sober," I shout.

He looks toward the water, taking in what I said. "You'll have to talk to my higher power about that," he says finally. "He's the only one who can turn an old, ornery alcoholic like me into an older, less ornery, sober alcoholic. He's the one to talk to about miracles."

26 ELLEN

Walking and living amidst us are members of a group who share basic assumptions about life and spirituality and self-improvement based on their recovery from alcoholism and addiction. . . . If they were not so anonymous and loose-knit, they would count as, well, what? Definitely not a religion or cult. Members agree on little, maybe nothing, other than the effectiveness of a spiritual way of life.

—CHRISTOPHER RINGWALD, *THE SOUL OF RECOVERY: UNCOVERING THE SPIRITUAL DIMENSION IN THE TREATMENT OF ADDICTIONS*

TWO DAYS AFTER Thanksgiving, I meet Ellen at a hospital in the Northeast for a Saturday morning meeting of Food Addicts in Recovery Anonymous (FA). Nearly three months ago, Ellen left Overeaters Anonymous and joined FA, a harder-line fellowship founded in 1998 by former OA members. In FA, Ellen says it's suggested that addicts stick to a strict food plan agreed upon with their sponsor, write the next day's food plan down each night, weigh and measure their meals, attend three FA meetings a week, call three other FA members, take thirty minutes of "quiet time" each day, pray every morning and evening, and read a page or two of *Alcoholics Anonymous*—also known as The Big Book—each night before going to sleep. (Many Twelve Step fellowships besides AA use The Big Book as a resource.)

"Seeing as though I'm allergic to being told what to do," Ellen told me a few days before the meeting, "it took a lot of courage for me to come to FA. I used to think FA was a cult—a bunch of *food Nazis*, I used to call them. But OA just wasn't working for me anymore. I love OA, but I was constantly struggling and obsessing about food. In OA, you define your own abstinence. But I'm an *addict*, and if I could make healthy decisions for myself around food, I probably wouldn't be a food addict in the first place. I needed a program with less wiggle room. And now, for the first time in my life, I'm eating without question, without guilt, without remorse."

Joining FA was a major ego deflater for Ellen, but one she suspects was good for her. While she doesn't talk to Marianna (her former OA sponsor) as often as she used to, in many ways Ellen's switch from OA to FA was in keeping with much of what Marianna had stressed during their weekly talks at Starbucks. Joining FA was an exercise in blind faith, in moving away from ego and the comforts of attachments. Marianna had long urged Ellen, a self-described "control freak," to practice surrendering control and being willing to experience change and loss.

Leaving OA was a serious loss for Ellen. In that fellowship, she was a recovery star. She sponsored many newcomers, and other members looked up to her. But in FA, Ellen was just another "bozo on the bus," as she put it. A *mute* bozo, no less. New members aren't allowed to share in meetings until they reach ninety days of FA abstinence. Ellen still has a week to go, so at the meeting she sits quietly next to me, listening as a parade of experienced FA members recount their Thanksgivings, the most challenging of holidays for most food addicts.

"I am so incredibly grateful, because it's the Saturday after Thanksgiving, and I didn't spend all of yesterday with a fork in front of the refrigerator!" one woman tells the crowd of about forty women and ten men. They come in all shapes and sizes, although many, like Ellen, look spry and healthy. If I didn't know better, I would think this was a gathering of the hospital's employees, not a meeting of compulsive overeaters. "I used to just kill myself preparing this abundance of food for my whole family," the woman continues, "and then the next day, when everyone was gone, was *my* day to eat. I wouldn't even get out of my nightgown. And I always made sure it was my nightgown so that there wouldn't be anything constricting my waist. I would just gorge and gorge, then nap, then gorge some more. I am so incredibly grateful that isn't my Thanksgiving experience anymore."

Several women recount bringing their own food to their family's Thanksgiving get-togethers, a decision that wasn't always well received by their loved ones. "My mom wasn't happy about *that*," reports one middle-aged FA member. "She said, 'Why can't you just have what we're going to have?' My niece was upset, too. She said, 'I can't believe you brought your own food!'"

A younger FA member—slim and strikingly beautiful, it's hard to imagine her at her pre-FA weight of 220 pounds—recounts her Thanksgiving with her food-addicted family. "My family is very hard-hit with this disease," she tells the group. "They're very, very large people. What was striking was just the physical difficulty they had maneuvering around the table. My cousin would say, 'Oh, I'd like to get that,' but then she'd say, 'Oh, never mind,' because she couldn't get through a space or around a chair. I'd be like, 'I'll get it,' because I could fit. Today, I get up and move because I can."

Like several of the previous speakers, she brought her abstinent meal to Thanksgiving dinner, which she finished in about half the time it took her family members to finish theirs.

"So I just sat there with gratitude," she says. "A couple of my cousins went outside to have a cigarette. Another had to go take his blood sugar. And everyone just ate and ate. I'm so grateful that I'm not a slave to a substance today."

Not all FA members eat the same thing, but abstinence in the program is defined as no sugar, flour, individual "binge" foods, or quantities other than what's agreed upon with a sponsor. Ellen calls her FA sponsor every morning to commit to what she'll eat that day.

One of FA's unofficial slogans is, "Spice up your life, not your food," and Ellen's food plan is typical in its simplicity: For breakfast, she eats six ounces of yogurt and six ounces of fresh fruit. For lunch and dinner each, she has four ounces of protein and six ounces of cooked vegetables, six ounces of potatoes or rice, six ounces of salad (with one tablespoon of oil and vinegar), and a piece of fruit.

In OA, Ellen abstained from sugar and white flour, but she took "considerable liberties" with quantities. She occasionally binged on sugar-free ice cream or a bag of potato chips, and she often grazed carrots and cucumbers as she prepared her family's dinner salad. She was also a slave to Dunkin' Donuts, she says.

"Every afternoon, I would have the same debate with myself," Ellen recalls. "I craved a latte, and even though it was sugar-free and decaf, it made me feel crappy. I would drive to Dunkin' Donuts against my will. It was like my car just drove me there."

The night before her first FA meeting, Ellen had her biggest binge in years. She loaded up on sugar- and wheat-free cookies from a health food store and then drove to McDonald's with her kids, where she bought fries for herself. Back at home, Ellen locked herself in her bedroom and stuffed herself sick.

Since joining FA, Ellen says she's had perfect abstinence and is at her ideal weight of 115 pounds. She's also stopped obsessing about food for the first time in her life. "I never used to think that was truly possible," she tells me after the FA meeting. "I heard people talk about it, but I didn't really believe that could happen, at least not for me. When I was in OA, I would ask Dru all the time, 'Am I ever going to get rid of my food obsession?' Dru would say, 'If you just get abstinent, you will.' That always pissed me off, because in my mind I *was* abstinent. But she would say, 'No, you're not. I hear the games you play when you call in your food every morning. You say things like, 'Oh, my abstinence is *pretty good*. Sure, I ate a few carrots while I was making the salad, but you know, that's okay.' I was in such denial until I got into FA, because I basically spent about two years in relapse without realizing it. I didn't put on a ton of weight, but it wasn't clean abstinence."

While she sometimes struggles to make three FA-related phone calls each day, Ellen has taken easily to the fellowship's other suggestions. She treasures her quiet time before her kids get up each morning, which she uses to pray and meditate. (While she still doesn't consider herself religious, Ellen is now proudly spiritual.)

"In OA, I would often wake up in the morning feeling crappy, but now I wake up feeling good, and I have a great morning," she says. "I'm nicer to my husband, nicer to my kids. And since I'm not overeating, obsessing about food, or beating myself up for overeating or obsessing about food, I'm just much more open to my feelings and whatever is actually happening in the moment."

That means crying on occasion (Marianna would be proud), although she's in much better spirits than during her radio station's format change, when she was overwhelmed with sadness and anger. Ellen has warmed to the new format, and ratings are up. Things are so good, in fact, that Ellen can't help wondering if she might soon plummet from her pink cloud of sobriety.

"Sometimes I think that this can't last, that I'll either get sick of the food I'm eating in this program, or that I'll try to go out and self-destruct this good thing I have going," Ellen tells me. "Some people will say, 'Oh, how can you eat that same stuff every day? It's so restrictive.' Basically what people are saying is, 'Don't you ever get a *treat*?' And by treat, they usually mean sugar. But I'm a food addict, and I can't eat sugar, because I can't stop at *one* treat. As much as you explain food addiction to people, they don't really get that. I have no control over certain foods. If I eat certain foods, I will ruin my life. So I have to live what some people see as a really radical life. But so what? I'm enjoying life today more than I ever have."

She laughs in disbelief. "Who would have thought that putting my chicken on a scale would give me a happy life?"

27 KATE

You know the expression, "Don't just sit there, do something"? For many addicts, we need to do the opposite in recovery. We're so used to doing anything we can to avoid feeling our feelings, so we need a new saying for addicts: "Don't just do something—sit there."

—An addiction counselor at a
treatment center I attended

AT A CORNER table at a Sizzler near Kate's house on the West Coast, Kate and three members of the online shoplifting support group meet for their monthly gathering. Since there are few Twelve Step meetings around the country for shoplifters, Kate and others make do with these informal get-togethers, where members sometimes drive hundreds of miles to attend.

It's a clear Saturday in early January, the first of these meetings since Christmas, the most dreaded of holidays for most shoplifters. And at our table, only two of the women made it through unscathed.

"I had a slip," Kate tells the group. Two weeks before Christmas, after fifteen months without shoplifting, Kate picked out four small, $3 kids' stick-on earrings and a jewelry box for her niece at Target. She dropped two pairs of earrings in the box and put the other two in her basket. When she got to the register, she told the cashier to put the two from her basket into the box.

"In my mind, I assumed that if she saw the ones in the box already, she would say, 'Oh, you forgot these, do you want me to ring them up?'" Kate says. "But she didn't see them, and I didn't tell her they were in there. Part of me wanted her to see them and save me, and part of me wanted to shoplift them."

From the moment she walked into Target that day, Kate tells us, she knew she didn't want to be there. "I was in a bad mood, and it's never a good idea for me to shop in a bad mood," she says, sitting upright in her chair, wearing jeans and a T-shirt. Even though Kate recently had her slip, she's in an unusually lively mood. This is the first time I've seen her with other recovering shoplifters, and the camaraderie and shared experience of this group brings out the extrovert in her.

"I was resentful that day that I had to be doing the shopping in the first place," she continues. "I resent that women always have to be the shoppers! If it's Christmastime or someone's birthday, does the guy hop in the car and go and buy the last-second card? No, he gets his girlfriend, wife, or mother to do it. Obviously that doesn't excuse my shoplifting, but that was the mood I was in."

"Oh, I relate to that," says Linda, a tall, proper woman in her fifties who looks like a high school librarian. "I really have to watch my mood before I decide to walk into a store."

About six months ago, Linda says, she had a migraine and went to buy aspirin at a Fred Meyer supermarket. When she got to the register, the line looked a mile long and the clerk was a "total moron." After waiting a few minutes, Linda put the aspirin in her purse and stormed out. But before getting into her car, she thought better of it and ended up returning to the long line, waiting her turn, and paying for the aspirin.

(Linda has been shoplifting since her early twenties, brazenly stuffing clothes from department stores into her shopping bag. "I was so un-stealth about it," she recalls, "that it's almost like I was trying to be caught." She eventually was, and her arrest scared her enough that she didn't shoplift again for fifteen years. Still, the urges never went away completely, and a year ago she started again.)

Like Kate, Linda had a slip over the holidays, shoplifting a calendar from a kiosk at the mall. "I had the money to pay for it and I felt like I wanted to pay for it," she tells us, "but there was nobody at the register to give my money to. And I just *had* to have this calendar. So finally I got tired of waiting."

The woman at the table with the longest period of shoplifting sobriety is Joan, a veterinarian in her forties. Like the others, Joan has been arrested for shoplifting, although she says she hasn't stolen anything in nearly three years. She credits her success to one pragmatic decision: she mostly stays out of stores. This Christmas, she made many gifts herself, and she bought the rest online. "Online shopping is my savior," she tells me.

Seated next to me at the table is Sarah, a pretty and talkative stay-at-home mom also in her forties. Sober for many years from drugs and alcohol and a regular at AA meetings, Sarah only recently joined the CASA online group. This is her first time meeting Kate and the others, and she can barely contain her excitement at being able to speak openly about a subject that has brought her so much shame.

"I still can't get over the fact that we're all here like this to talk about *shoplifting*," she says with a mischievous giggle. "If anyone looked over at this table, they wouldn't assume we were a bunch of criminals. They would probably think we belonged in *Better Homes & Gardens*!"

Sarah tells us that she hasn't shoplifted for a few weeks but that the urges are still strong. "I'm way more powerless over shoplifting than I am over alcohol," she explains. "And I'm a little worried about what's going to pop up now that I'm not shoplifting. The way I see it, shoplifting is just a symptom of the disease of addiction. Even if you take away the shoplifting—"

"We'd still be dysfunctional," Kate interjects.

"That's definitely true of me," Linda says. "I did food, and alcohol."

"I have an eating disorder," Joan says, "and it starts really revving up when I'm not shoplifting."

"And what's harder about this addiction is that it has such a stigma," Sarah tells us. "With alcohol, I can tell pretty much anyone about my addiction, and I don't feel shame. With this, there's no upside to telling people."

Sarah says it took all the courage she could muster to tell her former boyfriend. "I really thought he would be judgmental, but he was like, 'Oh, my mom's been arrested for that *twice*.' Then he confided in me that he sometimes shoplifts, too. He'd tell me how he would put a case of bottled water under his cart at Safeway, and if they noticed it, they noticed, and if they didn't, then he wouldn't pay for it. He didn't see that as a problem, but for me that was really dangerous. My behavior picked up when I was around him."

Joan interjects that she hasn't told most of her friends about her shoplifting, nor does she talk about it often with her husband, who she assumes would rather not hear about it. At this table, Kate is the most open with her husband about her struggles.

"But if it was up to me," Kate admits, "I probably never would have told Eric. My comfort zone is to just keep everything bottled up inside. So it's good that he keeps asking me how I'm doing. I'll say to Eric, 'I have three errands to run today,' and he'll call me in the afternoon and ask if I got in and out okay."

Over the course of our lunch, the women alternate between referring to their shoplifting as a problem, a moral failing, and an addiction. Sarah—who, ironically, has been in recovery from shoplifting the shortest time—seems the most comfortable calling shoplifting a true addiction, probably because of her experience in AA.

"This is an addiction unlike any other," she tells the group several times, although the others don't seem convinced.

"I don't know," Kate says. "I guess I sort of see it as an addiction, but mostly I still feel like it's a bad behavior. But it's crazy what I'm willing to risk. When I shoplift I'm risking my family. I'm risking my friends finding out. I'm risking going to jail. And I still do it."

"That's addiction," Sarah says. "That *has* to be addiction."

Joan chimes in. "There's definitely still a feeling that I have that it's a moral wrong."

"I was never really comfortable calling it an addiction until I read some books about it," Linda tells us. "I mean, I am powerless over it, so in that way it feels like an addiction."

But no one at the table seems comfortable calling themselves a shoplifting *addict*. "That has such a bad connotation," Sarah says. "I don't mind saying I'm an alcoholic and an addict, but I don't think I would be as comfortable saying I'm a shoplifting addict."

Across the table, Joan nods in agreement. "I think it's probably true that I'm a shoplifting addict," she tells us, "but I would never call myself that in front of other people. They would probably think I was offering up an excuse for my behavior, instead of taking responsibility for the fact that it's wrong. I don't think that way about alcoholics, but I do think that about shoplifters. It's amazing how hard I am on myself. For some reason, I can't accept that this isn't my fault."

———

In the months following our lunch at Sizzler, Kate struggles through a handful of strong urges to shoplift ("I don't want this slip to turn into a full-on relapse," she tells me) and posts regularly to the online support group. In this first posting, Kate responds to a woman who recently had a slip and then asked the board members how she might go about making amends for her theft.

I know what an awful letdown you feel—do recall that it was only one month ago that I was in your shoes. I sat before you, my friends, and described the situation I put myself in that day at Target. I hated myself for not being stronger and wished I could just forget about shoplifting. Now that you've had a day to reflect on what happened, can you see it as the mistake it was and move on?

As far as making amends, I suppose you could return the items to the store, thereby giving them back and also giving them up. That, however, would mean going back into a store which could lead to further relapse. A CASA member once suggested mailing cash anonymously to the store manager with a note of apology for shoplifting. A discussion of this topic ended I believe in some members feeling like it was a cop-out. I, however, believe that doing this is far better than doing nothing at all.

Another CASA member suggested donating the amount you stole anonymously to a reputable charity. It has been repeatedly noted that receiving any recognition of any donation you make would cancel out the intended purpose of making amends.

When the board quiets down for a few weeks, Kate, who's not a leader by nature, finds herself in the unusual position of urging her fellow shoplifters to post more. She even calls me a few times to express her frustration that the board has temporarily turned quiet. "Is everyone out shoplifting?" she jokes.

Things are awful quiet around here. Are we all on a mental vacation? I have been kicking around the idea of drafting a statement which I will like to offer to our local judicial and law enforcement offices informing them that a support group is available to shoplifters interested in stopping the behavior. Would any of you be willing to share your opinions about this subject with me?

In this last post, Kate responds to a woman who stole three cans of green beans from a Dollar Store and also recounts two challenging shopping trips.

Your post brought back so many memories for me. I remember mostly shoplifting things from discount places like the Dollar Store, Ross, and thrift stores, as well as shoplifting from the clearance merchandise of regular department stores. I worked on this issue in counseling and what I think is the biggest reason I risked everything for so little was because I never felt "worth" the good stuff.

In other news, yesterday while my son was in school, I ran several errands. Goodwill, Costco, Home Depot, Target, PetSmart and Blockbuster. While I encountered moments of frustration for various reasons, I resisted the urges to act out by shoplifting. Of course, I still thought about it. It is those thoughts I wish I could erase from my life permanently.

Then last night I met with friends for a couple hours, and on the way home I stopped at the grocery. It was nearly 10 o'clock at night, the place was virtually deserted, I got what I needed and paid for it. After I got out the door I saw the flowers . . . you know, those displays they put at the door to remind shoppers to buy flowers for someone they love . . . and for a moment I thought about scooping them up and going home. But I did not.

When I got home, my Eric & I shared about our day. I told him all the places I went and all I had accomplished and he asked how I did, i.e. did I shoplift? I felt relieved when I recounted for him what I have told you here. At the same time I reminded us both that the OLD me would have taken those flowers, but I resisted because I don't want to be her anymore. Shoplifting causes me to live my life in fear and shame and I don't want to live a life like that anymore either. Seems like such a simple choice, doesn't it? If only it were! So there it is . . . I didn't shoplift yesterday. Did you? Be safe today, my friends.

28 JODY

> *If it can be taken as a symptom of civilization*
> *when men's desires, hitherto exclusively con-*
> *fined to the bare necessities of life, pass beyond*
> *these limits, and the individual, no longer*
> *satisfied with the crude sustenance afforded*
> *by or wrested from nature, finds and delights*
> *in stimulants which mainly affect the nervous*
> *system, then a suitable background for such*
> *physical cravings must form part of the human*
> *constitution.*
>
> —LOUIS LEWIN, *PHANTASTICA*, 1931

AT A RESTAURANT near the beach only a few blocks from Jody's sober living community, a middle-aged waitress seats us close to a table packed with attractive college-age girls. "I figure you guys might like the scenery here," she says with a wink and a smile, handing us our menus and leaving us alone, presumably to gawk in peace.

Sadly, the scenery is mostly lost on us. I'm gay, and Jody's blind. "Man, I'm at such a disadvantage when it comes to picking up women." Jody tells me. "Everything depends on that eye contact, but when I look over at that table, I just see shapes, a big blur. I wouldn't know if any of them were checking me out. I never know what the fuck is going on!" Fortunately, Jody says he happens to be instinctively drawn to beautiful women. "My friends are like, 'Jody, how the fuck do you *always* get hot girls?'"

Jody walks without the help of a cane or a guide dog, meaning most people assume he can see normally. That creates problems when someone he meets runs into him again days or weeks later, waves or tries to make eye contact, and receives a blank stare in return.

"I can't tell you how many people have said to me, 'Jody, I thought you were the biggest snob, the biggest asshole. I waved, I walked right past you, and you pretended like you didn't see me,'" he says. "I'm pretty sure that I look like I can see a lot better than I can actually see. Everyone bases blindness on whether you run into shit. People are like, 'Nah, Jody's not *that* blind—he never runs into shit.'"

I made a similar assumption when I first met him, which likely explains why we've talked so little about his blindness. But Jody wants to talk about it tonight. As I try to delve into a discussion about addiction and trauma, he interrupts me mid-sentence. "I think my trauma was losing my vision," he says. "And I haven't dealt with it *at all*."

Jody knew from a young age that he had retinitis pigmentosa, and that it would just be a matter of time before he lost most, if not all, of his vision. Getting high temporarily blotted out the debilitating fear that he would be alone for the rest of his life, unlovable and unable to provide for himself.

"Ever since I was young, I've had the same old tapes running through my head," he says. "*I don't measure up. I'm not good enough. Nobody will love me.* Same old bullshit. And I think those tapes still really affect me today. I used to have the drugs and the gambling to block it out. I think I still try to block those messages out today with relationships and women. That's the way I prove to myself that I'm worthwhile, that I'm good enough."

At various times, Jody has attended blind support groups, but he's never stayed for long. "One time I called this guy who was supposed to be this bigwig in the blind community, someone who organized a lot of these groups," Jody recalls. "I told him, 'You know, I don't think I've ever really dealt with my blindness. How have you dealt with it?' Without missing a beat he said, 'Alcohol and pills.' He was dead serious. So I was like, 'Oh, well, then I've *definitely* dealt with my blindness."

After dinner, I drive Jody back to the sober living community, where we sit on white garden chairs in front of the apartment Dickie (the gambler who attended the GA conference with us) shares with Kevin and Ryan, two drug addicts in their twenties. It's a still, humid night, and Kevin and Ryan lounge around on their couch shirtless, chain-smoking and watching the NBA Finals. Dickie is working tonight, driving addicts from C.A.R.E.'s inpatient treatment center to Twelve Step meetings in the community.

It's been a few months since I last visited Jody in Florida, when he spoke at the GA conference about relapse prevention. Since then, he nearly relapsed. Life was going fine, he tells me, until he asked a yoga teacher to show him stretching exercises to loosen his hip flexor, which he hoped would help him with his newest passion, Brazilian Jiu-Jitsu.

After the stretches, Jody felt excruciating pain on his right side. "I was like, 'I think my kidneys are bleeding,'" he told the yoga instructor. "But she looked at me like it was no big deal. She said, 'Sweetheart, it's from the stretching. It's your psoas muscle.' I was skeptical that a muscle could hurt that much, but what the fuck did I know about psoas muscles?"

Jody went home, where the pain only got worse. But he wanted to tough it out without painkillers. "I'm an opiate addict—I've got no business taking narcotics," he says. His roommate agreed ("I don't want to see you going down *that* road," he told Jody), so Jody went to bed that night hoping to sleep it off. The next morning, he could barely get out of bed. He somehow made it to work, where he keeled over in anguish in front of the addicts during a lecture. That night, he rolled around the floor of his apartment in pain before grudgingly agreeing to be driven to the emergency room.

Jody told the doctor that he pulled his psoas muscle, but the doctor made a different diagnosis: kidney stones. To treat them, Jody would need to take pain medication until the stones passed through his urine.

"I'm like, 'Look, man, I'm a drug addict, an *opiate* addict, and I can't be relapsing over some fucking kidney stones,' I told the doctor. I was so scared. I felt like a dead man walking going into the pharmacy to get my script." Jody had his boss from C.A.R.E. with him, because she was going to keep the Vicodin. Jody didn't trust himself with the pills. "I told everyone, 'Listen, I'm going to say everything that goes without saying, because once I start taking these things, God knows what I'll be saying!' Everyone was like, 'You'll be fine, Jody,' but I didn't feel like I would be fine."

Jody hadn't forgotten the last time he took prescription medications with a potential for abuse, the episode when a well-meaning psychiatrist had suggested he take Adderall to help with his ADD, and Jody spent months on a heroin and crack binge.

"Ever since then," Jody says, lighting a cigarette as a white cat stretches on a bench near our garden chairs, "I have one major goal in life, and that's to never, ever spend another night in a treatment center's twin bed. That's my motto. NO MORE TWIN BEDS!"

Jody took the Vicodin for his kidney stones, and for a week he felt fine—no cravings, no depression, no wanting to take more than prescribed. The pain went away, and he assumed the stones had passed.

He also wondered—in the kind of wishful thinking common to addicts—if maybe he wasn't as much of an addict as he used to be.

But a few days later, the pain returned, so Jody ended up back on the painkillers. He made an appointment with a urologist, who told him that there was no guarantee the stones would pass on their own, and that they might need to consider surgery. But the doctor wanted to give it another week, so Jody ended up taking four Vicodin each day as prescribed for the next seven days.

And that's when everything changed, he says. Suddenly, Jody needed the Vicodin to function. He woke up every morning feeling terrible, and only a Vicodin pill could make him feel better. But that never lasted long—thirty minutes later he would "crash" until the next pill.

"Lo and behold, I was still an addict," he tells me with a laugh. "And I was so fucking scared. It all felt way, way too familiar. I'm a firm believer that with drug addiction, issues alone, or a bad childhood, don't make you a drug addict. I wholeheartedly believe that my body processes drugs differently than your body does. When I took the Vicodin, it interacted with my brain in a major, tangible way. I was taking them as prescribed, but it was affecting me like I'd been strung out on methadone for two years."

Jody is interrupted when a car pulls into the driveway, and the door to the apartment behind us swings opens. Ryan, who's headed to a 10 P.M. AA meeting with a friend, shuffles past us, his flip-flops smacking against the concrete. "I'll be back after the meeting," he tells Jody.

"Cool. Go get healed, bro," Jody says, taking a drag from his cigarette and watching as Ryan slumps into the passenger-side seat of the waiting car.

"So I was telling everyone that I wasn't doing well at all," Jody continues, "but evidently I wasn't being clear, because no one seemed all that concerned. I was scared to death that I would call the doc and ask for a prescription for a stronger narcotic, because I was afraid that once I did that, then things would get shady really fast. Then I would be powerless to stop the train wreck."

If Jody relapsed, he knew he would lose more than his sobriety. He would also lose his job. (It's a common fear—and a powerful motivator—for the thousands of addicts with sobriety who staff addiction treatment centers across the country.) But Jody made it through the tough patch and underwent a minor surgery designed to break the stones into smaller pieces, making them more likely to pass. The pain went away, and Jody stopped taking the Vicodin.

But he wasn't expecting what happened next: He went into a major withdrawal, and he felt more depressed than he ever had. He couldn't sleep, couldn't get in the shower, couldn't answer his phone, couldn't go to Twelve Step meetings. He somehow managed to get himself to work, but he was on autopilot, and he doesn't remember anything he did there those two weeks.

"I was so depressed that I basically gave up," Jody tells me. "I couldn't do anything to pull myself out of the depression. I wasn't capable. I wasn't reaching out. I was isolating. I was doing all the things you aren't supposed to do when you're that depressed and going through withdrawal."

Jody thinks he knows what caused the debilitating depression. "At some point through the experience of taking the Vicodin, my brain said, 'Oh, Jody's providing dopamine artificially again, so we don't need to make it anymore.' It was a Wednesday, and I remember telling people, 'If I'm still like this on Monday, I'm going to see a psychiatrist, because I may need to be hospitalized.'"

That Friday, Jody went to bed feeling more hopeless than ever. He managed a two-second prayer ("God, please help me"), but as he lay in bed, all he could think about was killing himself. "For the life of me," he says, "I couldn't figure out why anyone would want to be alive on this planet."

The next morning, though, he felt fine. The depression had lifted. "Did time heal it? Did my higher power heal it?" Jody wonders. "I have no idea, but it's a miracle that I didn't relapse through all of this. I know that if I was in Virginia when this happened, if I didn't have the structure and responsibility of this job, I would have gone off the deep end."

For Jody, the experience has crystallized the fragility of sobriety. "I don't think people realize how tenuous our recovery is," he tells me. "I bet there are a ton of people in AA who have rotator cuff surgery, get pain medications, and then go off the deep end. And they look at it like it's a relapse, like it's *their* fault. Man, it shouldn't be like that. Nobody can really wrap their heads around the fact that as true addicts, we're powerless. Throughout all of this people would say to me, 'Well, Jody, just take the medication as prescribed, don't fuck up, and you'll be fine.' But they really didn't get it. This addiction is way stronger than me! Even some people in AA meetings don't get it. They'll be like, 'It's all about your mind-set, your intent.' My intent? Are you kidding me? Do they actually think it's my *intent* to throw away my life, to lose my apartment, to lose my job, to end up on another twin fucking bed?"

Jody laughs as he says this, but he's more angry than amused. He stands up and stretches his legs, nearly squashing a small lizard resting on the pavement near his chair.

"People need to understand something about addiction," Jody says. "My addiction is *so much stronger* than my willpower. I didn't avoid relapsing because I'm a strong person or because my recovery is so much better than anyone else's. I have no idea why I didn't relapse through all of this, but it has nothing to do with having strong willpower. When drugs like Vicodin enter my system, all bets are off. And my brain doesn't differentiate between legal drugs and illegal drugs. My brain doesn't go, 'Don't be addicted to this, Jody, because it came from a *doctor.*' My brain goes, 'I need more of this, and I will do whatever I have to do to get it.' We need to start treating this like the disease it is. Man, we've got way too much morality around all of this. It's adding to the shame that fuels the addiction. And it's killing people."

But on this night, at least, it's not killing Jody, nor is it killing the addicts in the sober living community he manages. Ryan is headed to his AA meeting. Kevin is sprawled out on the couch in the apartment behind us, listening to meditation music and reading the AA Big Book before going to bed. Dickie is helping other addicts.

On this night, on this street, everyone is safe. "When you think about it," Jody tells me, "it's a miracle that any of us can stay sober for one fucking day. But we all did that today. I did it. You did it. Everyone in this community did it. Today, we're sober. And you know what?"

"What?" I ask.

"Today we're some of the luckiest sons of bitches on the planet."

29 BOBBY

God grant me the serenity
To accept the things I cannot change,
The courage to change the things I can,
And the wisdom to know the difference.

—The Serenity Prayer

IT'S A MISERABLE late spring afternoon, but as Bobby and I sit in my car facing the Castle Island Lagoon in Southie, with rain crashing against the windshield and airplanes rumbling low through the dark, blustery sky, he couldn't care less about the gloomy weather. Bobby is ten weeks removed from drugs, and he's radiating the boundless optimism and cheer of the newly sober.

"Life is good right now," he tells me with a smile. "Life is real good. And for the first time in a long time, I actually want to be clean more than I want to get high. I know I can do this. I know I can stay clean. I'm ready to live sober, and I say that without any reservations."

It's been thirteen months since I drove with Bobby and Margaret to get him Suboxone. He disappeared after that but called me out of the blue five months ago, asking for a ride to see the Suboxone doctor again. Bobby claimed to be doing well, but I didn't buy it. He told me he had a sponsor, but when I asked to speak with him, Bobby changed the subject. When I pressed him on whether he was using the Suboxone as directed, he conceded that he "occasionally" used heroin but was mostly relying on the Suboxone to stay clean. I suspected that it was the other way around—he was "occasionally" using Suboxone to avoid a painful withdrawal when he couldn't get his hands on heroin.

After that second trip to the hospital five months ago with Bobby, he promised to meet me the following night at a nearby AA meeting. I wasn't surprised when he didn't show up. By that point, I was used to it.

"Oh, I remember that night—I was smoking crack," Bobby tells me with a guilty cackle, seated in the passenger seat and wearing a black Nike T-shirt and gray sweatpants. He has gained some weight since I last saw him—he says he's eating more now that he's not taking drugs. "I knew I was supposed to meet you that night, but I was all fucked up. I was full of shit back then. You knew it. I knew it. You probably think I'm full of shit now, too. But I'm actually clean. No heroin. No crack. No alcohol. No Suboxone. Nothing."

I suspect he's telling the truth. He's been regularly returning my calls the last week, which he's never done before. He's been going to AA meetings daily, and after spending five weeks in inpatient treatment and twenty-six days at a halfway house, he's now living at Sober Surroundings, a sober house outside Boston where he's drug-tested three times a week. (Boston was home to the country's first lodging home for addicts. In 1841, the Washingtonian Society of Boston offered rooms under its meeting hall for struggling alcoholics.)

Even with the positive actions that Bobby's been taking lately, I'm not convinced when he tells me that he's willing to go to "any lengths" to stay sober. He certainly didn't do that at the halfway house, where he was asked to leave for not following the rules.

"I made it to all the mandatory house meetings," Bobby says, "but I was being written up for silly shit, like wearing my hat in the house. Basically, me and the guy at the front desk had a little personality conflict. He didn't like me, and he wanted me out of there. But now I'm in a better place."

He's undoubtedly in an easier place. At Sober Surroundings, there are no mandatory house meetings and few rules, and Bobby can live there as long as he passes his drug tests. But after more than a decade as an active addict and chronic relapser, and with only ten weeks of sobriety, Bobby desperately needs structure. A halfway house is an ideal place to practice the skills he doesn't have—following rules, learning to compromise, being a productive member of a community. But if he can't survive a halfway house, can he really be expected to survive the real world?

I pose that question to him, but he's not interested in exploring it. "It just wasn't the right place for me," he says. "I get structure by going to the gym, by talking to my sponsor, by going to AA meetings every day."

At a recent AA meeting, Bobby was surprised to spot his brother, Dan, sitting two rows behind him. "I did a double take when I saw him," Bobby tells me. "I smiled, and he smiled back. Since I've bounced back and gotten clean, it's really affected him. He's going to the gym, going to some meetings, trying really hard to get clean off the Oxys. I know he's going to do it."

Southie AA and NA meetings are packed lately, mostly with men and women trying to stay away from heroin—or, more often, from the pharmaceuticals they switched to when heroin started losing its purity a few years ago. "People are getting addicted to FDA-approved drugs more than illegal drugs now," Bobby says. "With pharmaceuticals, you know what's in them, and you know you're going to get a great high. Look at Anna Nicole Smith. She could have had any drugs she wanted, but what was her choice? Methadone and benzos." ("Benzos" is short for benzodiazepines.)

While Suboxone doesn't cause a high like methadone, it's a popular way to self-detox from stronger opiates. And in Southie, there's no need to worry if you don't have a doctor's prescription. There are plenty of people, like Bobby, willing to sell you some of theirs.

"There are a lot of guys around here who take opiates recreationally," he tells me. "You might not call them *junkies*, but they like having a few beers and taking a few pills and going home and banging their girlfriend, or whatever they do when they're high. But eventually they get addicted, and instead of going to detox or treatment, they just get the Suboxone and detox themselves. You don't get high from Suboxone, but you feel nice. And no one can tell you're on anything. It's a great safety net."

Bobby credits Suboxone with keeping him out of jail the last year. When he sensed withdrawal coming on and couldn't find heroin, he would pop a Suboxone pill to hold him over. He rarely did anything desperate or stupid. "I'd just take some Suboxone, be content, wait until it wore off, and then go get the real deal when I had some money in my pocket."

(Doctors who prescribe the drug know that some of their patients divert it, but many aren't overly concerned. "It's still getting used for its intended purpose," one addiction medicine doctor who has treated hundreds of patients with Suboxone told me. "It's not like people are getting high off of it, like they do with methadone. Compared to the harm of diverting Xanax or Klonopin or Valium, the harm of diverting Suboxone is pretty minimal. I'd rather someone get Suboxone on the street than not get it and overdose on heroin.")

I ask Bobby what motivated him to seek treatment, and why he believes he's been able to stay sober since. He thinks about my question for a few seconds while a middle-aged man in a yellow rain jacket walks on the sidewalk in front of us, his sopping Labrador pulling him along by the leash.

"It was something my father said," Bobby tells me, adjusting his body in the passenger seat. "I was at the house just hanging around, and one day my dad just looked at me, shook his head, and said, 'What a fucking waste.' Then he walked up the stairs and slammed the door to his room. I knew he was right, and I knew I had to stop living like I was living."

"How have you dealt with urges to use since you've been clean?" I ask him.

Bobby tells me about two close calls. In the first, he was talking to two addicts he used to use heroin with when the conversation turned—as it usually does, he says—to drugs. Bobby could feel himself feeding into the conversation.

"I was basically trying to see how far I could go without getting in trouble," he says. "One of the guys was like, 'Oh, but we can't talk too much about this now to Bobby, because he's doing so good,' but I could tell he just really wanted to tempt me. These guys are birdbrains. I know what they're trying to do. They're trying to drag me down with them. But for some reason I still want to be around them. Part of me still wants to be at that table with all the other birdbrains getting high. I don't understand that." (Bobby managed to extricate himself from that situation, going straight to the gym and "working out" his urge to use.)

Then, just last week, Bobby was hanging out at the L Street Tavern, a popular local bar featured in the film *Good Will Hunting*. It was a warm night, and it seemed like everyone he knew from the neighborhood—including a girl he likes—was out relaxing and socializing. Bobby desperately wanted a beer, but he settled instead on two Red Bulls.

What would have happened if he'd had a beer? "Well, it wouldn't be just one beer," he says. "It would be four or five beers, and then I'd go out looking for a line of coke, and by the end of the night I'd have a crack pipe in my hand. The next day I would feel so shitty that I would take an opiate to make myself feel better, whether it's dope or something else. Then I would get really depressed and wonder what the fuck happened. I'd be like, 'I had all this clean time, and I threw it away just to feel this *shitty*?'"

But Bobby didn't throw it away that night. Instead, he went to bed, got up early the next morning, worked out at the gym, and then helped his son with a school assignment about rocks and minerals. Bobby says both his sons are calling him more now that he's sober.

"When I'm using, I'm not thinking about my kids," he admits. "All I think about is where the fuck I'm going to get my next bag. Sometimes I'll say to myself, 'Once I get my next bag, *then* I'll go see my kids.' But that's bullshit—I still don't go even after I get the bag. It feels so good to be there for them now. They need me right now."

Bobby tells me that he's looking for a job, and that he's considering taking some classes at a community college. "The sad thing is that I've always been a smart guy, but when I was young I had no self-esteem," he says. Bobby got good grades in school, but he didn't think he would amount to anything, except maybe as a boxer. "I wish I knew then what I know now. I would have done pretty much everything different. When I look back at my life, I can't believe that it's turned out like this. It's a fucking nightmare what my life has been. A total nightmare."

He goes on like this for another minute, his voice full of regret. But then he cuts himself off, straightens himself in his seat, and looks at me. "I need to try and stay positive," he says. "All I need to do is not use, stay vigilant, and stay positive."

"That's a good attitude to have," I tell him.

"If I do that," he continues, "then I won't have any more regrets.

I want to be an inspirational story. It would be amazing if in a year I'm still sober, if after all the despair and the hopelessness, after you and everyone thinking that I'm a lost cause, after all that I manage to stay clean. That would be a great story. An inspirational story of hope about overcoming addiction that would show the world that recovery is truly possible, even for a no-good addict like me. Wouldn't that be a great story?"

"It would," I tell him. "But it would be an even greater *life*."

"Yeah, it would," he says softly, nodding his head as an American Airlines jet thunders low through the ominous Southie sky, a symbol of freedom in a neighborhood where so many people feel stuck. As we wait for the sound of the airplane to pass, I can't help thinking of Jack Leary, the beloved Southie probation officer who had many run-ins with Bobby over the years.

Last month, Leary—a relentless optimist who refused to give up on anybody, devoting his life to helping Southie addicts get sober— shot himself in the head. A neighborhood in mourning couldn't help wondering: Had Jack given up on himself, or had he given up on them? Had twenty-five years fighting addiction in Southie finally broken the man whom many called the neighborhood's patron saint?

"The ripple effect of Jack's goodness and love cannot be quantified," Mayor Thomas Menino said at Leary's eulogy. Bobby agrees, and he wonders what Southie addicts will do without Leary watching over them. "I bet you he single-handedly saved hundreds of lives," Bobby tells me.

A few minutes later, Bobby says he has to leave soon to meet his sponsor at a nearby AA meeting. "You want to come?"

I tell him I can't, that I have a sex addiction meeting for my own recovery. But as I drive him back to his parents' house, where he has a load of laundry in the washer, we make plans to meet the next night at an AA meeting in Boston.

"You'll definitely be there?" I say.

"I'll definitely be there," he tells me, opening the passenger-side door. "I won't leave you hanging like I usually do. I'll be there. I promise."

For the first time since I met him more than two years ago, I actually believe him.

30 TODD

That, of course, is the devil's bargain of addiction: a short-term good feeling in exchange for the steady meltdown of one's life.

—DANIEL GOLEMAN, *EMOTIONAL INTELLIGENCE*

"SO, I'VE MADE some big decisions since I last saw you," Todd tells me, standing next to his yellow SUV in the Gold's Gym parking lot in the city where he lives. It's a muggy, early summer morning, and he's just finished working out in a white tank top and tight blue athletic shorts.

It's been a few months since I last visited Todd and Julie. I was supposed to see Todd last month during one of his work trips to Boston, but he cut it short and flew home after only a day. "I have a bad cold," he told me at the time. But that wasn't the whole story. The truth was that Todd felt unattractive, and he couldn't perform for his clients.

He had started cutting down considerably on his steroid use about a month before the trip, moving from injectables to a less powerful steroid cream. He felt healthier on the low dose (he was less tense and sleeping more soundly), but his body dysmorphia kicked into overdrive.

"I wasn't taking enough for me to psychologically feel superior and in control," he tells me, leaning against the front door of his car. "No matter how good a client thinks I look, if I don't see it, it doesn't matter. My body dysmorphia is very powerful. I can't be confident, I can't be an exhibitionist like my clients expect. I can't put on a mask. Logically I knew that I looked fine in Boston, because I was maintaining my size and having great workouts. But logic didn't win out."

Rather than stay in his hotel for two days and "cry," Todd decided to go home, cancel his upcoming trips, and ponder his future. Maybe, he thought, this was a sign that he needed to slow down on the escorting and make some changes in his life. "I can't be going on work trips and just be sitting in my hotel room scared to see anybody!" he says, amazed that it had come to this.

It was his second disastrous trip in a matter of weeks. Before Boston he had flown to Washington, D.C., a city where he has many clients and usually makes good money. But when he checked into the hotel and looked at himself in his room's full-length mirror, he panicked.

"Different mirrors can make you look wide or narrow, and this one was making me look narrow," he says. "So not only did I have the body dysmorphia that was making me feel small, but this mirror was *actually* making me smaller. I felt like I was shrinking. The mirror confirmed all my worst fears, so I just shut down. I couldn't imagine having anyone touch me or see me."

Todd canceled his appointments and stayed in bed all day. The next morning, he put on baggy clothes before venturing outside to eat. Todd felt more confused and unsure of himself than ever. "Even when I was using crystal meth," he tells me, "I somehow managed to keep afloat and meet my commitments. What happened in D.C. was a real sign that something is wrong. But I'm not sure what it is."

I think I know. As I follow Todd to his apartment in my rental car, it occurs to me that he's likely in serious withdrawal from the high doses of steroids his body is accustomed to. He has many of the symptoms of steroid withdrawal: He's moody, depressed, and insecure. It's not uncommon for bodybuilders coming off steroids to change gyms or end romantic relationships, all in an effort to isolate and not be *seen*.

Interestingly, in his period of withdrawal Todd sounds more cogent and self-reflective than I've ever heard him. But that, too, may be a symptom of his withdrawal.

"*Seeming lucidity* is one of the things I see the most in guys coming off steroids," said Christian, the bodybuilding coach who first introduced me to Todd. "Guys can become much more cognitive and verbal and expressive as they go through the mood swings and depression of withdrawal. These guys have unusually insightful outpourings of thought, where they're really heightened in their sense of order, logic, and reason. They'll just suddenly start analyzing themselves to death and sounding like they know exactly what's going on and why they make certain decisions. Sometimes they're dead right, which is the killer. They seem so authentic, but I have to remember that they're also addicts in withdrawal, that they're living in an unreliable narrative."

And by using the steroid cream instead of quitting steroids cold turkey, Todd knows he may be dragging out that unreliable narrative, prolonging the pain and discomfort of withdrawal. He would prefer not to be using the cream, but he concedes that he's scared to stop steroids completely.

"Part of me knows that I need to stop, at least for a while," he tells me as we walk up the stairs in his apartment complex. "It's a dream of mine, but it's terrifying."

When we arrive at Todd's place, Julie is on her hands and knees in the main room, flexing suggestively in a string bikini and thong bottom in front of two 250-watt light bulbs and a camcorder mounted two feet off the floor. Over loud music (the Celine Dion song "One Heart"), Todd tells me that she's taping a four-minute segment for paid members to her Web site.

"If I ever got confident, I would do the same thing," he says before disappearing to the kitchen, returning a few minutes later with a plate packed with six scrambled eggs and some oatmeal with raisins (his standard post-workout meal).

"Welcome to my studio," Julie tells me when she's picked herself off the carpet and turned the camera and music off. Her skin is glistening with sweat. "I just worked out before this," she tells me, grabbing a towel. "Wow, am I sweating. This is hard. It looks easy, but it's hard!"

Todd gives Julie a quick kiss on the lips before inviting me into the guest bedroom, where he lounges on his side on the bed and pokes at his eggs. He looks tired. He also looks significantly older than I remember him. Did I just not notice before, or is more than a decade of steroids—compounded by a few years of meth and his current addiction to ephedra—finally taking a physical toll? With a body like Todd's, it's easy to overlook his face. And Todd's face is starting to look its age (forty-three). It's tan, hardened, and worn out.

As I look at him, I wonder how much longer he can keep taking steroids. How old is too old to be an escort? And for how long will his perceived self-worth depend on the subtle variances in hotel room mirrors? A few minutes later, as if reading my mind, Todd says, "As you age, there are things you need to change to make a graceful exit to the next part of your life. The clock is ticking."

I ask him what those changes might be. "I need to stop escorting full time—I'm clear about that," he tells me. "I need to find work that will lessen the stress of trying to perform and having to look a certain way." (In that vein, he's looking into personal training and doctor's assistant jobs and is considering going back to school.)

"I also need to get control of the caffeine and ephedra," he says. "I'm really struggling with those. I wake up, load up on both, and feel like Superman for a few hours. But by the end of the day, I'm depressed and miserable. So I'll say, 'Tomorrow, I'm going to stop this insanity,' but then tomorrow comes, and I do the whole pattern over again."

I ask Todd about steroids. "It seems like you're clear that you want to cut down on escorting and stop the ephedra," I tell him, "but you seem less willing to give up the steroids."

"You're right," he says. "I'm not as willing as I want to be."

It's easy to see why. Stopping steroids completely would mean being confronted with the terror of his body dysmorphia—the fear that he's never big enough, never good enough. Todd understands this, but self-knowledge has never been a match for addiction.

In the more than two years I've followed him, Todd has talked a lot about taking action to improve his life, but he's rarely followed through. He told me he would "get his life together" so he could compete in bodybuilding competitions, but when the time came, he was never ready. He committed early on to cutting down on ephedra, but instead he started using more. And a few months ago he said he would be off steroids completely the next time I saw him, but he's still on them.

I don't doubt that Todd meant everything he said when he said it, but Todd is an active addict, and addiction routinely trumps commitment. Still, Todd thinks he's ready for the biggest commitment of his life. I'm not prepared when he says this: "I'm at the stage of my life where I'm ready to be a father."

"A *father*?" I say, unable to hide my astonishment.

"Yeah, a father," he says. "Julie and I both want kids, but we're just waiting to make sure the marriage stays on solid footing and we've been together longer. Kids are serious—not something you want to jump into."

"Definitely not," I tell him.

"But I can't wait to be a dad. I think Julie and I would make great parents. I've always wanted to be a dad. I just got distracted by other things, including meth. But I'm ready to do whatever I have to do to be a dad. I'm ready for the next phase of my life."

I'm surprised by how uncomfortable the prospect of Todd and Julie as parents makes me. As I try to picture the scene—a half-naked Julie recording a segment for her Web site, Todd on the phone with an escorting client, steroids and ephedra in the medicine cabinet, and the baby asleep in its crib—Julie pokes her head in the room.

"What are you guys talking about?" she wants to know.

"Kids," Todd says.

"Oh," Julie says.

"I'm telling him that if things go well, we'll have a kid together. I think we're almost ready. We just need to get some things figured out and settled, and then we'll be ready. Don't you think, honey? Don't you think I would make a great dad?"

31 SEAN

We learned that powerless does not mean helpless.

—Hope and Recovery

SEAN PLOPS HIMSELF down next to me on a blue couch at an SLAA meeting near Fenway Park, where a Red Sox game is in progress. We can't hear the crowd tonight from here, but the walls of this street-level meeting space are so thin that we do know what our neighbors—a convenience store, and a car/limo dispatching company—are up to. The store cashier is watching a television show with a laugh track, and a dispatcher is yelling at somebody who displeases him.

This long, rectangular room is devoted to addiction recovery meetings, mostly for gay members of AA, SLAA, and Crystal Meth Anonymous. There are posters on the walls warning about the danger of crystal meth (*Would you inject brain cleaner and antifreeze?* reads one), a gay rainbow flag, and the words *Sober & Proud* over a big pink triangle. Nonetheless, some straight men, like Sean, come to the two SLAA gatherings here each week.

Attendance at this meeting is usually low during Red Sox games, when parking is nearly impossible. But tonight's turnout is especially bad. Sean and I are the only two here, and we're about to leave when Neil, a youthful forty-year-old and longtime SLAA member (he was Sean's first sponsor), shows up a few minutes late.

"Do my eyes deceive me?" Neil says with a smile, giving Sean a bear hug. "Welcome back! We missed you."

"Yeah, thanks," Sean says, awkwardly returning his hug. (Nearly a year of treatment has helped Sean become a bit more at ease socially, but he still has problems accepting and returning affection.) "It's good to be back. It's only my second day back in Boston."

"You're back for good?" Neil asks him.

"Yeah, for good. I missed these meetings so much. This was actually the second place I ever came for a meeting."

"I remember your *first* meeting," Neil tells him, sitting down on a green couch facing us. "I couldn't believe how young you were, but you jumped right in. You raised your hand and were like, 'Hey, so, how does this whole recovery thing work?'"

After opening the meeting with the Serenity Prayer, Neil asks Sean if he wants to be tonight's main speaker. Sean agrees, and for the next fifteen minutes he tells the story of how he ended up back in Boston. He had spent the previous few months in Florida, moving there after growing tired of Arizona, where he was spending most of his days playing pool. He intended to stay in Florida with his grandparents for only a month over the Christmas holidays before heading north to Boston, but instead he settled in.

"It was just really easy and comfortable living down there," he tells us. "I didn't have rent to pay, didn't have any expenses. So I just got lazy and stayed. And that's how I was able to be in relapse and not really realize it. I had people telling me to get out of bed, people cooking my meals, people cleaning my clothes. It was all really enabling. Part of me loves that comfort. That's what scares me about moving back to Boston. Now, suddenly, I'm responsible for everything again. In Florida, my family took care of me. I wasn't going to meetings. I was just spending all my time with my girlfriend, Jane. And that was a really fucked-up situation."

I got to see that for myself when I visited Sean two months ago. As we drove down a busy Florida street lined with bars and strip clubs on our way to pick up Jane in a nearby suburb, Sean regaled me with stories of their "dysfunctional relationship." But first, he pointed out a strip club with flashing neon lights. "When I was at treatment at Gentle Path," he said, "one of the strippers from that place was there, too. She was so hot! Every straight guy in treatment with me wanted to have sex with her."

Jane was Sean's first real girlfriend (he doesn't count Ann, the escort, as a "real girlfriend"), and while he suspected that he loved her, he worried that they were both "too fucked up" to make it last. There was the time, he said, when they got drunk and purposely had unsafe sex because they wanted to "make a baby," although they thought better of it the next day and got her the morning-after pill.

Another night, Jane got so drunk that she clawed violently at Sean's face while he slept. And many nights when they went out together, Sean said Jane would drink too much and would sometimes try to leave with other guys. "She's an active alcoholic," he told me, "but she won't admit it or get help." When I reminded him that he'd said the same thing about his mother, he was stunned. "Oh, wow, you're right," he said. "Fuck, it's like I'm dating my mom!"

A few weeks prior, Sean had gone to a nearby strip club with Jane. "It was her idea," he said. "I think she thinks those places are funny—and there's plenty of alcohol there. I've told her that I'm a sex addict, but I don't think she really *gets* it. I felt weird being there with her. I was like, 'This is really stupid. This is the kind of place I'll go when I'm depressed, not when I have a girlfriend.'"

Sean conceded that he'd brought plenty of his own dysfunction to the relationship. He wasn't going to SLAA meetings, and while his sex life with Jane seemed to be satisfying most of his urges, he still occasionally looked at Internet porn. But it was the neediness and obsessive energy he brought to the relationship that worried him most.

"I never really understood the whole love addiction thing," he said. "But I think that I'm definitely a love addict, because it's like I'm just totally enmeshed in the relationship. I spend all my free time with Jane, and I obsess about her a lot. It's the same kind of energy I have obsessing about sex. I probably just switched from sex addiction to love addiction."

Sean told me about the day early in the relationship when Jane hadn't answered her cell phone. Fearing that she was with another guy, Sean went "completely psycho," calling her hundreds of times and then driving to her house to ask her mother where she was. Jane was at a large outdoor music festival, her mother explained, so Sean sped there hoping to find her among the crowd. To his surprise, he did. But Jane wasn't with another guy, nor was she ignoring his calls because she didn't like him anymore. She was with a girlfriend of hers, and her cell phone had simply run out of power.

"Even though I know it's my addiction and obsession that's causing this, I still find myself not trusting her," Sean told me as we pulled up to Jane's house.

Jane is shaped a bit like an ostrich. Tall and lanky, with a long neck, she wore a blue Mickey Mouse T-shirt and short white shorts that showed off her pale and exceptionally long legs. As we drove to a restaurant after picking her up, I couldn't help remembering the last time I was in a car with Sean and a girl he liked. That was back in Boston, when he'd hung out with Ann during the break from treatment caused by Hurricane Katrina.

I was surprised by how much more I liked Ann than Jane. While Ann had a warm and meditative quality about her (and seemed reflective and intelligent), Jane struck me as emotionally immature and easily distracted. She was also fixated on finding alcohol, even leaving Sean and me at my hotel room for twenty minutes while she went looking for a liquor store. The following morning, as she smoked a cigarette while we waited for a table for brunch, I asked her how she'd reacted to Sean's announcement early in their relationship that he was a sex addict.

"I was, like, 'Whoaaaa,'" she said. "I was pretty shocked. But then I thought about it, and I was, like, 'Well, that's okay, because he's over it now.'"

Over it now? I stole a glance at Sean, but he looked away. I wondered if Sean had explained his sex addiction to her that way, or if that was just her wishful thinking. "I did ask him a lot of questions about it, though," Jane continued. "When he told me that he watched a lot of porn, I asked him if he had ever watched gay porn."

"I told her yes, just joking around," Sean said. "That really freaked her out."

"But I still don't get how you define sex addiction," she said. "I mean, if you define it as just *really* liking sex, then I could be a sex addict, too!"

It was clear that Sean hadn't explained his sex addiction to her, nor, he told me the next day, had he come clean to her about going on her computer to look at pornography. "It's definitely not the most honest and healthy relationship," Sean said.

As was his pattern, Sean asked me several times during my visit what I thought about his situation. I didn't know what to tell him. Part of me agreed with his mother, who told me that Sean was just making up for lost time.

"He's trying to find himself," she told me during a telephone conversation, adding that her relationship with Sean has improved in recent months. "He's living the life and doing all the things that most kids do at seventeen or eighteen. He's with his first girlfriend and trying to see what a relationship is about. He's just a few years behind most guys his age."

Another part of me hoped Sean would move back to Boston, where I remembered him being happiest, and where I suspected he would start working on his recovery again.

In the two months after my visit, Sean called me many times, seeming more eager to leave Florida with each call. On the last call before announcing that he would indeed move back, he sounded more sure of himself than he had in a long time.

"If I don't make a change," he told me, "I could see myself getting stuck down here and waking up one day when I'm forty and being like, 'Shit, look how much of my life I threw away, look at how much potential I had.' I really think I need to get back to Boston, get a job, get back to school, and start going to meetings again. The truth is, I date Jane because I like her and it feels good to have someone, but I'm not really in love."

Still, Sean had a hard time letting go of the relationship, even inviting her to join him for the drive up to Boston (she flew back to Florida once they arrived). "I'm trying to come up to Boston to get healthy, but I'm still holding on to this fucked-up relationship," he told me on the phone from a hotel room during their drive north. I asked him where Jane was. "Where do you think?" he said, laughing. "She's out looking for a liquor store."

In the weeks following the meeting near Fenway Park, Sean attends a meeting nearly every day and stays with an SLAA friend while he looks for a job and an apartment. Sean calls me often, usually to tell me how happy he is to be back in Boston. "This is the best decision I could have made for myself," he says.

Still, the stress of the move—and his sadness over the end of his relationship, as unhealthy as it was—gets the best of him during his second week, when he logs on to his SLAA friend's computer and looks up escort services. A few days later, he pays $300 to meet one in person. Minutes after the encounter, he calls me on his cell phone.

"Fuck!" he shouts into the phone. "I just did it."

"Did what?" I ask him.

"I just saw an escort. I'm so fucking *mad*." Sean sounds angrier than I've ever heard him. I try to calm him down, but there's no use. He's inconsolable. "I can't believe I did that. Why the hell did I do that? My day was going fine. Nothing was wrong. But then it just happened. Fuck! I'm so fucking mad!"

When he takes a breath, I ask him whom he's mad at. "I'm mad at this stupid girl that I just gave all my money to," he says. "I'm mad at the addiction. I'm mad that I went to treatment for almost nine months, and I'm still acting out! And part of me is mad that I moved back to Boston. I mean, I never saw a prostitute in Arizona or Florida. I can't fucking believe that I just did that. What the hell is wrong with me?"

"Nothing is wrong with you," I tell him. "We're addicts. What we do doesn't make sense. But you're okay. You had a slip, but you're okay."

"I hardly have any money, but I go and spend $300 to see a prostitute?" he says. "Fuck! I wanted to take the money back and run out of there so bad. I can't believe I went and did that. I can't believe what this fucking addiction has me do. Am I ever going to get better? I don't feel like I'm ever going to get better."

I can relate to everything he's feeling—the rage, the confusion, the hopelessness. But if there's any Twelve Step fellowship that truly lives the *Progress Not Perfection* slogan, it's SLAA. "You're already getting better," I tell him. "You've been getting better since you came to your first meeting. But this is a journey. You'll be getting better your whole life."

"Fuck that—I want to be better now," he says.

Later that day, I meet up with Sean at an SLAA meeting. I'm not surprised that he came. While some sex addicts hide out in shame after a slip, or continue to act out for weeks, months, or years before coming back to a meeting, that was never Sean's style when he lived in Boston. He always showed up and got honest.

At the meeting, Sean and I sit and listen as another young SLAA member—a gay nineteen-year-old who was sexually abused when he was seven and started cruising public places for sex when he was twelve—tells the group that he has sixty-two days of sobriety. "I'm feeling better about myself than I ever have," he says. Another member is celebrating one year.

There is hope in the room, and after listening to a dozen people share, Sean raises his hand to speak. "Hi, my name is Sean, and I'm a sex addict."

"Hi, Sean!"

"I had a major slip today," he tells the group. "I saw a prostitute. I was really mad at myself most of the day. I was also angry at her, angry at this addiction, angry that I've done so much work to fight this addiction, but it's still here. I'm feeling a little better tonight. I'm still sort of mad, but at least I'm not mad at myself. Maybe that will hit me tomorrow, but right now I'm not beating myself up or feeling shame. I'm still sort of numb from the acting out, so I'm not sure what I'm feeling. But just being here helps."

By the end of the meeting, Sean is in much better spirits, and he volunteers to read The Promises, which were first published in The Big Book and have subsequently been adopted by other Twelve Step fellowships. The meeting's chairperson passes the printout of The Promises to the man to his left, who then hands it to me. I hand it to Sean, but not before I try to make him laugh.

"Don't fuck up," I whisper to him. (At the meeting near Fenway Park, Sean had so badly mangled the first paragraph of The Promises that he'd had to start over.)

"Shut up," Sean tells me with a smile.

With the room at attention, Sean leans forward in his chair, clears his throat, rests his elbows on his thighs, and holds the paper gently with both hands.

"If we are painstaking about this phase of our development," he begins, "we will be amazed before we are halfway through. We are going to know a new freedom and a new happiness. We will not regret the past nor wish to shut the door on it. We will comprehend the word serenity and we will know peace. No matter how far down the scale we have gone, we will see how our experience can benefit others. That feeling of uselessness and self-pity will disappear. We will lose interest in selfish things and gain interest in our fellows. Self-seeking will slip away. Our whole attitude and outlook upon life will change. Fear of people and of economic insecurity will leave us. We will intuitively know how to handle situations which used to baffle us. We will suddenly realize that God, or our higher power, is doing for us what we could not do for ourselves. Are these extravagant promises?"

"We think not," the group responds in unison.

"They are being fulfilled among us—sometimes quickly, sometimes slowly," he reads. "They will *always* materialize if we work for them."

32 JANICE

It seems you're allergic to drugs. Every time you use them, you break out in handcuffs.

—ATLANTIC CITY SUPERIOR COURT JUDGE
MICHAEL CONNOR, SPEAKING TO AN ADDICT
FACING DRUG CHARGES

JANICE SITS CROSS-LEGGED on her queen-size bed, cradling a small boom box on her lap and swaying to the Percy Sledge song "When a Man Loves a Woman." She pokes playfully at her three grandchildren sprawled on the bed in her cramped $135-a-week room, which is painted yellow and has one small window that she's covered with a sheet. Janice shares this ground-floor Bronx apartment—it has one small bathroom and no common area—with a middle-aged black man who keeps to himself.

The oldest of the grandkids with Janice today, nine-year-old Tocarra, sketches in a pink journal, her legs dangling over the faux linoleum floor. (She's just finished applying red polish to her fingernails, and the room still smells of polish.) Tyree, who is seven, shuffles a deck of cards in preparation for taking on Tocarra in "I

Declare War," a game of chance where players split a deck in two and pit their cards against each other one by one, with the winner taking the loser's card based on whose is higher.

Dequan, who is four, begs Tyree to let him play, too. "But you don't know *how* to play, Fat Fat," Tyree tells him. (Dequan has several nicknames—including Fat Fat and Football Head—relating to his unusually large skull.)

Janice's room came furnished with the bed, a nightstand, a chair, a wooden pole for her to hang her clothes, and an unfinished wooden shelf where she keeps her certificate of graduation from Odyssey House. After two and a half years in treatment, she finally completed the program three weeks ago. She never passed her GED, but the court decided she could leave treatment without it as long as she attends GED classes while living on her own. She took the test for a third time a few days ago.

"This time, I really believe I passed it," she says, rubbing Dequan's head and bellowing the words to the Spinners song "A One of a Kind Love Affair." (Janice has been baby-sitting the kids since last night, when her daughter dropped them off on her way to a concert.) "The test didn't seem so hard this time. Math was still tough, though. I guessed at a lot of them. I hate math."

A minute later, she changes the subject. "But can you believe I'm finally free?" she practically sings. "Shoooot, sometimes I thought I'd be stuck in there forever!"

"Do you miss anything about treatment?" I ask.

"Whaaaat?" Janice says. "Well, I do miss my friends there. They all helped me get to where I am today. The Friday night I left, everyone followed me downstairs and gave me big hugs. Nearly squeezed me to death."

Janice almost wasn't allowed to leave that night. "The heavens just opened up, and the rain was coming down in buckets," she recalls. With poor visibility on the roads, the Odyssey House staff didn't want Janice's kids driving to the center to pick her up. But the rain finally stopped, and she was allowed to leave. "Believe me, I would have busted out of there if they had tried to stop me!"

Janice doesn't plan to stay in this apartment for long, and she's made little attempt to make it feel like a home. The walls of her room are bare. Only her nightstand reveals anything about her personality: It's stacked with books—including two paperback romance novels and an adventure novel by Clive Cussler—and a framed sign that reads, *Relax. God's in Charge.*

Soon, Janice says she'll begin looking for a bigger apartment with a fellow Odyssey House graduate. But can she afford one? Janice makes $271 a week after taxes as a full-time cook's assistant in a nursing home. Even her current rent is difficult to afford on that salary.

A few days before my visit, Manhattan Deputy Chief Assistant District Attorney Rhonda Ferdinand—who monitored Janice's progress through treatment—told me that she was worried about Janice's living situation.

"It's one of my pet peeves about the way housing works for people like Janice," she said. "It's hard to recuperate your life as a person in recovery if you can't find housing that's safe and affordable. Janice is working hard, she's working *full time*, but she's only making minimum wage, and all she can find is an overpriced tiny room that's not in the best area. At least she's not living where she used to use crack—we would never allow that. But I always worry about housing, because that's the kind of stressor that could prompt Janice to start using again. What if she moves into a place with a fellow recovering addict, and that person relapses and can't pay her share of the rent? They could both be evicted and end up on the street."

To help ensure that Janice stays clean, she's required to attend outpatient treatment three nights a week for the next six months.

There, she's regularly drug-tested and attends individual and group therapy.

If Janice does relapse, she could face jail time. "It really depends on what kind of relapse it is," Ferdinand told me. "It usually goes one of two ways with people addicted to crack. In the better scenario, they use once and then regroup. If that happens to Janice, she'll be upgraded to a five-day-a-week outpatient program. But if it's a binge and she disappears, then we have to issue a warrant for her arrest and go find her." (Ferdinand doesn't buy the line that relapse is an inevitable part of recovery. "I tell everyone, 'Relapse is a conscious decision you *don't want to make.'"*)

Janice insists—as she has since I first met her at Odyssey House— that she will never use drugs again. "And in six months," she says, "I'll be done with treatment, and the charges against me will be dropped."

In the meantime, she's most excited about the prospect of cable television. In a few days—the same day Janice turns fifty-eight— the cable company will come to deliver her cable box, which will allow her to watch her two favorite channels, HBO and Black Entertainment Television. Right now the television is tuned to a network station broadcasting the war movie *Black Hawk Down*, but Janice muted the sound of gunfire and death in favor of her mixed tape of love songs.

"I have to pay $11 extra a month for HBO," she says, rubbing Dequan's head again, "but life wouldn't be worth living without it." Janice will be at work that day, so her son, Mark, has agreed to be here when the cable person arrives. "Mark knows I'll kill him if he's not here when he's supposed to be," Janice tells me. "Nobody messes with my cable television."

I last saw Mark and Janice two months ago at one of her regular appearances at the Criminal Court in downtown Manhattan. As part of her mandated treatment in the Drug Treatment Alternative-to-Prison program, Janice regularly appears before Rhonda Ferdinand and Judge Patricia Nunez. (She'll need to keep coming to court until she finishes outpatient treatment.) For each visit while she was in Odyssey House, Janice's counselor wrote a letter summarizing her progress.

Mark arrived late that morning, but it didn't matter. The court was moving at a snail's pace, and Janice's name wouldn't be called for another two hours.

"These benches are hard as hell," complained J.R., one of Janice's counselors, who escorted her to court and passed the time reading the *Daily News*. "And the problem is, I don't have much natural cushion!"

"Well, these benches are hurting me—and I've got lots of cushion," Janice quipped.

Mark didn't say much in court but seemed riveted by the parade of addicts—most black or Hispanic, and many in the DTAP program—who were called before Judge Nunez. A 1997 appointee of Mayor Rudolph Giuliani, Nunez was equally adept at playing good and bad cop, congratulating those who were working hard toward their recovery and scolding those who weren't.

Nunez appeared to take her cues from Ferdinand, who has worked in the Office of Special Narcotics since 1985 and is generally regarded as one of the state's leading experts on alternatives to incarceration. Ferdinand beamed with joy in court as she congratulated a young black woman for completing inpatient drug treatment, passing her GED, and securing a job.

"I've come to know her well," Ferdinand told Judge Nunez, "and I know I won't be seeing her again in the criminal justice system." Nunez congratulated her profusely ("I am so proud of you," she said several times) before dismissing the woman's case.

Things didn't go nearly as well for several other addicts. One man, who Ferdinand told the judge was disrupting his treatment program, was ordered back to jail. "I'll give you a week in Rikers to think about things," Nunez told him.

She then urged one middle-aged man who barely failed his GED not to give up ("You're almost there! You'll pass it next time!") and dismissed charges against a young woman who successfully completed treatment and earned her GED. "You'll be able to be a great mom to your little boy," she told the woman, who cried with joy and then hugged Ferdinand.

A few minutes later, Ferdinand turned to look at Janice, mouthing the words "I'm sorry" for the interminable wait.

"I really have to go to work," Janice told me. "I hope it's not too much longer."

"You're telling me," J.R. said, shifting his weight on the bench. "I'm dying here."

Finally, Janice's name was called. She hurried to the front of the courtroom, stopping in front of a wooden desk about ten feet from Judge Nunez, who sat perched behind a mammoth wooden table underneath a sign that read, IN GOD WE TRUST (although the letter *I* was barely visible, so it actually read *N GOD WE TRUST*). Ferdinand stood to Janice's left and scanned the latest progress report letter written by J.R. It read, in part:

Janice has been in residential treatment thirty months and has successfully met most of her short-term treatment plan objectives. Although Janice has been in this treatment process for an extended length of time, she continues to participate in all treatment services on a daily basis.

Janice is a full-time employee and verbalizes her fondness and appreciation for employment. Janice has a bank account, makes regular deposits, and budgets appropriately. Janice's housing situation is another objective where she expends conscientious effort. She continues to work with our housing specialist and has submitted applications for low income housing.

She attends GED classes four times per week, after attending a full day of employment. She has verbalized a commitment to obtaining a GED. However, it may be in Janice's best interest to allow her to pursue the GED after she completes residential treatment.

Our clinical team has reviewed Janice's treatment progress and have found that she continuously displays exemplary behavior and possesses an attitude of sincerity and commitment toward remaining free of active addiction. Since her inception in the program, all of her random urine samples have been screened by Bellevue Laboratories and all have been negative for any use of illicit chemicals or alcohol.

Janice has utilized her time in treatment and taken full advantage of the services offered both directly and on referral. She has been a role model for all of her peers. We believe that, upon accomplishing her housing needs, she is ready to reenter the larger society as a law-abiding, productive citizen.

"She's doing excellent," Ferdinand told Nunez. "She's working, she's looking for a place to live, and she's working toward her GED."

"You look fantastic," Nunez told Janice.

"Thank you, Judge," Janice said with a wide smile.

"You're doing great work. Keep it up, okay? The end is in sight."

"Oh, don't worry, Judge. I will."

And with that, the next case was called.

As we left the courtroom, Janice grabbed my arm. "I'm almost free!" she said, looking happier than I had ever seen her.

After listening to her mixed tape of love songs, Janice bundles her grandkids in sweaters and hooded jackets—it's frigid outside—and asks them if they're in the mood for McDonald's. It's a silly question; they're always in the mood for McDonald's.

The kids hurry out the apartment's front door and push open the tall red gate that leads to the sidewalk. Janice's street is quiet. The "drug activity," she tells me, is a few blocks away. Across the street from her house, Janice points out a newly built five-story brick building. "That's going to be a senior citizen center," she says. "They have to have a kitchen, so I might apply to work there. Wouldn't be much of a commute."

Safely arrived at McDonald's, the kids trade their Happy Meal toys and chase each other around the table. Janice, meanwhile, updates me on her love life. In hushed tones, she tells me about her boyfriends.

"That's right—I have *two*!" she says with pride.

The older of the pair, Bruce, is sixty but still lives with his mother (Janice affectionately refers to him as a "mamma's boy"). They've dated on and off for sixteen years, starting when both of them used crack. He recently stopped on his own, although she wishes he would go to treatment. "A place like Odyssey House would do him a lot of good," she tells me. "If he starts using again, he won't be seeing any more of me."

Janice met her second boyfriend, a fifty-eight-year-old crack and heroin addict named Robert, at Odyssey House. They flirted there but only started seriously dating after he graduated from the program ten months ago.

"Does boyfriend number one know about boyfriend number two?" I ask her.

"Whaaaat?" she says, giggling. "No way. They both want to claim me, but neither has said, 'Let's get married.'"

"Do you *want* to get married?" I ask. Janice has loved a handful of men in her life, but she's never been married. Crack always took precedence over love.

"I might," she tells me. "I don't think I would marry Bruce, but if things go well with Robert, who knows? Shoooot, now that I'm clean, anything is possible."

Will Janice ever use drugs again? It's impossible to say, but I doubt it. Of all the addicts I followed for this book, Janice is one that I worry about the least. Is my confidence in her misplaced? Perhaps. I'm normally wary of addicts who promise to stay away from drugs "forever"—we addicts have broken so many promises that they cease to be meaningful. All we can commit to is staying sober *today*. When we keep the focus on today, we tend to stay sober long-term.

Ferdinand was surprised when I told her how confident I was in Janice's continued sobriety.

"I hope your intuition is right," she said, "but I worry about Janice, just as I worry about so many people when they come out of treatment. They have a much better chance than people who don't get treatment, but it's still an uphill battle. If Janice stays clean for six months now that she's out, her prognosis for continued sobriety is pretty good. A good sign is that Janice wants to be remembered positively as someone who was there for her family and friends."

Ferdinand can't help taking a little credit for Janice's focus on her legacy. When she first met Janice a few years ago, she said she gave Janice "the talk."

"It's what I tell many addicts, especially those who are getting up in age," Ferdinand told me. "I said, 'Janice, you basically have two options now. You can continue taking drugs, which means you will eventually die, probably on the street or in a crack house, and your kids and grandchildren won't even know. Or, you can devote yourself to your recovery and be there for yourself and the people who matter to you in the remaining years you have. When you close your eyes for the last time, what do you want people to say about you? What do you want your legacy to be? Do you want them to say you were a crack addict, or do you want them to say you were a loving mother, sister, and grandmother who made a positive impact on the lives of the people around you? This is your chance. Which way do you want to go?'"

On our walk back to Janice's apartment, I ask Janice if she remembers Ferdinand's lecture. "Oh, hell yes," she says. "I was crying my eyes out. But I decided to go the right way, didn't I? I'm done with drugs. Shoooot, how can I be a good grandmother if I'm on crack? I can't. So no more crack for me."

CONCLUSION

*In the end, when we don't stand up and speak
out, we hide behind our recoveries, we sustain
the most harmful myth about the disease—that
it is hopeless.*

—William Cope Moyers, author of *Broken:
My Story of Addiction and Redemption*

IT IS SOMETIMES said that addiction, if left untreated, will likely lead
a person to one of three unenviable ends: jail, a mental institution, or
death. From that perspective, the time I spent with Bobby, Marvin,
Todd, Ellen, Sean, Janice, Jody, and Kate must be considered a rousing success. No one died. No one ended up in an insane asylum. And
no one went to jail (except Bobby, who spent only five days there).

I also avoided these fates, although, like a majority of the addicts
I followed for this book, I did not stay sober for the duration of this
project. In fact, during one stretch, I had the worst relapse of my
life. Until that point, I had never completely bought into the idea
that addiction is a *progressive* illness—that my addiction is "doing
push-ups" even when I'm sober, waiting patiently for its chance to

reappear, stronger and more determined than ever to destroy my life. But I don't doubt it now.

In my relapse, my addiction consumed me in ways it never before had. For entire weeks I could barely function. I isolated from my friends. I stopped going to therapy. I stopped taking my dog to the park. I lied—to everyone, about everything. And I felt perilously close to losing my mind. While I had long seen my addictive behavior as insane, I now felt insane.

As the main text of the SLAA fellowship describes, I felt "the terror of irrevocably losing sanity, of slipping over the edge of an abyss beyond which any stability and life purpose would be forever out of reach." Still, I didn't stop.

One morning, I woke and vowed to get through the day sober. But by mid-morning, I was headed across town to meet somebody for sex. On my drive there, I looked around in disbelief at all the people who seemed to be going about their normal lives. Some walked to work. One man ran with his dogs. Another did tai chi in a park. How, I wanted to know, could they not be having sex right now? Didn't they know that sex was the most important thing in the world? What were these poor people thinking?

The problem, of course, was *my* thinking. What the hell was happening to me? Why couldn't I stop chasing sex? Why, on many days, did I not *want* to stop? Who was I? Was I really the person doing these things? If that wasn't me, why did I keep doing them? And where did I get off writing a book about addiction when I was so thoroughly engrossed in my own addiction? What kind of hypocrite does *that*?

I feared headed for a similar fate as Luther Benson, an alcoholic who in 1877 wrote the book *Fifteen Years in Hell* from a locked ward at the Indiana Asylum for the Insane. A temperance lecturer who toured the country trying to convince alcoholics to stop drinking, Benson routinely got drunk after his speeches. Eventually his reputation was destroyed and he lost his mind. But what seemed to eat at him the most was his hypocrisy. How had his noble ambitions (to get sober and help other addicts) been so perverted by his addiction?

"Depraved and wretched is he who has practiced vice so long that he curses it while yet clings to it," Benson wrote.

I could relate to Benson's belief that he "could live neither with alcohol nor without it," as William White put it. During my relapse, I felt the same way about my sexual acting out. On most days, I chose what Ellen—the food addict—calls "the safe unhappiness" of active addiction over the scarier unhappiness of withdrawal. Acting out clearly makes me miserable, but it's a misery that can feel familiar and oddly comforting.

My friends in recovery expressed grave concern as I became increasingly isolated and depressed. "Are you trying to kill yourself?" one asked me. "I'm not going to sit by and watch you destroy your life," another said. Many nights they called again and again, threatening to show up at my house if I didn't answer my cell phone. To get them off my back, I lied. "I'm working on my book," I would say. Was I really using a book about addiction as cover for my addiction?

My lies became more egregious (and my shame more paralyzing), causing some friends to pull away. Others got angry. My exceedingly patient therapist hinted that if I didn't start at least "trying to stop," that she would have to kick me out of group therapy. One group member wondered if writing this book might be adding fuel to my addiction. Maybe, he said, fear over coming out publicly as a sex addict was turning me into *more* of a sex addict.

"Are you sure you want to do this?" he asked me several times. "Is having the whole world know going to help your recovery?" I wondered the same thing, but my lack of sobriety handicapped my attempts to think clearly.

I shared my struggles with most of the addicts I followed for this book. Kate and Ellen expressed support and motherly concern, often trying to shift the focus to me during our talks. Bobby listened intently as I explained sex addiction to him, but he seemed genuinely baffled that anyone would choose sex over drugs. Jody, like any good addiction counselor, urged me not to beat myself up. He reminded me that wallowing in shame would only make me act out again.

I was the most open about my struggles with Sean, probably because we suffer from the same addiction. In the midst of my relapse, he called me often and made many suggestions, including that I get a cell phone without Internet capability, as he had done two years before. Like many sex addicts in recovery, I had purchased Internet blocking software—the kind designed for kids—for my computers. The software worked well. So well, in fact, that I started using my cell phone to go online and look at pornography.

It's not easy to find a cell phone without Internet capability. A well-meaning Sprint customer service representative couldn't, for the life of her, understand why I would want such a phone. When I insisted, she said I could simply have Internet capability removed from my current phone. And she was right—I could do that. I already had done that, three times in the previous two months. But it's a solution that doesn't work so well for sex addicts. In the midst of a relapse, I had simply called Sprint to have the Internet reinstated.

I eventually found an antiquated cell phone without Internet capability. That same day, I changed my number and deleted an e-mail account I was using to meet people for sex. These were positive actions, but I suspected it would take more than a day's worth of willingness for me to get sober and have the life I claimed to want: one of honesty, integrity, joy, friendship, and true intimacy.

I had been sober before, but now the prospect seemed monumental—and, on many days, unlikely. What would it take for me to recover? Maybe, a friend suggested, I could look for answers—and hope—in the lives of the addicts I followed for this book.

————

Recovery without hope is not possible, at least not for me. Fortunately, I can find it in Janice's miraculous transformation from a homeless crack addict with false pride into a strong, sober woman with integrity and a life purpose. I can find it in Ellen's ability to stay thin—and, more importantly, in her willingness to seek humility and a spiritual way of life.

I can find it in Kate's dramatic reduction in shoplifting, which she credits to breaking through isolation and connecting honestly with others in her online community. I can find it in Marvin's four years of sobriety, in Jody's resolve never to sleep on another twin bed, and in Sean's penchant for rarely giving up for long, no matter how much he falters.

I can even find hope in the stories of the two addicts—Bobby and Todd—who routinely made me want to scream, "Why won't you just stop?" My strong reaction to their struggles likely says as much about me as it does about them. I reacted so intently, I suspect, because I saw so much of myself in their maddening propensity for denial, rationalization, self-delusion, and broken promises. If there's anyone to whom I often want to scream "Why won't you just stop?" it's me.

But Bobby's and Todd's stories, like my story, are not without hope. The fact that Bobby is still alive is a testament to his strength—or, as his godmother, Margaret, once told me, "to someone upstairs looking out for him." And it's important to remember the progress Todd has made—he has managed to stay off meth and has cut down on his steroid use. As AA has long professed, recovery is about progress, not perfection.

As I look back on this book, I am not short on hope. But *answers*?

Can I claim, as many self-described "addiction experts" routinely do, to have debunked or otherwise solved the mystery of addiction? Can I boast, like the dozens of people who e-mailed me these last few years pitching miracle addiction cures ("You can't write a book about addiction and not include *this*!" they exclaimed), to know "the truth" about addiction and recovery?

I cannot. If anything, writing this book further complicated addiction in my eyes. Is addiction a disease like hypertension or diabetes, or is it instead a malady of the spirit? Or is it, as many suggest, a cruel combination of both? Will we ever effectively combat addiction with medicine, as we have been "on the brink of" doing for much of the past two centuries? Why do some people recover from addiction, while others die from it? And why did Bobby and Janice become addicted to drugs while Sean and I became enslaved by sex? I don't know. Others may claim to know, but I can't, in good conscience, join them.

What I can do—and what I hope others suffering from addictions will also do—is try to learn from the addicts I followed for this book. Bobby, Marvin, Todd, Ellen, Sean, Janice, Jody, and Kate are the true addiction "experts." They have much to teach us—addicts and nonaddicts alike—about addiction and recovery.

At Odyssey House, I learned that treatment—if given the time it needs—tends to work. Odyssey House isn't a fancy place (no "recovery yoga" classes, no serene views), but it might just be the model for how to effectively treat addiction, particularly in economically disadvantaged addicts and those with drug-related convictions.

We've historically "treated" those like Janice in two ineffective ways: We've either locked them in prison, occasionally offering cursory rehabilitation there but more often hoping they'll be scared straight and return to their drug-infested communities with a newfound resolve to "Just Say No." Or, we've mandated them to short-term treatment programs, barely scratching the surface of their problems before patting them on the back and returning them to their drug-infested communities—but not before reminding them to avoid the "people, places, and things" that might cause them to relapse.

The DTAP program recognizes the absurdity of both approaches. It understands that recovery rarely happens in thirty days and that it is about far more than stopping the addictive behavior. Recovery demands that addicts learn "all the adult things you weren't doing because you were too busy getting fucked up," Jody once told me. Long-term treatment allows for that kind of process. (I once told Janice that I wished there were free long-term treatment center for sex addicts. "I'd be the first person to sign up," I said, and I meant it.)

If Janice taught me the value of surrendering to treatment, no matter how long it takes, Ellen taught me the importance of surrendering to something other than my oversized ego. From the moment I met her, I related strongly to Ellen's knee-jerk take on the world: That she knew what was best for her—and for everyone else. Ellen was a driven, cynical, self-described "know-it-all" before starting OA, and that life philosophy had not served her well. She weighed three hundred pounds, and she was miserable.

For Ellen—and, I suspect, for me—recovery depends on the aggressive and consistent pursuit of self-acceptance and humility. Neither trait comes naturally to us, or to most addicts. Marvin may have put it best. "I'm an egomaniac with an inferiority complex," he said.

So how does an egomaniac with an inferiority complex change his ways? Not easily, to be sure. "For me," Ellen told me recently, "it only happened by working the Twelve Steps harder than I've worked at anything in my life. I had to shut up long enough to learn to have faith in something other than my distorted thinking."

Are the Twelve Steps the only roadmap to sobriety? Certainly not. AA concedes as much. "Upon therapy for the alcoholic himself, we surely have no monopoly," The Big Book states. But for millions of Americans, working the Twelve Steps is a critical safeguard against the return of addictive thinking, namely the delusion that we know what's best when it comes to our addiction.

Kate's safeguard—her daily act of humility—is to reach out to her online support community. She parks herself in front of her computer and gets honest, whether she feels like it or not. Understanding how critical connection and accountability are to her recovery, Kate took the initiative to organize monthly face-to-face gatherings of recovering shoplifters in her area.

I expect that the next step for Kate—one that will ensure an emotionally rich life, not just a sobriety that feels restrictive—will be to begin healing from her sexual abuse. I had a surprisingly strong reaction to her unwillingness to face her trauma. I remember several times wanting to shake her and shout, "But, Kate, you're not going to get better unless you face this!"

Once again, I likely was projecting onto Kate what I feared about myself. I could certainly see the trauma in others, but had I ever truly faced mine? In some ways, I was envious that Kate had a clear target—her sexual abuse.

I have no recollection of being sexually or physically abused. My childhood trauma—an authoritarian and emotionally withdrawn mother who never said she loved me, a father who said he did but who I didn't believe truly *knew* me, a sexual identity that I thought made me inherently unlovable, and a staggering loneliness that I desperately tried to mask with overachievement—always struck me as less tangible, less easily faced.

But if I believe anything about addiction, it's that its roots can usually be found in childhood. (In one study of 872 boys, low self-esteem at eleven mostly predicted drug dependency at twenty.) Not every young victim of physical, sexual, or emotional abuse develops an addiction, just as not every addict had a terrible childhood. But if neuroscientists truly want to combat addiction, a good start would be to develop a pill that buffers kids against the struggles and mistakes of their families.

The addicts in this book certainly suffered their fair share of abuse and trauma: Kate was ignored by her mother and molested for years by a family member. Janice was raped when she was nine and then sent away by her mother at fourteen. Sean grew up feeling alone, isolated even from his own mother, who he says drank too much and emotionally abused him. Jody grew up knowing that he would soon go blind (and worrying that his drug-addicted father might die). Marvin—although he maintains that his childhood was mostly "happy"—had an active alcoholic father. And Bobby grew up in a family, and a neighborhood, where it was common to medicate unhappiness with alcohol and drugs.

The trauma isn't as easy to find in Ellen's story. "There was no emotional, physical, or sexual abuse that could easily explain why I turned to food," she told me the first time we met in person. "I was definitely born into a food-addicted family, and I do think that for whatever reason, I wasn't always heard or responded to in a way that would have been ideal growing up. But for me, I really think it came down to genetic predisposition. I believe I was born a food addict."

Was I born a sex addict? I doubt it, but who knows? It's conceivable that I have two strikes against me (genetic predisposition to addiction, and childhood trauma), making my recovery more challenging than someone with, say, a genetic predisposition but a happy childhood, or no genetic predisposition but a traumatic life.

Whatever the case, an intellectual understanding of addiction will not keep me sober. For proof, look no further than Jody, who relapsed while running a treatment center. As a longtime addict and addiction counselor, Jody has spent more time than most probing the complexities of addiction.

"I've spent a lot of time psychoanalyzing myself and other people, trying to figure out how the hell we all ended up fucked up in this way," he told me one night as we made the rounds of his sober living community. "But I try to stay away from all of that now, because it doesn't lead me anywhere good, and I need to focus on the fucking solution."

"And what is the fucking solution?" I asked him.

"How the hell should I know?" he said. "But dude, seriously, for me the solution is pretty simple. I need to ask for help, help others, stay honest, and try like hell to feel my feelings. If I do those things, the odds are pretty good that I won't relapse, fuck up my life, and end up on another fucking twin bed."

A few months later, as I sat down to write this conclusion, Jody was rewarded for his sobriety—and his many years helping other addicts—when he was offered and accepted the executive director position at A Sober Way Home, an addiction treatment center in Prescott, Arizona. "Talk about a place where the blind will be leading the blind!" Jody joked when I call to congratulate him.

Two weeks later, I checked in with him again. "Save any souls yet?" I wanted to know.

"Oh, we're trying," he told me. "I'm only one blind dude, and this is only one treatment center, but we're going to save some lives before we're done."

I don't doubt that he will, but Jody recognizes that he can do only so much. "You can have the best treatment center in the world," he once told me, "but nothing will really change in this country until people in recovery, and those who care about people in recovery, decide that they've seen enough heartbreak, enough needless death. People in recovery need to stand up and demand to be counted. We don't have nearly enough people out there screaming until something changes, until we start devoting real money and resources to fighting this disease. Where are the millions of addicts in this country who are sober and have turned around their lives? They need to be

on the front lines of this war, but they're at their AA and NA meetings in church basements, talking to each other. And that's great,
and that's important, and personal recovery depends on it, but man,
that's not enough anymore! I mean, when will we wake up and flip
the fucking script?"

THE TWELVE STEPS OF ALCOHOLICS ANONYMOUS

1. We admitted we were powerless over alcohol—that our lives had become unmanageable.
2. Came to believe that a Power greater than ourselves could restore us to sanity.
3. Made a decision to turn our will and our lives over to the care of God *as we understood Him*.
4. Made a searching and fearless moral inventory of ourselves.
5. Admitted to God, to ourselves, and to another human being the exact nature of our wrongs.
6. Were entirely ready to have God remove all these defects of character.
7. Humbly asked Him to remove our shortcomings.
8. Made a list of all persons we had harmed, and became willing to make amends to them all.
9. Made direct amends to such people wherever possible, except when to do so would injure them or others.
10. Continued to take personal inventory and when we were wrong promptly admitted it.
11. Sought through prayer and meditation to improve our conscious contact with God *as we understood Him*, praying only for knowledge of His will for us and the power to carry that out.
12. Having had a spiritual awakening as the result of these steps, we tried to carry this message to alcoholics, and to practice these principles in all our affairs.

NOTES

Introduction

Page
  3 *"on the installment plan"*: Sara Mayfield, *Exiles from Paradise*, p. 116.
  6 *"communicating enormous love"*: Solomon, *The Noonday Demon*, p. 233.
  6 *"My primary loyalty was to sex"*: Ryan, *Secret Life*, p. 4.
  7 *"syndrome model" understanding of addiction*: Shaffer to BDL.
  8 The use of a substance or activity: Fellowship-Wide Services, *An Introduction to Sex and Love Addicts Anonymous*, pamphlet, p. 4.
  8 *the world's most abused substance*: Courtwright, *Forces of Habit*, p. 19.
  8 *"intoxicates, without inviting the police"*: Ibid., p. 189.
  8 *Nurses who drank two to three cups*: Ibid., p. 93.
  9 *shoot heroin dealers in the head*: Ibid., p. 187.
 10 *"Merchants, capitalists, and the political elites"*: Ibid., p. 91.
 10 *For most of the 1800s*: Brodie and Redfield, *High Anxieties*, p. 3.
 10 *Americans drank more alcohol*: Rorabaugh, *The Alcoholic Republic*, p. 10.
 10 *"When I was in Virginia"*: Ibid., p. 7.
 10 *One man who did*: White, *Slaying the Dragon*, p. 2.
 10 *although the word itself*: Ibid., p. xiv.
 10 *"religious, metaphysical, and medical"*: Ibid., p. 3.
 10 *should be placed in a "sober house"*: Ibid., p. 4.
 11 *"I am aware that the efforts"*: Ibid., p. 2.
 11 *"In my judgment"*: Ibid., p. 9.
 11 *"around stereotypes of the opium-smoking"*: Brodie and Redfield, *High Anxieties*, p. 3.
 12 *"The country eventually fell sway"*: White, *Slaying the Dragon*, p. 31.
 12 *nearly 23 million Americans*: 2006 National Survey on Drug Use and Health by the Substance Abuse and Mental Health Services Administration (SAHMSA).
 12 *another 61 million smoke cigarettes*: Ibid.
 12 *More than 70 percent of abused and neglected kids*: "No Safe Haven: Children of Substance-Abusing Parents," 1999 report by the National Center on Addiction and Substance Abuse (CASA) at Columbia University.
 12 *In 2007, the economic cost*: National Institute on Drug Abuse, 2007 estimate.

12   *"What funds terrorism"*: Califano, *High Society*, p. 1.

13   *"tolerance for delay"*: Twerski, *Addictive Thinking*, p. 16.

13   *"We live in a society whose whole policy"*: Merton, *The Seven Storey Mountain*, p. 133.

13   *"Addiction is not, as we like to think"*: Peele, *Love and Addiction*, p. 182.

14   *Half the participants called it a personal weakness*: From an internal 2005 report prepared for Faces and Voice of Recovery and the National Council on Alcoholism and Drug Dependence.

14   *In a 2004 poll*: Poll of 801 American adults conducted by Peter D. Hart Research Associates and the Coldwater Corporation.

14   *Even the family members*: "USA Today/HBO drug addiction poll," *USA Today*, July 19, 2006.

15   *"Can you imagine the power"*: Carnes to BDL.

15   *"Like a cattle prod"*: Fellowship-Wide Services, *Sex and Love Addicts Anonymous*, p. 69.

Chapter 1

Page

16   *The drug is at once*: Brodie and Redfield, *High Anxieties*, p. 9.

Chapter 2

Page

22   *Alcohol, and not the dog*: Milkman and Sunderwirth, *Craving for Ecstasy*, p. 44.

23   *In an AA newsletter*: National Center on Addiction and Substance Abuse, *Women Under the Influence*, p. 138.

23   *The wives of some early AA members*: Ibid., p. 137.

24   *"The laughter within AA"*: White, *Slaying the Dragon*, p. 147.

Chapter 3

Page

27   *A junkie is someone*: Matt Zoller Seitz, "Sunshine Daydream, With Pointed Point of View," *New York Times*, December 26, 2007.

29   *While at least 12 million Americans*: 2006 National Survey on Drug Use and Health by SAHMSA.

29   *"an all-purpose cure-all"*: Owen, *No Speed Limit*, p. 203.

30   *"The ones who first"*: Ibid., p. 92.

Chapter 4

Page

33   *When we drug ourselves*: Pressfield, *The War of Art*, p. 26.

Chapter 5

Page

39   *Every addiction arises*: Tolle, *The Power of Now*, p. 152.

Chapter 6

Page
44 *Over the past century*: Brodie and Redfield, *High Anxieties*, p. 4.

Chapter 7

Page
48 *People who claim*: Solomon, *The Noonday Demon*, p. 223.
53 *Of the more than 23 million people*: 2006 National Survey on Drug Use and Health by SAHMSA.
53 *"We can build a better system"*: Hoffman and Froemke, *Addiction*, p. 202.

Chapter 8

Page
54 *Shame is the motor*: Hazelden Meditations, *Answers from the Heart*, p. 5.

Chapter 9

Page
58 *The spiritual life is not a theory*: AA World Services, *Alcoholics Anonymous*, p. 83.
59 *"the greatest social architect"*: AA World Services, *Pass It On*, p. 368.
59 *AA has more than a million members*: Official AA estimate, 2007.
59 *was mostly dead a decade later*: White, *Slaying the Dragon*, pp. 12–13.

Chapter 10

Page
67 *Who could even imagine*: Alexander and Roberts, *High Culture*, p. 3.
72 *forced his way inside*: Tal Abbady, "Man, 40, Dies After Taser Shock," *South Florida Sun-Sentinel*, July 18, 2005.
72 *It was the state's twenty-seventh death*: Antigone Barton, "Drugs Shadow Taser Deaths," *Palm Beach Post*, August 14, 2005.
72 *The State Attorney's Office*: Edward Sifuentes, "State Cleared in Man's Death After Taser Use," *South Florida Sun-Sentinel*, December 1, 2005.
72 *"He was not always"*: Tal Abbady, "Man, 40, Dies After Taser Shock," *South Florida Sun-Sentinel*, July 18, 2005.
73 *Even the country's drug czar*: Torgoff, *Can't Find My Way Home*, p. 275.
74 *"in a park across the street"*: Reinarman and Levine, *Crack in America*, p. 22.
75 *there were no crack dealers*: Ibid., p. 23.
75 *they manipulated a black*: Ibid., p. 23.
75 *Nearly two-thirds of Americans*: Ibid., p. 24.
75 *"a threat worse than any nuclear warfare"*: Torgoff, *Can't Find My Way Home*, p. 355.

Chapter 11

Page
77 *I would distrust anyone*: Hoffman and Froemke, *Addiction*, p. 174.

Chapter 12

Page

80 *Like the alcoholic, the junkie*: Malcolm X, *The Autobiography of Malcolm X*, p. 265.

81 *half-million Americans incarcerated*: Bureau of Justice Statistics cited by the Sentencing Project's 2005 report, "Incarceration and Crime: A Complex Relationship." The international comparison is based on statistics compiled by the International Centre for Prison Studies, at the School of Law at King's College, University of London.

81 *A five-year study*: "Crossing the Bridge: An Evaluation of the Drug Treatment Alternative-to-Prison (DTAP) Program," a 2003 CASA report.

82 *"This program in which failure"*: Ibid.

82 *"The way to get the intensive"*: Hoffman and Froemke, *Addiction*, p. 202.

Chapter 13

Page

89 *Drug dealers are to dopamine*: Courtwright, *Forces of Habit*, p. 111.

91 *Most showed a preference*: Wood RI. Anabolic-androgenic steroid dependence? Insights from animals and humans. *Front Neuroendocrinol*. 2008 Jan 3; [Epub ahead of print] PMID: 18275992.

91 *unlike with classic addictive drugs*: Triemstra JL, et al. Testosterone and nucleus accumbens dopamine in the male Syrian hamster. *Psychoneuroendocrinology*. 2008 Apr;33(3):386–94.

91 *It also leads to aggressive*: Grimes JM, et al. Alterations in anterior hypothalamic vasopressin, but not serotonin, correlate with the temporal onset of aggressive behavior during adolescent anabolic-androgenic steroid exposure in hamsters (Mesocricetus auratus). *Behavioral Neuroscience*. 2007 Oct;121(5):941–48.

91 *"tickle the same part"*: Pope to BDL.

91 *Give an animal a drug*: Peters K, et al. Androgen overdose: behavioral and physiologic effects of testosterone infusion. *Neuroscience*. 2004;130:971–81.

91 *Human steroid users*: Kanayama G, et al. Past anabolic-androgenic steroid use among men admitted for substance abuse treatment: an underrecognized problem? *Journal of Clinical Psychiatry*. 2003 Feb;64(2):156–60.

91 *In a large study*: Ibid.

92 *Steroid users also have high rates*: Kanayama G, et al. Risk factors for anabolic-androgenic steroid use among weightlifters: a case-control study. *Drug and Alcohol Dependence*. 2003 July 20;71(1):77–86.

Chapter 14

Page

99   *Who cares to admit complete defeat?*: AA World Services, *Twelve Steps and Twelve Traditions*, p. 21.

101 *fastest-growing age group*: U.S. Census Bureau report, "65+ in the United States: 2005."

101 *Between 2002 and 2005*: Warren Wolfe, "For Aging Drug Users, It's Hard to Kick the Habits," *Minneapolis Star Tribune*, December 10, 2006.

101 *For those in their forties and fifties*: Mike Males, "This Is Your Brain on Drugs, Dad," *New York Times*, January 3, 2007.

102 *number of people older than fifty*: "The Aging Baby Boom Cohort and Future Prevalence of Substance Abuse," a 2002 SAHMSA report.

102 *"Very few people have thought"*: Provet to BDL.

102 *More than 80 percent*: CASA report, "Under the Rug: Substance Abuse and the Mature Woman," 1998.

107 *"Alcoholism isn't a spectator sport"*: Rebeta-Burditt, *The Cracker Factory*.

108 *"My life's purpose of sobering up Bill"*: Al-Anon Family Group Headquarters, *How Al-Anon Works for Families and Friends of Alcoholics*.

108 *Beebe was sentenced to*: Joe Pisani, "A Story of Rape, Repentance and Forgiveness," *Stamford Advocate*, March 23, 2007.

109 For the readiness to take: *Twelve Steps and Twelve Traditions*, p. 87.

Chapter 15

Page

110 *I admire addicts*: Chuck Palahniuk, *Choke*, p. 185.

113 HEROIN DIGS ITS HOOKS: Brian MacQuarrie, "Heroin Digs Its Hooks Into South Boston," *Boston Globe*, March 5, 1997.

113 *gangs of gun-wielding kids*: Paul Tough, "The Alchemy of OxyContin: From Pain Relief to Drug Addiction," *New York Times Magazine*, July 29, 2001.

113 *In 2002, nearly 90 percent*: Hoffman and Froemke, *Addiction*, p. 31.

114 *Between the summers of 2001 and 2002*: Ric Kahn, "By Sad Stats, Southie No. 1," *Boston Globe*, January 11, 2004.

114 *Southie has*: Massachusetts Department of Public Health, "Substance Abuse Mortality: Age-Adjusted Rates by Neighborhood, Boston, 2001–2003."

114 *"I feel kind of hopeless"*: Ric Kahn, "By Sad Stats, Southie No. 1," *Boston Globe*, January 11, 2004.

114 *The city's per capita rate*: Massachusetts Department of Public Health, "Substance Abuse Mortality: Age-Adjusted Rates by Neighborhood, Boston, 2001–2003."

114 *Between 1993 and 2005*: Massachusetts Organization for Addiction Recovery.

114 *The increase coincided with a dramatic*: Ibid.

114 *Of the nearly 25,000 people*: Governor Mitt Romney's 2006 budget recommendations, Budget.doc H1-06-202.

Chapter 16

Page

117 *"This ritual undermines"*: White, *Slaying the Dragon*, p. 145.

124 *That distinction belongs to*: Schwartz, *Never Satisfied*, p. 204.

124 *"could hardly get through the crowd"*: www.tops.org.

124 *By 1958, TOPS boasted thirty thousand members*: Schwartz, *Never Satisfied*, p. 207.

124 *Its local chapters had colorful names*: Ibid.

125 *"My doctor says that dieting"*: Lina Goldberg, "Between the Sheets: The History of Overeaters Anonymous and Its Food Plans," unpublished research paper.

125 *"I believed that I was not so weak"*: Ibid.

125 *Rozanne was stripped of her position*: Ibid.
125 *OA approved three "disciplined" food plans*: Ibid.
125 *OA scrapped the Grey Sheet*: Ibid.
125 *other OA members have left*: Ibid.
126 *"We all knew—because it was common knowledge"*: Torgoff, *Can't Find My Way Home*, p. 314.
126 *"can now be entirely dispensed with"*: White, *Slaying the Dragon*, p. 109.
127 *"food, sex, and surfing" could be addictive*: Smith to BDL.
128 *Americans are the fattest people*: Crister, *Fat Land*.
128 *Two-thirds are either overweight or obese*: "Prevalence of Overweight and Obesity Among Adults: United States, 2003–2004," National Center for Health Statistics.
128 *between 2000 and 2005*: Roland Sturm, "Increases in Morbid Obesity in the USA: 2000–2005," *Public Health*, July 2007.
128 *"Right now the line between"*: Wang to BDL.
129 *Weight is more strongly inherited*: Gina Kolata, "Genes Take Charge, and Diets Fall by the Wayside," *New York Times*, May 8, 2007, in an excerpt from her book, *Rethinking Thin: The New Science of Weight Loss—and the Myths and Realities of Dieting*.

Chapter 17

Page
130 *Our physical appearance, our mannerisms.* Fellowship-Wide Services, *Sex and Love Addicts Anonymous*, p. 73.
138 *"We don't blame [heart patients]"*: Bill Moyers, *Close to Home* series on addiction, PBS.
140 *"Most gay people have been enormously"*: McNaught, *Now That I'm Out, What Do I Do?*, p. 48.
141 *"teenagers are suffering every day"*: Griffin-Shelley, *Adolescent Sex and Love Addicts*, p. 7.
141 *"it is time that a diagnosis"*: Ibid.
142 *There is "no scientific data"*: Schmidt quoted in *Substance Abuse: A Comprehensive Textbook*, p. 505.
142 *"alcoholic drinking and addictive drug use"*: White, *Slaying the Dragon*, p. 96.
142 *"primary maternal identification"*: Ibid., p. 96.
142 *"fear of castration"*: Ibid.
142 *"latent homosexuality"*: Ibid.
142 *"Every drinking-bout is tinged"*: Ibid.
143 *"In rather doctrinaire fashion"*: Tiebout, *Harry Tiebout*, p. 89.
143 *"a symptom that had itself become"*: White, *Slaying the Dragon*, p. 98.
144 *"there are many behaviors, including sex"*: Martin to BDL.
144 *"inhibitory circuitry"*: Constance Holden, "Behavioral Addictions: Do They Exist?", *Science*, November 2, 2001.
144 *"People don't exactly throw money at you"*: Carnes to BDL.
145 *"The guy who sees a woman standing"*: Ibid.
146 *"Clinton allegedly broke down in tears"*: Eric Pooley, "Kiss but Don't Tell," *Time*, June 24, 2001.

146 *"It's much harder to be a straight sex addict"*: BDL attended the conference.

146 *sex researcher Jeffrey Parsons found three main types*: Parsons J.T., et al. (in press). Explanations for the origins of sexual compulsivity among gay and bisexual men. *Archives of Sexual Behavior.* [Epub ahead of print] PMID: 17882541.

147 *"We had a lot of guys who said"*: Parsons to BDL.

147 *"Thirty years ago no one could stand up"*: Walker to BDL.

Chapter 18

Page

149 *In my own life, as well as in the lives*: From an unpublished essay by Michael Grohall.

152 *Allen reportedly bought hundreds*: Tim Funk, "Ex-Bush Adviser Pleads Guilty," *Charlotte Observer,* August 5, 2006.

155 *One of the first shoplifters to gain*: Jon Grant, "Kleptomania," *Clinical Manual of Impulse-Control Disorders,* 2005.

155 *"It is not that we need so much more"*: Abelson, *When Ladies Go A-Thieving,* p. 55.

155 *In 1898, the* New York Times: Ibid., p. 3.

155 *A 1901 study titled "Les Voleuses des Grand Magasins"*: Ibid., p. 46.

156 *Oh, don't we live in curious times*: Ibid., p. 2.

156 *In 1967,* Life *magazine published*: Ibid., p. 202.

157 *Retailers lose about $13 billion a year to shoplifters*: National Retail Federation 2007 survey.

157 *About two-thirds of this group are women*: Shulman to BDL.

159 *"Cancer can be viewed as an invasion"*: Cupchik to BDL.

Chapter 19

Page

166 *Acknowledging the existence of something larger*: P., *Turning It Over,* p. 6.

Chapter 20

Page

179 *I know of no class of people*: Keeley, *Opium: Its Use, Abuse, and Cure.*

189 *"With the scientific advances we're making"*: Torrington to BDL.

190 *When some of the top scientists in Britain*: "Ethical Aspects of Developments in Neuroscience and Drug Addiction," Foresight Brain Science, Addiction and Drugs Project, 2005.

191 *In the early 1900s, some doctors*: White, *Slaying the Dragon,* p. 89.

191 *Indiana passed a law banning marriages*: Ibid.

191 *These extreme measures came only after*: Ibid., p. 93.

191 *One study found that nineteen*: Ibid., p. 67.

191 *White recounts other failed treatments*: Ibid., p. 95.

191 *"But it has never lived up to its promise"*: Alexander to BDL.

192 *Alexander took sixteen lucky rats*: Alexander B, et al. Effect of early and later

colony housing on oral ingestion of morphine in rats. *Pharmacology Biochemistry and Behavior*, 1981;15:571–76.

192 *unnecessarily stressed during childhood*: Dube SR, et al. Childhood abuse, neglect and household dysfunction and the risk of illicit drug use: the adverse childhood experience study. *Pediatrics*, 2003;111(3):564–72.

193 *Studies show that animals stressed*: Vazquez et al. Maternal deprivation increases vulnerability to morphine dependence and disturbs the enkephalinergic system in adulthood. *Journal of Neuroscience*, 2005;28:4453–62.

193 *living in an enriched environment*: Meaney et al. Environmental regulation of the development of mesolimbic dopamine systems: a neurobiological mechanism for vulnerability to drug abuse? *Psychoneuroendocrinology*, 2002; 27:127–38.

193 *"We know from human twin and family studies"*: Uhl, GR, et al. Substance abuse vulnerability loci: converging genome scanning data. *Trends in Genetics*, 2002;18(8):420–25.

195 *Studies in both animals and humans*: Volkow ND, et al. Dopamine transporter occupancies in the human brain induced by therapeutic doses of oral methylphenidate. *American Journal of Psychiatry*, 1998;155(10):1325–31.

195 *obese subjects have lower levels of D2 receptors*: Wang et al. Brain dopamine and obesity. *The Lancet*, 2001;357(9253):354–57.

195 *Volkow increased the level of dopamine D2 receptors in rats*: Thanos, PK, et al. Overexpression of dopamine D2 receptors reduces alcohol self-administration. *Journal of Neurochemistry*, 2001;78:1094–1103.

195 *Studies of people with Parkinson's*: Driver-Dunckley, E. Pathological gambling associated with dopamine agonist therapy in Parkinson's disease. *Neurology*, 2003;61(3):422–23.

195 *researchers at the Wake Forest School of Medicine*: Morgan, D, et al. Social dominance in monkeys: dopamine D2 receptors and cocaine self-administration. *Nature Neuroscience*, 2002;5:169–74.

196 *"The field has wasted a lot of time on dopamine"*: Koob to BDL.

197 *"We're open to medications that will actually work"*: Schwarzlose to BDL.

Chapter 21

Page

199 *About three million Americans*: Marianne Szegedy-Maszak, "The Worst of All Bets," *U.S. News & World Report*, May 15, 2005.

199 *Another few million*: Ibid.

201 *$15 billion-a-year online gambling industry*: Emily Flynn Vencat, "Caribbean Hold 'Em," *Newsweek*, October 1, 2007.

201 *"Gambling is the future of the Internet"*: Steven Crist, "All Bets Are Off," *Sports Illustrated*, January 26, 1998.

201 *a Lehigh University sophomore*: ABC News, July 25, 2006.

201 *a Long Island bookkeeper and mother of three*: Richard Weird and Dave Goldiner, "Mother Embezzled Millions to Fund Lottery Addiction, Authorities Say," *New York Daily News*, August 23, 2006.

202 *A 1997 study of Minnesota's*: Stinchfield and Winters, *Treatment Effectiveness*

of Six State-Supported Compulsive Gambling Treatment Programs in Minne-sota, Fourth and Final Report, University of Minnesota Medical School, 1996.

202 *a national survey found that*: Volberg, *When the Chips Are Down*, p. 11.

210 *In a study of 3,639 college students*: McCabe SE, Screening for drug abuse among medical and nonmedical users of prescription drugs in a probability sample of college students. *Archives of Pediatrics and Adolescent Medicine*, 2008;162(3):225–31.

Chapter 22

Page

214 *I once had a dad who would pick me up*: NPR, April 4, 2007.

216 *The U.S. prison population more than doubled*: Reinarman and Levine, *Crack in America*, p. 42.

216 *By 1990, roughly 25 percent*: Ibid.

216 *black Americans are still ten times more likely*: "The Vortex: The Concentrated Racial Impact of Drug Imprisonment and the Characteristics of Punitive Counties," Justice Policy Institute, December 4, 2007.

223 *"Autobiography in Five Short Chapters"*: Nelson, *There's a Hole in My Side-walk: The Romance of Self-Discovery*.

Chapter 23

Page

228 *Being confronted with the thinking of an alcoholic*: Twerski, *Addictive Think-ing*, p. 7.

Chapter 24

Page

235 *Relapse is not a failure of treatment*: Hoffman and Froemke, *Addiction*, p. 28.

Chapter 25

Page

244 *Remember that we deal with alcohol*: AA World Services, *Alcoholics Anony-mous*, p. 58.

Chapter 26

Page

249 *Walking and living amidst us*: Ringwald, *The Soul of Recovery*, p. 214.

Chapter 28

Page

262 *If it can be taken as a symptom of civilization*: Lewin, *Phantastica*, p. 2.

Chapter 29

Page

271   *Boston was home to the country's first*: White, *Slaying the Dragon*, p. 47.

276   *"The ripple effect of Jack's goodness"*: Bryan Marquard, "He Helped When 'Chips Were Down,'" *Boston Globe*, April 14, 2007.

Chapter 30

Page

278   *That, of course, is the devil's bargain of addiction*: Daniel Goleman, *Emotional Intelligence*. TK.

Chapter 31

Page

284   *We learned that powerless does not mean helpless*: Anonymous, *Hope and Recovery*, p. 3.

Chapter 32

Page

293   *It seems you're allergic to drugs*: John Froonjian, "Unequal Treatment," *Press of Atlantic City*, October 2, 2004.

Conclusion

Page

303   *In the end, when we don't stand up*: Jodi Mailander Farrell, "Addiction Recovery Moving 'Out of the Basement' into Public Health Arena," *North County Times*, January 6, 2007.

304   *"the terror of irrevocably losing sanity"*: Fellowship-Wide Services, *Sex and Love Addicts Anonymous*, p. 69.

304   *"Benson routinely got drunk"*: White, *Slaying the Dragon*, p. 7.

305   *"Depraved and wretched is he"*: Ibid., p. 8.

305   *"could live neither with alcohol"*: Ibid., p. 7.

309   *"Upon therapy for the alcoholic himself"*: AA Word Services, *Alcoholics Anonymous*, p. xxi.

310   *In one study of 872 boys*: Taylor et al. Self-derogation, peer factors, and drug dependence among a multiethnic sample of young adults. *Journal of Child and Adolescent Substance Abuse*, 2005;15(2):39–51.

BIBLIOGRAPHY

AA World Services. *Alcoholics Anonymous.* New York: AA World Services, 2001.

————. *Pass It On: The Story of Bill Wilson and How the AA Message Reached the World.* New York: AA World Services, 1984.

————. *Twelve Steps and Twelve Traditions.* New York: AA World Services, 1985.

Abelson, Elaine. *When Ladies Go A-Thieving: Middle-Class Shoplifters in the Victorian Department Store.* New York: Oxford University Press, 1992.

Al-Anon Family Group Headquarters, Inc. *How Al-Anon Works for Families and Friends of Alcoholics.* Virginia Beach: Al-Anon Family Group, 1995.

Alexander, Anna, and Mark S. Roberts, eds. *High Culture: Reflections on Addiction and Modernity.* Albany: State University of New York Press, 2003.

Anonymous. *Hope and Recovery: A Twelve Step Guide for Healing from Compulsive Sexual Behavior.* Center City, Minnesota: Hazelden, 1994.

Assael, Shaun. *Steroid Nation: Juiced Home Run Totals, Anti-Aging Miracles, and a Hercules in Every High School: The Secret History of America's True Drug Addiction.* New York: ESPN Books, 2007.

Bien, Thomas, and Beverly Bien. *Mindful Recovery: A Spiritual Path to Healing from Addiction.* New York: John Wiley & Sons, 2002.

Brodie, Janet Farrell, and Marc Redfield, eds. *High Anxieties: Cultural Studies in Addiction.* Berkeley: University of California Press, 2002.

Califano Jr., Joseph A. *High Society: How Substance Abuse Ravages America and What to Do About It.* New York: Public Affairs, 2007.

Carnes, Patrick. *Don't Call It Love: Recovery from Sexual Addiction.* New York: Bantam, 1991.

————. *Out of the Shadows: Understanding Sexual Addiction.* Center City, Minnesota: Hazelden, 2001.

Cheever, Susan. *My Name Is Bill: Bill Wilson—His Life and the Creation of Alcoholics Anonymous.* New York: Simon & Schuster, 2004.

Colleran, Carol, and Debra Jay. *Aging and Addiction: Helping Older Adults Overcome Alcohol or Medication Dependence.* Center City, Minnesota: Hazelden, 2002.

Courtwright, David T. *Dark Paradise: A History of Opiate Addiction in America.* Cambridge: Harvard University Press, 2001.

―――. *Forces of Habit: Drugs and the Making of the Modern World*. Cambridge: Harvard University Press, 2001.

Crister, Greg. *Fat Land: How Americans Became the Fattest People in the World*. New York: Houghton Mifflin, 2003.

Downs, Alan. *The Velvet Rage: Overcoming the Pain of Growing Up Gay in a Straight Man's World*. New York: Da Capo, 2006.

Fellowship-Wide Services, Inc. *Sex and Love Addicts Anonymous*. Norwood, Massachusetts: Sex and Love Addicts Anonymous, Fellowship-Wide Services, 2004.

Ferguson, Gary. *Shouting at the Sky: Troubled Teens and the Promise of the Wild*. New York: St. Martin's, 1999.

Finnegan, William. *Cold New World: Growing Up in a Harder Country*. New York: Random House, 1999.

Frey, James. *A Million Little Pieces*. New York: Nan A. Talese, 2003.

Goleman, Daniel. *Emotional Intelligence: Why It Can Matter More Than IQ*. New York: Bantam, 1997.

Goode, Erich. *Drugs in American Society*. New York: McGraw-Hill, 1972.

Griffin, Kevin. *One Breath at a Time: Buddhism and the Twelve Steps*. New York: Rodale, 2004.

Griffin-Shelley, Eric. *Adolescent Sex and Love Addicts*. Westport, Connecticut: Praeger, 1994.

Hartigan, Francis. *Bill W.: A Biography of Alcoholics Anonymous Cofounder Bill Wilson*. New York: Thomas Dunne, 2000.

Hazelden Meditations. *Answers in the Heart: Daily Meditations for Men and Women Recovering from Sex Addiction*. Center City, Minnesota: Hazelden, 1989.

Hoffman, John, and Susan Froemke, eds. *Addiction: Why Can't They Just Stop? New Knowledge. New Treatments. New Hope*. New York: Rodale, 2007.

Hollander, Eric, Dan Stein, Robert Simon, and Robert Hales. *Clinical Manual of Impulse-Control Disorders*. Arlington, Virginia: American Psychiatric Publishing, 2005.

Kaminer, Wendy. *I'm Dysfunctional, You're Dysfunctional: The Recovery Movement and Other Self-Help Fashions*. New York: Addison-Wesley, 1992.

Keeley, Leslie. *Opium: Its Use, Abuse, and Cure*. Manchester, New Hampshire: Ayer Company Publishers, 1981.

Klein, Alan M. *Little Big Men: Bodybuilding Subculture and Gender Construction*. Albany: State University of New York Press, 1993.

Kolata, Gina. *Rethinking Thin: The New Science of Weight Loss—and the Myths and Realities of Dieting*. New York: Farrar, Straus and Giroux, 2007.

Kurtz, Ernest. *Not God: A History of Alcoholics Anonymous*. Center City, Minnesota: Hazelden, 1991.

LeBlanc, Adrian Nicole. *Random Family: Love, Drugs, Trouble, and Coming of Age in the Bronx*. New York: Scribner, 2004.

Lehr, Dick, and Gerard O'Neill. *Black Mass: The Irish Mob, the FBI, and a Devil's Deal*. New York: Public Affairs, 2000.

Lowinson, Joyce, Pedro Ruiz, Robert Millman, and John Langrod. *Substance Abuse: A Comprehensive Textbook*. Philadelphia: Lippincott Williams & Wilkins. 2004.

McNaught, Brian. *Now That I'm Out, What Do I Do?* New York: St. Martin's Press. 2001.

Maltz, Wendy. *The Sexual Healing Journey: A Guide for Survivors of Sexual Abuse*. New York: Quill, 2001.

Maran, Meredith. *Dirty: A Search for Answers Inside America's Teenage Drug Epidemic*. San Francisco: HarperOne, 2003.

Marinick, Richard. *Boyos*. Boston: Justin, Charles, 2004.

Martin, Peter R., Bennett Alan Weinberg, and Bonnie K. Bealer. *Healing Addiction: An Integrated Pharmacopsychosocial Approach to Treatment*. Hoboken, New Jersey: John Wiley & Sons, 2007.

Mayfield, Sara. *Exiles from Paradise: Zelda and Scott Fitzgerald*. New York: Delacorte Press, 1971.

Meier, Barry. *Pain Killer: A "Wonder" Drug's Trail of Addiction and Death*. New York: Rodale, 2003.

Melody, Pia, Andrea Wells Miller, and J. Keith Miller. *Facing Love Addiction: Giving Yourself the Power to Change the Way You Love*. San Francisco: HarperOne, 1992.

Merton, Thomas. *The Seven Storey Mountain*. New York: Harcourt, 1999.

Milkman, Harvey, and Stanley Sunderwirth. *Craving for Ecstasy: How Our Passions Become Addictions and What to Do About Them*. San Francisco: Jossey-Bass, 1987.

Moran, Martin. *The Tricky Part: One Boy's Fall from Trespass into Grace*. Boston: Beacon, 2005.

Moyers, William Cope, and Katherine Ketcham. *Broken: My Story of Addiction and Redemption*. New York: Viking, 2006.

National Center on Addiction and Substance Abuse at Columbia University. *Women Under the Influence*. Baltimore: The Johns Hopkins University Press, 2006.

Nelson, Portia. *There's a Hole in My Sidewalk: The Romance of Self-Discovery*. New York: Atria, 1994.

Owen, Frank. *No Speed Limit: The Highs and Lows of Meth*. New York: St. Martin's, 2007.

P., Homer. *Turning It Over: A Third Step Guide for Recovering People*. Center City, Minnesota: Hazelden, 1999.

Palahniuk, Chuck. *Choke*. New York: Anchor, 2002.

Paul, Pamela. *Pornified: How Pornography Is Transforming Our Lives, Our Relationships, and Our Families*. New York: Times Books, 2005.

Peele, Stanton. *Diseasing of America: How We Allowed Recovery Zealots and the Treatment Industry to Convince Us We Are Out of Control*. San Francisco: Jossey-Bass, 1995.

Peele, Stanton, and Archie Brodsky. *Love and Addiction*. New York: Penguin Group, 1976.

————. *The Truth About Addiction and Recovery.* New York: Fireside, 1992.

Pope, Harrison G., Katharine A. Phillips, and Roberto Olivardia. *The Adonis Complex: The Secret Crisis of Male Body Obsession.* New York: Free Press, 2000.

Pressfield, Steven. *The War of Art: Break Through the Blocks and Win Your Inner Creative Battles.* New York: Warner Books, 2003.

Rebeta-Burditt, Joyce. *The Cracker Factory.* New York: Bantam Books, 1986.

Reinarman, Craig, and Harry G. Levine, eds. *Crack in America: Demon Drugs and Social Justice.* Berkeley: University of California Press, 1997.

Ringwald, Christopher D. *The Soul of Recovery: Uncovering the Spiritual Dimension in the Treatment of Addictions.* New York: Oxford University Press, 2002.

Rorabaugh, W. J. *The Alcoholic Republic: An American Tradition.* New York: Oxford University Press, 1981.

Ryan, Michael. *Secret Life: An Autobiography.* New York: Pantheon, 1995.

Schwartz, Hillel. *Never Satisfied: A Cultural History of Diets, Fantasies and Fat.* New York: Free Press, 1986.

Shavelson, Lonny. *Hooked: Five Addicts Challenge Our Misguided Drug Rehab System.* New York: New Press, 2001.

Sheff, David. *Beautiful Boy: A Father's Journey Through His Son's Meth Addiction.* New York: Houghton Mifflin, 2008.

Sheff, Nic. *Tweak: Growing Up on Methamphetamines.* New York: Atheneum, 2007.

Shulman, Terrence Daryl. *Something for Nothing: Shoplifting Addiction and Recovery.* Haverford, Pennsylvania: Infinity, 2004.

Simmons, Roy, and Damon DiMarco. *Out of Bounds: Coming Out of Sexual Abuse, Addiction, and My Life of Lies in the NFL Closet.* New York: Carroll & Graf, 2006.

Solomon, Andrew. *The Noonday Demon: An Atlas of Depression.* New York: Scribner, 2001.

Sultanoff, Barry, and Roger F. Klinger. *Putting Out the Fire of Addiction: A Holistic Guide to Recovery.* Lincolnwood, Illinois: Keats, 2000.

Tiebout, Harry. *Harry Tiebout: The Collected Writings.* Center City, Minnesota: Hazelden Press, 1999.

Tolle, Eckhart. *The Power of Now: A Guide to Spiritual Enlightenment.* Novato, California: New World Library, 1999.

Torgoff, Martin. *Can't Find My Way Home: America in the Great Stoned Age, 1945–2000.* New York: Simon & Schuster, 2004.

Trimpey, Jack. *Rational Recovery: The New Cure for Substance Addiction.* New York: Pocket Books, 1996.

Twerski, Abraham J. *Addictive Thinking: Understanding Self-Deception.* Center City, Minnesota: Hazelden, 1997.

Volberg, Rachel A. *When the Chips Are Down: Problem Gambling in America.* New York: Century Foundation, 2001.

Volpicelli, Joseph, and Maia Szalavitz. *Recovery Options: How You and Your Loved Ones Can Understand and Treat Alcohol and Other Drug Problems.* New York: John Wiley & Sons, 2000.

Weiss, Robert. *Cruise Control: Understanding Sex Addiction in Gay Men*. Los Angeles: Alyson, 2005.

White, William. *Slaying the Dragon: The History of Addiction Treatment and Recovery in America*. Bloomington, Illinois: Chestnut Health Systems/Lighthouse Institute, 1998.

X, Malcolm. *The Autobiography of Malcolm X*. New York: Ballantine Books, 1992.

ACKNOWLEDGMENTS

Many thanks to my agent, Todd Shuster, and to my editor, Bob Bender, for being first-class human beings.

A number of people read this book in various stages and offered valuable suggestions. Particular thanks to Dustin Lewis, Dave Ford, Jim Lopata, Christopher Nutter, and Bruce Shenitz.

I was blessed with a terrific research assistant, Andrew Tolve, and a life-saving fact-checker, *The New Yorker*'s Madeleine Elfenbein.

A number of addiction experts—some quoted in this book, some not—were particularly helpful and generous with their time. Special thanks to Carol Colleran, Pat Taylor, William Moyers, Matthew Torrington, David Powell, David Smith, Debra Jay, Larry Wells, Joe Kort, Nora Volkow, Sharan Jayne, Dru Myers, Robin Cato, and Rip Corley.

Thanks to the staff at Odyssey House, particularly John Roberts and Isobelle Surface, for the gift of access.

Thanks to my parents, Dennis Lewis and Benedicte Denizet, for their love and support. My father was my first editor, encouraging my writing in high school despite my inability to differentiate between *there* and *their*. My mother was also supportive of my writing, particularly of the plays I wrote in high school, and to this day she still asks me when I'm going to quit fooling around with this nonfiction stuff and write for the theater. Soon, Mom, soon.

Thanks to my late grandfather, the French writer and economist Jean Denizet, for believing in me—and for letting me hang around his office.

I would also like to thank the many friends, writers, editors, colleagues, and mentors who have helped me throughout my career and the writing of this book. They include David Brudnoy, Christian Matyi, Michael Clisham, Erik Sachs, David Wiegand, Dasha Trebichavska, Jose Pares-Avila, Corey Johnson, Ilena Silverman, Gerry Marzorati, Sheila Glaser, Adam Moss, Lauren Kessler, Maer Roshan, Dan Woog, Doug Most, Laurel Leff, Jason Bellini, Robert McClory, Margaret Engel, Shawn Leavitt, Mark McGrath, Scott Heim, Michael Lowenthal, Lynn Carey, Randy Myers, Amanda Curtin, Agathe Bennich, Tron Bykle, Evelyn Lincoln, Brian Shure, James Doty, David Watt, Andrew Murray, Gregg Keller, Christopher Rice, David Aronstein, Douglas Foster, George Flaherty, Henry Belanger, Tom Levine, Jennifer 8. Lee, Jenny Pritchett, Neil Savage, Michael Joseph Gross, John Mecklin, Jimmy Hester, Shana Naomi Krochmal, Martha Stookey, Kerry Lauerman, Mark Dennis, Larry Keane, Paul Payson, Seth Meschter, Jim Gibb, Jody Hotchkiss, Tim Schoonover, Brandon Andrew, Therese Henderson, Eric Bell, Sequoia Wild, Michael Grohall, Laura Phillips, Regina Brown, Bill Blue, Hanya Yanagihara, Jon Barrett, Alan Light, Corby Kummer, Jon Marcus, Michael Leslie, Patrick Lentz, Sandro Frattura, Patrick Mabray, Nick Street, Jay Doyle, Roger Schachtel, Kate Goldberg, Christopher Muther, David Salerno, Jodie Valade, Josh Eriksen, Rachel Dowd, Daniel McLaughlin, Nick Denton, Clayton Fleming, Alexandra Hall, Michael Blanding, James Shank, Peter Ian Cummings, Mim Udovitch, Jeremy Yellen, Teddy Greenstein, Nancy Gertner, Erik Piepenburg, Jesse Wilson, David Boyd, Billy Burgess, Joe Folan, Elizabeth Levy, Earnie Gardner, Michael Borum, David Bussiere, Brendan Little, Eric Kleiman, Keegan Kautzky, and Julia Landis.

INDEX